Elisabeth Luard, prize-winning food writer, novelist, natural-history artist, has never obeyed the rules. In 1963 and just turned twenty-one, she married Nicholas Luard, co-founder of *Private Eye*. Within six years, she had four children and moved to a remote valley in southern Spain. Twelve years later, with her family well on the way to adulthood, she turned to full-time writing.

She is the author of a number of successful cookery books, including the much-acclaimed *The Rich Tradition of European Peasant Cookery* which was recently screened on the BBC, and *The Flavours of Andalusia*, for which she won the Glenfiddich Award in 1992. She is a regular contributor to the *Sunday Telegraph*, is the cookery editor for *Woman's Journal*, and for many years wrote the food column in the *Scotsman*. Her first novel, *Emerald*, was chosen for the W.H. Smith 'Thumping Good Read' Award in 1995. The sequel to *Family Life*, *Still Life*, is now available from Bantam Press. She divides her time between London, Wales and the Hebrides.

'A magnificent and poetic writer, Luard's not-so-simple tale of family life is quite literally a triumph. She and her writer husband take their four children to a valley in Andalusia where they 'go native' with great success. Luard is a housewife who emerges as an award-winning food writer and artist. In some of the most poignant and moving writing this year, she chronicles the discovery that her daughter Francesca is under a death sentence, and its inevitable tragic conclusion' *Daily Express*

'Robust, wise, light but never flippant . . . Unspeakably moving. You leave it with a strengthened sense of what families are: hostages to fortune, doorways to the worst grief, and yet a rough, undesigned shelter from it. Few writers have so well described the solid nourishment of family life. She deserves a medal' Libby Purves, *The Times*

'This tenderly written, passionately felt memoir . . . Exotic, colourful and filled with old-fashioned adventure . . . An account of enterprise touched with magic . . . Filled with details of festivals, meals and anecdotes, plus a scattering of recipes, it exudes the rich whiff of escapism. Nevertheless, the author has to face the challenge of recording the death of a beloved daughter. Writing with admirable courage, she contributes memorably to the literature of family life' Elizabeth Buchan, *Mail on Sunday*

'Most people will find the closing chapters of this book too painful to read; certainly any comment from the critic would be otiose. It remains only for us to salute Francesca's courage . . . The main impression one gains of this family – and especially of Elisabeth Luard – is of vigour and courage . . . The book is not just an account of family life; it also bears witness to the journey through life from early marriage to maturity, from the dizzy days of the early Sixties to thoughtful middle age, of a woman who has been a full-time and devoted mother and who is now a professional writer and painter. For her weapons she had, among others, courage, stamina, imagination, tenacity and a certain conviction of her own rightness' Teresa Waugh, *The Spectator*

'It is enthusiasm, good humour and an obvious belief in the power of family life to unite and regenerate that inspires her narrative . . . In 1991, Francesca, the family's eldest daughter, tested positive for the HIV virus, and shortly before Christmas 1994, she died of AIDS-related cancer. The final three chapters of *Family Life* not only describe her family's response to her condition, but also contain her own account of diagnosis, illness and the onset of death . . . Eloquent, humane and all too brief, hers is a highly intelligent and remarkably sentiment-free record of illness. And when Elisabeth Luard reprises the story – recipes suspended and jaunty tone muted – her faith in the good in life, the power of the family to absorb grief and to renew itself, is clearly shaken, but not destroyed. The end of the book sees her planning a family picnic to commemorate Fran's life; one cannot help feeling it will consist of more than sandwiches beside a dusty road' *The Times Literary Supplement*

'Lovely book . . . with its moving and gripping and sad ending' *Valerie Grove*

'A captivating account of the peripatetic upbringing of her four children . . . Tragedy strikes when her elder daughter dies in her twenties, but Luard still manages to close this most unusual book with a positive affirmation of life' *Woman and Home*

'For two-thirds of this book, the tone is doughty, engaging . . . Then, with juddering suddenness, it swoops into darkness. Francesca, the first-born daughter . . . becomes infected with HIV while still in her twenties. Her mother gives over a chapter of the book to Francesca's first-person account of her diagnosis and illness. Francesca's voice is crisp, straight-forward, without sentiment and unbearably moving' Penny Perrick, *Sunday Times*

Family Life

Birth, Death and the Whole Damn Thing

ELISABETH LUARD

CORGI BOOKS

FAMILY LIFE
A CORGI BOOK : 0 552 14544 0

Originally published in Great Britain by Bantam Press,
a division of Transworld Publishers Ltd

PRINTING HISTORY
Bantam Press edition published 1996
Corgi edition published 1996

5 7 9 10 8 6

The poem 'O Come All Ye Faithful' reproduced on p.303 is from *Selected Poems*
by Christopher Logue. Reproduced by kind permission of Faber & Faber Ltd.

Set in Bembo by Hewer Text Composition Services

Corgi Books are published by Transworld Publishers Ltd,
61–63 Uxbridge Road, London W5 5SA,
in Australia by Transworld Publishers,
c/o Random House Australia Pty Ltd,
20 Alfred Street, Milsons Point, NSW 2061,
in New Zealand by Transworld Publishers,
c/o Random House New Zealand,
18 Poland Road, Glenfield, Auckland
and in South Africa by Transworld Publishers,
c/o Random House (Pty) Ltd,
Endulini, 5a Jubilee Road, Parktown 2193.

Reproduced, printed and bound in Great Britain by
Cox & Wyman Ltd, Reading, Berkshire.

For my beloved family – my husband Nicholas and my children, Caspar, Francesca, Poppy and Honey.

Acknowledgements

ON BEHALF OF MY FAMILY, I ACKNOWLEDGE A GREAT DEBT OF gratitude to all those Good Samaritans who helped us or tolerated us or taught us on our somewhat eccentric way – and among our relations, most especially my mother-in-law, Susan Spencer; among good companions, most particularly Venetia Parkes. On behalf of myself, to Ursula Mackenzie and Broo Doherty, my editors at Bantam Press, for their sensitivity and encouragement throughout what sometimes seemed an impossible task, and to my agent Abner Stein for his unfailing kindness and affection. On behalf of my daughter Francesca, to her beloved friends for the happiness, support and love they brought her – and continue to bring to her family.

Contents

CONTENTS

Prologue

I SHALL DECLARE MY HAND IMMEDIATELY: I HOLD NO TRUMPS IN THE card-game of life. This book is no self-improvement manual. It is simply one woman's account of how one family, shaped by time, place and social habit, coped with the business of reaching adulthood.

We were an unusual family only in that, as a writer, my husband Nicholas – and later, I, too – had the ability to earn a living in ways which did not tie us down geographically. We could choose where we lived and we moved our household often. In all other respects we were ordinary. Neither rich nor poor by the standards of western society in the second half of the twentieth century, and obliged, like most of humanity, to make our choices and cut our coat according to the cloth.

We grew up together, my children and I. In this we share the experience of every other family in every other corner of the world. It is, after all, an ordinary business, done by ordinary people. We fall into it so easily – by a trick of biology, or nature, or whatever heavenly godfather – or cosmic sadist, as C.S. Lewis had it in a rare moment of despair – dictates the continuation of our species. No special training is needed. Joy and sorrow, birth and death, none of us can avoid these things. If there is a mystery about successful family life, it is of our own making. We learn all the lessons we need in our own childhood: we have only to remember. Here are no secret journeyings through unchartered territory, only the experience common to us all.

If a family is welded together by the ties of blood, nature's most powerful guarantee of common cause, then each individual in this small unit – just as each nation in an alliance of nations – has to find his or her own balance. There are no rules to ensure success, except perhaps common sense. Maybe it starts with good housekeeping – women's business. It was no accident that the practical Isabella pawned the family jewels to send Christopher Columbus across the ocean. Who but a woman would sell her treasure to replace the spices in her store cupboard? Who but a man would risk his life on so foolhardy an adventure?

Humanity forms clans, it finds security in flocks. Few of us would choose the life of the lone hunter, the solitary gatherer, still less when we have children. We depend on co-operation, whether as a primitive hunting tribe, as a nation, a community, a family. We do not spring from random seed scattered on cold earth, but select our partners, make our shelter, feed our young. Nature dictates this is no short-term arrangement. We nurture our children until they are able to fend for themselves, we care for them all our lives, we hope for their care in return when we grow old. Our responsibilities do not end with a single generation: we recognize our ancestors, we expect to be ancestors ourselves.

I am no great believer in the intervention of the State in the family. I believe that family life is of its nature a matter for amateurs – those who work for love rather than duty or profit. Bringing up a family can never be a profession. It is a labour of love, a twenty-four-hour, seven-day-a-week vocation. Our children are our stake in the future, now and always. Whether they till the soil, work in the market-place or hope by their endeavours to change the world, their labours will pay for us in our old age – emotionally as well as financially.

If I learnt anything from those years when my children were growing to maturity, it was to trust not intellect but instinct, that delicate blend of nature and nurture. Even as a very young woman and new mother, I knew that if I loved my children, I would do right by them. I knew, too, that small things count – delivering what is promised, keeping faith. I understood that reliability is the most important factor in a child's security. Food, shelter, basic education are essential, but once these have been provided, a contented mother makes a contented child. Many a child has paid too high a price for the price its parents chose to pay, in money or in kind.

So I learnt not to ask too much of any of us, not to push myself or my children too hard, to look for the good in all things as well as searching out the bad. It's hard to know where to draw the line. Young children will always try the limits of parental tolerance – they need to test the length of the rope. In my time I tugged it along with the best.

If I admit to one single guiding principle in bringing up my family, it was to follow my own star. I had done so myself since I was a small child, half-orphaned by my father's death in the Second World War. I was sure of one thing only, that if the path chosen seemed right for me, it must be right for those whose welfare was as central to my happiness as my own. Loving my children came easily to me; I remembered myself as a child, I saw myself in them. With fortune and a fair following wind, families are best equipped to teach each other how to love – there's so much to give, so much to receive. The heart is not a repository for sentiment, but a muscle which needs regular exercise.

There were six of us when I first began this account of family life. Now we are no longer six but five. Just before Christmas a year ago Francesca, the second of my four children and the eldest of my three daughters, died at the age of twenty-nine.

Fran, as we called her, was the peacemaker of the family, the calm eye of any storm – although she could whip up a fine old whirlwind herself. Contentious, demanding, seeking perfection, strong in her certainties, yet kind to those weaker than herself, generous to anyone in trouble, patient with those she loved, wise and gentle when such virtues were needed. If the final chapter is devoted to her, it is not to commemorate her dying, but to celebrate her living. In life, she was as bright and as beautiful as any of us can hope to be. In death, her absence from our lives is the hardest thing we have ever had to bear. Yet there was great joy in her last days, illumination in the light shed by her brief star, solace in the strength she drew from those she loved, comfort in her choice of companions on that final pilgrimage.

I continue to learn from my children, and hope they continue to learn from me. As a daughter of the Sixties – the decade when everything was called into question – I have always had faith in the power of all of us to change. A one-time part-time flower child, I find myself perfectly in sympathy with my children's preoccupations in the Nineties. They, too, need to change the world.

Meanwhile, I have discovered no panacea for the troubles which afflict humanity – unless it is that a meal shared round the kitchen table serves both as a celebration of the good times and a comfort in times of trouble. At the end of it all, I can only echo the words of that wise old clergyman, the Reverend Sydney Smith (now there was a man for good advice):

'Take a short view of life. Look no further than dinner or tea.'

CHAPTER ONE

Starting Out

'It takes two to speak the truth. One to speak and one to hear.'

Henry David Thoreau (1817–1862)*

BY ALL ACCOUNTS, THE FIFTIES WERE DULL YEARS.

I wouldn't know. I reached my majority in the first year of a glamorous new decade. The Sixties were the bright dawn of youth, and we, the new generation, had caught the scent of freedom on the breeze. We were the war babies, the children who grew up in the aftermath of battle. Our memories of childhood were dislocated, our dreams disturbed by the scream of sirens, the whine of bombs, the smell of air-raid shelters, the incomprehensibility of loss. Many of us were left fatherless; we were a whole generation thrown into

*From *A Week on the Concord and Merrimark Rivers.*

5

confusion. But our surviving parents were surely as bewildered, as amputated, as we were.

For want of that lost generation, old men still clung to power. Fewer women sat in the Houses of Parliament than in Lady Astor's day. In spite of the travails of the suffragettes, in spite of wartime land-girls and munition-factory workers, few young women thought of a serious career.

Our mothers advised us to marry well – but, above all, to marry early. Young women like myself, provided with a modest dowry and the kind of education guaranteed to keep us in our places, were expected to choose a husband from among our own class. It was our daughterly duty to relieve our parents of the obligation to provide for our welfare. Those who didn't deliver were for ever doomed to barren spinsterhood, long-term dependents destined – under the iron rules of primogeniture – for the scrap heap.

We, the new generation, weren't so easily deceived. Our hero was Jack Kennedy, our liberation, the contraceptive pill. As a daughter of my time, I had no intention of following the old rules. I was no shrinking demoiselle. If sexual intercourse began too late for Philip Larkin, it was not too late for me. I had made no plans for marriage, I had no intention of falling in love. I booked myself into art school – the City and Guilds in Kennington – where I spent the mornings. In the afternoon I needed to work for a living. I knew Christopher Booker, the first editor of *Private Eye*, and the infant magazine needed help in the office – nothing creative, of course, but it passed the day and brought home a modest slice of bacon: in my case five pounds a week.

Soon after its launch, the magazine hit a bumpy patch. We needed refinancing and we went to the only source of funds who might be able to help us – Nicholas Luard, proprietor with Peter Cook of the Establishment Club, whose satirical cabaret drew blood from the same targets as we fired at in the pages of the magazine. Nicholas strolled into our garret of an office one day and that was it – love at first sight.

All I can say in my defence was that I was only nineteen and he was without doubt the most beautiful young man I had ever seen: tawny eyes, broad shoulders, a boxer's biceps, narrow hips. He was a former Guards and Special Forces officer with a first from Cambridge and a fellowship to an American Ivy League university (as if I cared). I made no secret of my intentions.

'I think I'll just warn you now,' I announced on our first date, 'that we'll be better off going through life with each other than without each other. And now I shan't mention the matter again.'

How can I explain it? I can't, of course, but like a lemming plunging over a cliff, I couldn't help myself. I was smitten – star-blasted, moon-crazy, just like in the fairy stories. Other ladies, certainly more sophisticated than me, admired him too. Wiser than my nineteen years, I retreated to Mexico where my stepfather had been posted to the embassy. I thought it politic to give my beloved time and space to miss me.

Three months later, bearing gifts, he followed.

Nicholas maintains it was the altitude which prompted him to propose marriage. I say it was the tequila which inspired me to accept. And then again it might have been the papaya with lime, or the Mexican *seviche*, pickled fish with chilli and coriander, or even the tacos stuffed with iguana and chocolate.

Whatever it was, we made public our intention to be wed. To my surprise, my mother pursed her lips in disapproval. No doubt, looking back on that time now, Nicholas was hardly what she had in mind for her eldest daughter: a young man running a subversive theatre club with the notorious Lenny Bruce topping the bill, who was also the owner of a satirical magazine actively engaged in prodding the soft underbelly of all that she held dear. Back in Britain, my future mother-in-law, more pragmatic in such matters, greeted our news with relief. At least I offered her the prospect of some much longed-for grandchildren.

We had little idea of what married life might bring, my beloved and I. We had been together alone only briefly – a stolen week spent on a Greek island, counting the world well lost, but fearful our friends, families or workmates might discover and assume a serious romance. The blue sea and the warm sands claimed our days. For the rest of the time, we did all those things which people do when they are together and in love.

Twisting the arm of a cousin who was a canon at Westminster Abbey, I secured St Margaret's, Westminster, for the wedding. A week before it was due to happen, I discovered we had failed to have the bans called. No need to worry, the deacon soothed. For twenty-five guineas – five weeks of my wages – the Archbishop of Canterbury would be happy to issue an indulgence, a special dispensation.

Mexican Seviche

You can make this raw-pickled fish salad with any firm-fleshed fish, as long as it's perfectly fresh. Lime-juice is important to the flavour.

―――――――――――― SERVES 6 AS A STARTER ――――――――――――

1 lb/500 g filleted white
fish, diced
Juice of 4 limes
2 ripe tomatoes, skinned and
diced
1 mild onion, skinned and
finely chopped

1 green chilli, de-seeded and
chopped finely
1 small bunch fresh coriander,
chopped finely
Salt
Olive oil

1. Combine all the ingredients and set them in the fridge in a covered bowl for a few hours, or in a cool larder to marinate overnight. The fish will turn opaque – effectively cooking it. Stir it every now and again.
2. If it's very liquid, drain it a little. Finish with a trickle of olive oil. Serve with tortilla chips and lettuce leaves for scooping.

Turn in your grave, Martin Luther, I thought grimly, but I paid without argument.

The February day dawned bright and sunny, in memory at least. We arrived at the altar simultaneously, I in hand-stitched white organdie from Norman Hartnell, Nicholas handsome in a morning coat — rented, of course; his youthful radicalism didn't allow him to own one. That was his chief concession to formality. He drew the line at printed invitations. Instead word of mouth had to do, and the church played host not only to our highly respectable families and somewhat less respectable friends, but also to a motley crew of low-lifers from Soho — the regulars from Muriel Belcher's Colony Club, the French Pub, Wheeler's in Old Compton Street, all of whom could scent the free champagne to follow at half a mile's radius on a foggy London night.

'I do,' I said, as no-one had raised just cause or impediment to our union.

'Speak up,' said Nicholas and we walked back down the aisle.

The press were out in force at the church door. Satire was hot news, *That Was the Week That Was* was the latest sensation on television, *Private Eye* was already breaking the Profumo scandal, and our marriage was a major story. Nicholas was quite used to such attentions, but I'd never in my life seen such a barrage of flash bulbs. Good heavens — my side of the church sucked its collective teeth if I rated so much as a decorous portrait in *Tatler*.

My husband was made of sterner stuff. 'I don't like you in hats,' said Nicholas, removing the bridal veil.

The photographers were explosively appreciative. The *Evening Standard* gave us the front page, briefly consigning the Duchess of Argyll's scandalous divorce to page two. 'King of Satire Weds Red-headed Heiress,' they splashed. Although it must have read well, regrettably it was a little short on fact. Nicholas had certainly earned his non-conformist spurs, and I was indeed the great-granddaughter of a considerable self-made fortune, but most of it had long since gone. My delightful grandfather had seen to that at the gaming tables in Monte Carlo.

I wasn't much of an heiress and I wasn't even red-headed.

Abandoning the rented Rolls, we made our way to the reception at Claridge's in a rapidly hailed taxi with the press in hot pursuit. Dizzy with clamour and champagne, I remember little of that afternoon, only random images: Richard Ingrams and Willie Rushton, heads together, plotting insurrection or perhaps just *Private Eye*'s next cover; French-Pub veterans Frank Norman and Jeffrey Bernard negotiating with the barman for the remainder of the drink; the bridal bouquet caught by Kim Waterfield, otherwise known as Dandy Kim, fresh from incarceration in a French jail for reasons I shall not explore since I value his friendship still; a gorgeous young actress with a baby whose paternity, as the *Daily Mirror* disclosed the following day, she coyly ascribed to the bridegroom.

In other words, a bit of a curate's egg. The egg wasn't made more palatable for my mother by the arrival during the toasts of an immense Moroccan, naked apart from a slave's loincloth, bearing a silver samurai sword – a gift from one of Nicholas's noble but absent friends.

My grandmother – she indeed had been an heiress – gave us an open-ended honeymoon at the Paris Ritz as a wedding present. Before we left London, we had heard distant rumblings that Randolph Churchill, the belligerent son of Sir Winston, was infuriated by a *Private Eye* article suggesting his father, the old warlord and national icon, hadn't been as saintly in his political youth as his biographers portrayed him.

Three days after we reached Paris, a panic-struck telegram arrived from *Private Eye*. The magazine had finally drawn blood. Randolph Churchill had issued writs for libel. He'd briefed all the country's top libel barristers, and the magazine wanted Nicholas to come back to take charge of its defence. The telegram didn't come a moment too soon.

If honeymoons were programmed into fruit machines, they'd come up lemons. The aftermath of a wedding isn't the proper time to gamble on the happiness of the two leading players by leaving them alone together. The odds are against from the start. The whole enterprise begins with a' roaring hangover, and a champagne hangover is the worst of all. Both parties have already endured the strain of unaccustomed social intercourse with family members only glimpsed at weddings and funerals. And then, anyone in their right mind is well aware that when the honeymoon is over, serious married life begins. That shadow lies over every honeymoon.

By the end of our three days we had done it all. We had bickered gently all round the Louvre. We had quarrelled vigorously at the Folies Bergère. We had even retired hopefully to our first-floor suite, but the expectations engendered by its satin upholstery and lace-edged sheetings served more as reproach than encouragement. Three days, in a nutshell, is probably two too many.

Nicholas thankfully returned to face the music of Randolph Churchill's writs – and I to set up house in his bachelor flat in Hyde Park Square. Here, new surprises awaited my innocence. Wifedom, I had been taught at nanny's knee, was the summit of female achievement – a chance to escape from the confines of home and parents. However, any female who had already laid claim to the privileges of the free and single was in for a rude awakening when she became a wife.

We women had had the vote for forty years. Sylvia Pankhurst hadn't chained herself to the railings in vain. We had minds of our own, and we were at least considering how to use them. We could, in theory, choose the size of our families and when to give birth. Nevertheless the machinery for the ultimate expression of physical affection is custom-made for procreation. Given half a chance it does the job with admirable thoroughness. As with sex, so with babies – it happens if you do nothing to stop it. At least I was better informed than my mother, who once told me that she confidently expected her first-born to make his entrance through her navel.

It sort of crept up on me, that first pregnancy, and in no time at all I was wishing it might creep away again. In my defence, I might say that I fell pregnant with remarkable ease. As my grandmother put it, the women of our family had only to hang a pair of trousers over the end of the bed, and that was all that was needed.

Perhaps I wasn't really in the mood for it. At just-turned twenty-one, I had only lately lost my schoolgirl puppy-fat. No Twiggy, mind you, but let's say I could cut a dash in a miniskirt with the best, particularly with my favourite Charles Jourdan thigh-high scarlet leather boots. In short, with my ironed-flat curls and my Vidal Sassoon bob, I was the very picture of the fashionable King's Road miss.

My rapidly expanding waistline put a swift end to all that. All too soon I was the shape of things to come. I gave up the unequal struggle immediately, wore long skirts, hid my hair under hats the size of lampshades, and sported a neckline which displayed my bosom, my only asset in which I could justifiably take pride.

A nightclub may not be the ideal place in which to nurture a foetus, but with a husband in the business, where else could I find myself of an evening? At the Establishment Club, Lenny Bruce had been replaced by Barry Humphries, hell-bent on introducing a bemused audience to his new creation, Dame Edna Everage. Upstairs in the bar, the playwright Michael Hastings had given Gerald Scarfe his first one-man show, dominated by a huge lampoon of Harold Macmillan. In the basement, Dudley Moore was banging the piano with the encouragement of Trog cartoonist George Melly. Upstairs again, Annie Ross was entertaining the equivalent of Princess Diana's county set with Christopher Logue's subversive lyrics set to music by Stanley Myers.

We took our rest and recreation after the show at the newly opened Annabel's in Berkeley Square. The wheel was already turning: the Establishment Club, hotbed of anarchy, had a recipro- cal admission arrangement with Mark Birley, purveyor of high-class entertainment to those very people most at risk. Here we all hung out with unsuitable company – Henry Miller's publisher Maurice Girodias, Alex Trocchi, Bill Burroughs.

To my delight I discovered there was no need to be a wallflower. Pregnant ladies have their charm, and I was whirled round the dance floor by admirers who had never given me a second glance before – the painter, Lucian Freud, was my favourite. Naturally I was grateful both for the attention and the exercise, but the memory still makes me a little uneasy. If dancing is indeed the vertical expression of a horizontal desire, biologically it makes no sense. Something, perhaps, to do with stable doors and bolted horses.

To those who didn't live there, London was the only place to be. Never mind that the Kray brothers ran the East End, that slum- landlord Peter Rachman gathered his rents with slavering Alsatians, and that the police felt free to plant bricks in the pockets of those they suspected of wrongdoing. *Time* magazine had hailed the birth of the swinging city, and everyone crowded in. The hub of the action was to be found somewhere between Soho, London's red- light district, and the flourishing new boutiques down the King's Road.

To those of us who lived there it was still a small town: everyone knew everyone else. You bumped into Larry Olivier and John

Osborne in the Royal Court's bar. No-one had yet become too famous to speak to anyone else. When Nicholas and his partner, Peter Cook, organized a concert for Amnesty International at the Albert Hall, they had a word with the Beatles. As bill-toppers, George Harrison recommended a new bunch of bad boys, the Rolling Stones. Peter's then-wife Wendy and I – the one as pregnant as the other – took one look at Mick Jagger and volunteered to throw a party afterwards, which we did in a huge borrowed King's Road studio. Paul McCartney brought his guitar. John Lennon spun a record by a new singer called Cat Stevens. A group called Pink Floyd arrived uninvited and offered to play. Sex and drugs were for others, but at least I could still rock 'n' roll.

The food was possibly a little exotic for the guests, brought up in the austerity of the postwar years. Wendy and I cooked huge cauldrons of rabbit stew – both of us had just discovered Elizabeth David – and I think we rather overdid the Mediterranean seasonings. Half the denizens of Chelsea were belching garlic and picking spikes of rosemary out of their gums for weeks.

At least it had a rare and unfamiliar flavour. So did that unforgettable moment in the early Sixties when our son, Caspar, was born.

Anyone who hasn't travelled the rocky path to motherhood can have no idea of how quickly one thing follows another. From that first moment when realization dawns that the little flutter in the midriff can no longer be ascribed to an Indian take-away, to the final weeks when there is absolutely no doubt that a pair of mating elephants has taken up permanent residence in the oesophagus, it's one long battle. But then, no-one in their right mind really wants to hear about varicose veins, belly buttons which pop out like a chorus girl's nipples, or that peculiar sense of loss when eye contact can no longer be made with the toes.

Of course there *were* times when, metaphorically speaking, it was all hearts-and-flowers and pink bunny rabbits in the undergrowth; times when it *was* turn left by the hawthorn tree, over the stile, and you'll find yourself in a field of buttercups. There were even times when there was a certain togetherness in the agitation which seizes the most placid of foetuses when its carrier climbs into a nice warm bath. A few – but not many.

Rabbit with Rosemary

For a party, bump up the quantities to match, and serve with plenty of bread for people to mop their fingers. If anyone chokes on a rabbit bone, thump them hard on the back. Live dangerously.

─────── SERVES 3–4 AS A MAIN DISH ───────

2 lb/1 kg rabbit joints
4 tablespoons olive oil
4 garlic cloves, skinned and crushed
1 onion, peeled and chopped
3 oz/75 g salt-dried ham or lean bacon, diced

2 red sweet peppers, de-seeded and sliced lengthways
1 lb/500 g tomatoes, scalded, skinned and well chopped
2–3 rosemary twigs
Salt and pepper

1. Chop the joints into bite-sized pieces – I do this with a heavy knife tapped through the bone by a sharp blow with a hammer.

2. Heat the oil in a deep casserole. Put in the rabbit pieces, garlic and onion and cook them gently until they take up a little colour. Push to one side and add the ham or bacon and the peppers. Fry them for a few moments. Put in the tomatoes and boil it all up. Add the rosemary twigs.

3. Turn down the heat, lid tightly and simmer for 30–40 minutes, until the meat is tender and the sauce well-reduced – remove the lid at the end of the cooking time and allow the mixture to bubble up and concentrate the juices.
Taste and add salt and pepper.

4. Serve with forks and plenty of bread for the juices.

The most curious effect of pregnancy is not in the body but the mind. '*Mens sana in corpore sano* – my arse', as Eliza Doolittle said with such memorable emphasis in *My Fair Lady*. Raging hormones turn the most intelligent, sensitive of females (such as myself) into a soft-brained, self-obsessed airhead, concerned not with the welfare of family and friends, but with the daily management of her own recalcitrant digestive system. Everything else goes to the wall.

Heartache is replaced by heartburn. The details of the long dark night of the small intestine, the agonies caused by the imperfect absorption of anchovy-and-peanut-butter sandwiches, are of no interest except to the sufferer.

I was well aware that my condition was somewhat out of step with the times. Many of the women whose intellect I admired considered the whole business of breeding a little uncerebral, not quite the stuff of New Woman whose role model was Germaine Greer – the queen of the blue stockings.

As a wife, I was relegated to second-class citizenship – not by my beloved, I hasten to add. He was far too sensible for that. And yet small inconveniences soon reminded me that whatever arrangement had been reached between the two of us as consenting adults, society saw otherwise. I needed a new passport to travel in my married name. Secure in the possession of official proof of my changed status, I took myself and my completed application forms to the appropriate queue in Petty France. Too late did I notice the uncompleted box at the end: 'Husband's signature is required'.

The absurdity, the injustice of it rankles still.

'Presumably,' I asked sweetly when it came to my turn, 'There is a space on my husband's form for his wife's signature?'

The supervisor, on hand to deal with troublemakers, regretted my situation – but boxes must be completed according to the rules. I might be as miss or madam as I chose but without my husband's signature there could be no passport. Or, as he put it, we might have every Tom, Dick and Harry wanting one, mightn't we? I forbore to point out that none of the gentlemen he'd named was likely to have a husband to sign for them. Instead, I passionately put to him my pennyworth to his pound: surely he wouldn't have me bring Her Majesty's good name into disrepute by travelling, swollen with child, on a spinster-lady's passport?

He gave me a frosty smile but declined to answer. Her Majesty's good name was, it seemed, a matter of supreme indifference to Petty France. Rules were rules.

I returned to the waiting-room benches, sat down, and thought.

Whatever their protests, our elders were most certainly not our betters. The Profumo affair had confirmed what we already knew – our politicians were as ready to drop their trousers as the rest of us, and were perfectly willing to lie about it in the highest chambers in the land. Thirty years after its first publication, a senior QC was that very day arguing that the naughty bits in *Lady Chatterley's Lover* made the book a hazard to the nation's wives and servants. It was hardly surprising that wives couldn't travel abroad without the permission of their owners, as we were clearly supposed to view our husbands.

There was a simple solution. I went round the corner to the cafeteria, and scrawled my husband's signature as best I could in the space provided. When I returned to the passport counter, the clerk eyed me with deep suspicion. He didn't believe for an instant I'd found my spouse wandering on the street outside, but he knew the times were changing and he gave me my passport all the same.

In these liberated days of equal rights, my daughters find such stories no more than tall tales from the dark ages. Their disbelieving laughter, the best proof of progress, warms my heart.

CHAPTER TWO

Baby talk

'Go to the shower-bath with a low temperature. Attend to the
effects coffee and tea have on you. Make no secret of low spirits
but talk of them freely.'

The Reverend Sydney Smith*

FIRST BABIES ARE ALWAYS LATE, THE USUAL EXPLANATION BEING
that daft new mothers have no idea when they conceived.

Mine was no exception. It was late autumn, and I was already way
over time. I spent my mornings catching falling leaves in Hyde Park
in the hope of a jump-start. Seven days of trying to crank up the
engine makes a person give up in despair. And then, just when I was
consoling myself with the notion I was destined to make history as

*Advice to a young lady in low spirits (c. 1830).

17

the first woman to endure a twelve-month gestation, my waters burst. Seconds out, round one. This is not something for which you can cancel the tickets.

In the early Sixties, the middle-class urban mother gave birth in a nursing home. Mine was run by Irish nuns. There were forms to be filled, name-tags to be affixed – as if, like mislaid luggage on a flight to Rio, you might find yourself delivered to Hong Kong.

As we all know who've been through it, the modern way of birthing is hideously undignified and ferociously uncomfortable. It may be safer to have a baby in sterile surroundings under medical supervision, and no doubt it's more convenient for the professionals, but in the name of all us amateurs, I would truly like to know when the business lost its humanity. What did we do to deserve all those steel forceps and iron stirrups?

There are a lot of people involved in the labour business. All have clearly defined duties. All except one, the expectant father. Not to put too fine a point on it, he's nine-month-old history. As for the birth, he can take it or leave it.

In medieval times, fathers were encouraged to go into sympathetic labour, surrounded by attentive ladies spooning in chicken soup. There's a great deal to be said for the arrangement: at one stroke, you solve the catering problems, keep Dad out of the path of the boiling kettles, and nail him firmly to his future obligations. After all that, it would be a brave man who asked for a blood test to prove paternity.

Nicholas was accorded no such privileges. Once his wife was safely delivered into the hands of the experts, he was a man without a role, a cherry without a cake. Unsettled by the gynaecological small print, like many a father before him, he took to drink. For the next few hours, he wandered in and out of the delivery room with a hip-flask sticking out of his pocket. Occasionally he inspected the non-business end of the problem.

'Feeling better now?' enquired the sole begetter of my predicament.

You must be joking. In between well-timed womb-clenchings, I told him quite graphically where to put it. I was not feeling at my best. My vocabulary would have done credit to a gang of East End brickies.

'My, my – she's a lovely girl. But the language!' said the Irish nun as she clamped on the gas-and-air.

By now panic had moved in. I delivered myself of something along the lines of an expletive-deleted, 'Can I go home now, please? Promise I'll try again next year.'

Nine months too late. We were locked together, my unborn and I, trapped at the wrong end of a cul-de-sac, struggling blindly towards a non-existent street light.

My personal medical man – snake-oil merchant, purveyor of powder-of-sympathy – checked in briefly at the cocktail hour. His dinner-jacket proclaimed a long and bibulous evening.

'Are we ready to push?'

Funny how medical men use the plural. We all know perfectly well there's only one of us directly involved.

We struggled on through the long evening, our rhythms ragged, our vocabulary hideous, our pelvis unbending. There is no orifice in the female anatomy adequate to the task, at least not without a hacksaw.

And then, oh joy, the final heave.

A cry, a surprisingly robust wail – a boy, a girl, who cared? If they'd told me I'd given birth to a baby camel I wouldn't have been in the least surprised. The view from my end of the affair did not encourage further speculation. Even through the rose-tinted glasses of brand-new motherhood, the fruit of my labours was a terrible mess: a bundle of aquatic debris which looked nothing so much as a small hairy dolphin roped to a plastic bag. As for the accompanying debris, *that* was straight out of a Hitchcock movie, or perhaps the aftermath of a prizefight in a strawberry-jam factory – and to hell with the Queensberry Rules.

What I had in mind was something altogether more *finished* – say, a handful of swaddling clothes, the odd manger, maybe a shooting star.

By now, the powder-of-sympathy squad was out in force, clipping, stitching and making with the swabs. Nicholas, patrolling the business end, accepted congratulations, the champion taking a turn of the ring. Seven and a half pounds of baby boy tipped the scales. Nicholas checked extremities. Ticking off lists seems to come naturally to men – Army training, I expect. Ten toes, ten fingers, all the bits between. Cigars all round.

And then, dear heaven, someone thought to lay my infant in my arms. I cannot readily explain the romance of that first encounter with my sweet son. How to define the joy? A newborn baby does not tug at every heartstring. There are many who are impervious to the softness of cheek, the perfection of fingernails, the single tear which dews an eyelash. Not me.

He was simply the loveliest creature I had ever seen. Tall now, broad-shouldered, tousle-haired, keen-eyed and smiling, he remains so today. I see him and my heart turns over.

Not that it was all rosebuds and pink cherubs then; our interests did not immediately coincide. What Caspar Edward Timothy had in mind was a little light refreshment. He was always one to know what he wanted. I, on the other hand, was more than ready for a little rest and recreation.

The Irish nuns were in no doubt about who took priority. A large pink hand, rough as a navvy's, reached out and grabbed a handful of breast.

'Come along dear. All our mothers do.'

With the greatest respect to the Virgin Mary, experience counts. This thing is easier said than done. I had never seen anyone breast-feed a child before, but I learnt fast. As a teacher, nature beats nurture into a cocked hat. It's no accident that the sprat-sized, newborn kangaroo can find its way through its mother's fur into the pouch to clamp itself onto her nipple. An infant pointed in the right general direction has an extraordinary talent for sorting itself out.

Breast-feeding, for those who need to know such things, is thoroughly convenient. There's no shopping involved. The container doesn't need sterilizing and can't be left behind in the station waiting-room. In short, here is a cheap well-balanced meal in a portable, planet-friendly, self-warming storage container.

There's an unexpected bonus to breast-feeding. To put it delicately, the pump action seems to pull the relevant muscles for reproduction back into place – you can feel them tightening up. Happily for my relationship with my children, I found breast-feeding sexy. Indeed, for a month or two after the business of childbirth any alternative activity would have been too painful to contemplate.

Practically speaking, the new mother does not need a husband, she needs a mother. Mine was a no-nonsense monthly nurse provided by my mother-in-law. We settled into Nicholas's bache-lor flat, all four of us together, the baby in a wooden cradle in the living-room, the monthly in the back bedroom, lately vacated by the lodger, the famously unwell Jeffrey Bernard. The monthly nurse was not nearly so entertaining as the lodger, but at least she didn't lust noisily after Fenella Fielding, the occupant of the next flat up, or return home in the small hours without any small change for the taxi in the company of a lady unlikely to be anyone's wife.

The monthly nurse, unlike Jeff, reminded me of my own old nanny. And like my old nanny, at the end of her allotted time, she took steps to transfer responsibility. By the time she left for new pastures, I knew how to bathe and handle my infant.

With the monthly nurse's departure, I was flying on my own. When the bell tolls in the nuclear family, it tolls for thee. Nicholas declared himself happy to be a father, but he was hardly the stuff of surrogate motherhood. Young men had not, in these years before equality of opportunity, grasped the nettle of shared parenting. Having established that nappy-changing was not his area of expertise, he went about the business of the hunter-gatherer, or bringing home the bacon, or whatever young men of his generation called what they did. Mostly he did it elsewhere.

He was willing, within reason, to discuss with near-strangers which of his first-born's physical characteristics could be attributed to him. The nose? The chin? Colour of hair? Eyes? Perhaps, and then again – and then again perhaps not. Content to let the hand that rocked the cradle rule the world, Nicholas followed the traditions of his forefathers and left the day-to-day disposables to the distaff.

I had no such option. Not for me the newly claimed privileges of the sisterhood. Domestic affairs were my domain – assisted, in the periods when I was tumbling in and out of hospital during the cycle of my pregnancies, by a series of scatty mother's helps and young nannies. When the going gets tough, the tough get going. There's never been a more ridiculous question than, 'Do you work, or are you just a mother?'

Neither the monthly nurse nor the kindly Irish sisters had told me that the dependent offspring and I would be locked into a shared digestive tract. Or that if I ate anything which disagreed with the infant with whom I was meal-sharing, it would come out in spots – lumpy ones with little blobs on – all over. Except, of course, those bits hidden from public view by the nappy. It's no joke wheeling out a pramful of the Great Plague.

Ah well. Our evening gin and tonic had to go. So did our spinach. So did our beetroot and our breakfast of cheese on toast. Our Guinness and our Chinese take-aways seemed to go down both of us a treat. Fermented malt and monosodium glutamate are not generally considered a suitable diet for the nursing mother, but they suited us just fine – along with delicious Vanilla Flan and Bread-and-Milk Pudding. There seemed to be no rules: trial and error was the only way.

Public opinion is not on the side of maternal instinct. Most citizens of the big city disapprove of mothers suckling their babies, however discreetly, anywhere but behind closed doors at home. The odds are they've never seen such a thing before, unless as a delicately denatured image of the Virgin and Child tastefully framed in gold leaf. I often wondered whether anyone would have made the connection if I had chosen the National Gallery as a mother-and-baby room, and settled down to suckle my own infant beneath, let's say, the painted maternal attentions of one of Leonardo's Madonnas.

Public disapproval is the universal lot of the public suckler. Disapproval makes a mother anxious. Anxiety in the suckler leads to indigestion in the suckled. There is nothing babies dislike more than indigestion. Indigestion keeps both of you up all night, and after the third night on guard duty, I would find myself sorely tempted to pick the offender up and give it to someone else – anyone else, Attila the Hun for preference. This, I dimly grasped, was the moment to lay the infant back in its cot and retire as far away as possible. Out of earshot is out of mind.

Dr Spock thought otherwise, but then he would, wouldn't he? He's a man, after all. His was the doctrine of baby-knows-best and feeding on demand. Mine was the doctrine of cottonwool-in-the-ears and unplug the baby alarm. This reaction is not hormonal. It is normal.

I preferred to feed my infant last thing at night, after midnight if possible. Then I could sleep till morning, maybe to half past seven or eight. Between us we came to a mutual arrangement: my instincts told me that if I did those things which suited me best, I would be content, my digestion suitably tranquil, and my offspring would reap the rewards, albeit second-hand. At seven months, we called it a day.

It was not so much the arrival of a pair of razor-sharp teeth (note for nursing mothers – a suckling infant will let go if you hold its nose), it was more my increasing reluctance to find myself playing second fiddle to a soft-boiled egg.

Vanilla Flan

All babies love this – and it's just as good for pregnant ladies and nursing mothers. It's soft and sweet and nourishing.

———————————————— SERVES 4–6 ————————————————

1 pint/600 ml milk
2 tablespoons honey
A short length of vanilla pod

1 whole egg
5 egg yolks

———————————————— FOR THE CARAMEL ————————————————

3 tablespoons sugar

1 tablespoon water

1. Put the milk and honey to infuse with the vanilla on the side of the stove.
2. Make the caramel by melting the sugar and water together in a small pan and cooking it until the sugar caramelizes. Take it off the heat as soon as it turns a rich beech-leaf bronze – once the colour turns it will be black in no time. Pour the caramel into individual moulds or a small pudding bowl and roll the caramel round the sides.
3. Fish the vanilla pod out of the milk and scrape most of the sticky little black seeds from the inside of the pod back into the milk. Whisk in the eggs and pour the mixture into the individual moulds or bowl.
4. Set the filled moulds or bowl in a baking tray. Pour in enough boiling water to come halfway up the sides. Bake in a moderate oven, 325°F/140°C/mark 3, for 45–60 minutes, when the custard should be firm. If the temperature is too high, the custard bubbles and acquires watery little air holes.
5. The flan keeps well in the fridge in its container. Turn it out onto a plate when you are ready to serve. It will collapse into a soft hillock of creamy custard. The caramel provides its own sticky little sauce.

Bread-and-Milk Pudding

This is also known as Manchester Pudding and Queen of Puddings, and probably much else besides. For a more sophisticated version, whisk the egg-whites with 2 tablespoons of caster sugar, and finish the pudding with a layer of soft meringue.

──────────── SERVES 2 AND THE BABY TWICE ────────────

1 pint/600 ml milk
2 eggs
2 tablespoons sugar
4 oz/100 g finely grated fresh
breadcrumbs

1 teaspoon grated lemon zest
3–4 tablespoons damson or
blackcurrant jam (the sharper
the better)

1. Beat the milk with the eggs and sugar and stir in the breadcrumbs and lemon zest.
2. Spread the jam in the bottom of a pie dish. Pour the custard mixture over the top.
3. Bake in a moderate oven – 350°F/180°C/ mark 4 – for 25–30 minutes, until set and golden. Grown-ups can have it with thick cream. Babies like the soft eggy part.

CHAPTER THREE

More baby talk

'Compare your lot with other people's.'

The Reverend Sydney Smith★

THEY *DO* SAY IT'S JUST AN OLD WIVES' TALE THAT YOU CAN'T conceive when you have a child at the breast. I'm not so sure. As soon as I stopped breast-feeding, I was back in trouble with the trousers–over–the–bed routine: pregnant again.

This second time, there were problems. We did not yet know it but as breeding partners, Nicholas and I were unequivocally incompatible after the birth of our first child. In those days, no-one had thought to test future parents' blood groups. My blood group is rhesus negative, Nicholas's rhesus positive – with no

★Advice to a young lady in low spirits (*c.* 1830).

possibility of producing a rhesus-negative child. After the first birth, the combination of the two bloods triggers antibodies in the mother. The antibodies identify any subsequent product of the same combination as an interloper. Medical advances being swift, what was once a fatal combination has now become a minor inconvenience – but thirty years ago, we were still at the sharp end of the research into the problem.

Our eldest daughter, Francesca, was the first of our children to be affected by the incompatibility of our blood groups. For the first few days she hung onto the world by her tiny blue fingernails. She had had to be rushed from the nursing home, clasped in her father's arms, through the ice-bound darkness of a January night to the intensive care unit at Queen Charlotte's Maternity Hospital. It was four days before she was declared out of the wood, and by then I had had myself transferred to the hospital to be near her.

In the premature mothers' ward, at least we were all in the same boat, anxiously monitoring the news. We were kept permanently busy. A baby in intensive care needs mother's milk, supplied by a mechanical wet-nurse in constant need of priming. We were there to provide the necessary. An electric milking machine did a circular round of the ward. A kind of reverse tea trolley, it was not so much one lump or two, as 'Your turn next, dear.' I will leave you to imagine sizes and shapes, but it was not far removed from what's applied to Daisy of a morning in the milking shed.

Nevertheless it gave us all something else to worry about rather than what was happening to the product of nine months' hard work. I think we all laboured under the delusion that *our* babies would get *our* milk.

Beyond this minor activity, machinery took over in the baby ward. As parents, we could do nothing. Our tiny girl-child was only visible through glass: albeit, we told each other for encouragement, the most tenacious scrap of infant determination in the unit. They were anxious days for both of us, until the fragile little creature was finally released into my safe keeping. By now, I was absolutely confident. At twenty-three I was an old hand with babies. I had the catering down to a fine art – the all-in-one supper was minestrone.

One thing followed another. I fell pregnant again. This time the antibody count hit the jackpot: it soared. By a happy coincidence, the

Everyday Minestrone

Vary the vegetables as you please. Rice or cooked haricot or borlotti beans can replace the pasta. In summer, courgettes, young leeks, peas, broad beans, green beans replace the root vegetables; if so, the cooking times will be shorter, so egg noodles or vermicelli can replace the macaroni.

—————— SERVES 2 ADULTS AND 3–4 BABY MEALS ——————

3 tablespoons olive oil
1 onion, skinned and chopped
1 large carrot, scraped and diced
A few celery tops, washed and chopped
½ teaspoon dried thyme
1 sage leaf (for the digestion)
1½ pints/1 l water or good home-made stock

1 small turnip or bit of swede, peeled and diced
1 parsnip, peeled and diced
1 large potato, peeled and diced
3 oz/75 g macaroni
A couple of good handfuls of spinach or other greens, washed and shredded
Salt

1. Warm 2 tablespoons of the oil in a saucepan and gently fry the onion, carrot and celery until the vegetables soften. Sprinkle in the thyme, and the sage, add the water and the diced turnip, and bring it all to the boil. Season with salt.

2. Let it all simmer for 15 minutes.

3. Add the diced parsnip and potato and the macaroni and bring it all back to the boil. Let it simmer for another 15–20 minutes, until everything is soft.

4. Stir in the green vegetables, and bring it back to the boil. The soup should be thick – more of a stew, really.

5. Whack the baby's portion in the liquidizer and give it a good whizz. When reheating it for a second infant helping, make sure you give it a good bubble and then let it cool, rather than just warming it up. Adults can have their minestrone with freshly ground pepper, grated cheese and croûtons.

laboratory at Queen Charlotte's Maternity Hospital had been donated by my great-grandfather, the old philanthropist through whom, had it not been for my grandfather and the seductive allure of the *salles privées* at Monte Carlo, I might indeed have been an heiress.

I'm sure the old man, a tobacco baron whose fortune equipped half the hospitals in London, would have been tickled pink to know that his gifts saved the lives of at least some of his great-grandchildren.

I had to spend one out of every two weekends in hospital while the baby's blood was changed in the womb. The vehicle for transfusion was a thick-needled syringe which would have scared an elephant. I, the size of an elephant, was equally scared. You might have expected something more sophisticated – a miniaturized channel-tunnel borer or a laser beam maybe. But no. What amounted to needles on the end of a salmon-rod was what was available, and I was not complaining. The ward was full of women who were in after the fifth miscarriage, so with two in my nursery I was, as everyone frequently pointed out, the lucky one.

Not this time.

Peter Astrolabe was born and died. For six days he fought the battle, and on the seventh he slipped away. We never knew why or how, except that there was ever-present danger in what was a bold but always high-risk attempt to thwart nature. I remember little of those days and nights of the waiting and the hoping. Later, when it was all over, we gave ourselves whatever comfort we could to help us to accept what had happened. So many things could have gone wrong. There is no adequate epitaph for the death of a child, and no sense in searching for one.

The human mind can cope with anything but the loss of hope. I tried again. Each time I reappeared pregnant the word rippled round the hospital. I swear they sold tickets. This time the crunch came for me when they installed colour television monitors to track the intra-uterine transfusions.

There was much excitement among the experts. As usual I was wheeled into the operating theatre, horizontal in my tie-fastened white hospital smock, confidence boosted by a syringeful of pre-op medication. The patient was supposed to be hazy but awake. I was more breezy than hazy.

I counted the masked green-clad audience. Twenty-two pairs of eyes stared into mine. Some of them wore spectacles. Some of them had mascara'd eyelashes. One of them whose blue eyes I recognized was the surgeon. Suddenly I felt it only proper to be introduced to those with whom I was about to share periscopic views of the most intimate parts of my anatomy. Anyone who's ever been in a similar situation will understand. The patient is naked and known, the observers are gowned and anonymous. It's like being a stripper at a peep-show without even the fragile dignity of a *nom de plume*. I couldn't even pretend to be Fifi les-deux-Eglises: my name was written in bold capitals at the foot of the bed.

I sat up. 'That's enough,' I announced. 'You all know who I am. I don't know who *you* are. I refuse to co-operate until everyone takes off their masks and tells me their names and why they're here.'

Pethidine-boosted, the strong wine of truth in my veins, I was not to be denied. One by one the audience nervously stepped forward, removed their masks, and explained themselves. Eighteen second-year students and two trainee midwives made up the throng. I lay back. It was a victory, maybe only a small one, but still a victory. I felt better.

Not for long. The whole business was painful and risky, but there was no alternative. It was the only way I could have children. Soon for me those sessions became normal.

Poppy was the next to be born: a scrap of blond-haired, four-week-premature determination with the blue eyes she inherited from her two grandfathers. As she struggled with constant changes of blood in the first two weeks of her life, we held our breath. Then she won her battle and there were three in the nursery.

To this day I share with my daughters the legacy of tiny needle-scars from those pre-birth transfusions, a sharp reminder of the price paid sometimes to win and sometimes to lose. In those days it wasn't easy for any of us. The surgeons were the equivalent of First World War pilots, doing their best with string and balsa-wood machinery as they tried to bring the kite – the child – home safely on a wing and a prayer.

By the time I came to a halt, the consultants, for whom I was providing a large proportion of the available statistics on rhesus-negative births, would have been grateful if I had done a little moonlighting and produced a rather less explosive combination of blood groups.

Honey, my fifth child, was the last of the survivors. The hospital, expecting trouble after seven difficult months, opted for a Caesarean. They soothingly proposed a general anaesthetic. They should have learned their lesson. Once more under the influence of the blessed pethidine, I insisted on an epidural so I could be propped up on a pillow and see the action.

She was my daughter. I had made her. Whether she lived or not, a little mess was a small price to pay for a ringside seat at her birth. Honey emerged fighting, perfect and unmarked, but so strangely navy blue I wondered briefly if there was African blood in either of our families. I held her for no more than an instant, a scrap of dark-haired, open-lunged energy, before I handed her over. It was all I needed. I knew she'd survive.

She was taken away to an oxygen tent in the now familiar intensive care unit for Queen Charlotte's premature babies. Watching over her a few hours later Nicholas was appalled to see Sister Penrhys, the white-haired doyenne of the unit, ignore the child as she tended to the others.

'She's a good one,' Sister Penrhys said crisply. 'Most of these others are going to die – they need me. Not her, she's going to live.'

She spoke with the wisdom and experience of forty years. And so it proved. The navy-blue skin turned back to shrimp-pink. The one-and-three-quarter-pound infant gained weight as fast as an ocean-bound salmon. At last we took her home in triumph. Honey Abigail Stonewall joined the other three in the nursery.

Four children is enough, one might think. No. Six months later, I was pregnant again. It was time for strengthening lentil soup all round.

What happened this time was almost more than any of us could bear. Boychild – for lack of a more formal baptismal name – was my swansong. Even when the doctors searched for the heartbeat after the final transfusion, and found none, I did not believe them. Perhaps it was my very unwillingness to accept defeat – the thought that the experts might somehow be mistaken – that carried me through that last labour. The truth was a day and night in coming. The child was indeed stillborn. Recovery then was harder than it had ever been, lacking even the diversion of the usual post-natal attentions. The milk round rattled past my cot. The nurses drew the curtains round my cubicle. Victory has many parents. Defeat is an orphan.

Lentil and Spinach Soup with Eggs

This is the perfect vegetarian one-pot meal, suitable for all the family (the baby's portion goes in the liquidizer). It's quick to prepare, too: lentils are the only pulse vegetables which don't need soaking.

——————— SERVES 2 AND THE BABY TWICE ———————

8 oz/250 g lentils
(the greeny brown ones)
2 pints/1 l water
2 tablespoons olive oil
1 onion, skinned and chopped

3–4 cloves
2 garlic cloves, skinned and chopped
Salt and pepper

——————— TO FINISH ———————

8 oz/250 g spinach, washed and shredded
2 tablespoons olive oil
A little grated lemon zest

1 tablespoon chopped fresh marjoram, oregano or parsley
3 eggs
½ teaspoon ground cumin
1 tablespoon paprika

1. Put all but the finishing ingredients into a roomy pan. Bring to the boil, turn down the heat and leave to simmer for an hour, until the lentils are quite soft (this may take a little longer.)
2. Stir in the spinach and let the soup simmer for another 10 minutes.
3. Stir in another tablespoon of the olive oil, the grated lemon zest and herbs. Taste and adjust the seasoning.
4. Meanwhile, soft boil the eggs – bring them to the boil from cold, take them off the heat and leave for 6 minutes.
5. For the adults, peel the eggs and drop each into a bowl of soup, to be mashed in and trickle each portion with the remaining olive oil worked to a thin scarlet paste with the cumin and paprika.

Nicholas, romantic and distraught, decided that water was a more fitting cradle for a stillborn child than cold earth. He managed to charter a British Rail tugboat, hired a whisky-priest, tucked the four older children into their warm woolly vests, and took the whole lot, with the tiny coffin, down to Portsmouth to have the burial service conducted at sea.

Boychild Luard went to his rest in the grey and stormy waters of the English Channel.

Still in hospital I had the report of it all at second-hand. The four siblings, wide-eyed and pink-cheeked on their return from what had clearly been a great adventure, said it was exciting but very rough and windy, and that Honey, the youngest, had refused to throw her posy of spring flowers into the waves. Wrestling with her on the tossing boat, Nicholas had almost managed to throw her overboard too. Somehow the gesture restored the balance: there was, at least, a vivid memory of laughter to share.

The first thought after such a disaster is that another child will replace the loss. Good sense prevailed. Four children were a great gift – won against all the odds – and they needed a mother to share their childhood.

We had to be content. I hung up my hospital gown and swore it was for good.

CHAPTER FOUR

Round the kitchen table

*'What is sauce for the goose may be sauce for the gander but is
not necessarily sauce for the chicken, the duck, the turkey or the
guinea hen.'*

Alice B. Toklas*

THE KITCHEN HAS ALWAYS BEEN THE HEART OF OUR FAMILY'S DAILY
existence. It's certainly where we all feel most at home. And it's
always the place where visitors – whether my own children, their
friends or our friends – still seek me out first.

My own cooking career started very early indeed. Long before I
was of school age, I spent as much time as I could in the basement
kitchen of my mother's London house. In those postwar days the

*From *The Cookbook*.

green-baize door still had servants behind it, and we children were more welcome downstairs than up.

The nursery was a no-man's land for my brother and me, the domain of the latest starched dragon who had been engaged to keep us out of the grown-ups' hair. The two of us were a hardship post, and known in London's small community of nannies as 'tearaways'. 'Father killed in the war, you know – no discipline.'

Until the arrival of our kindly (and permanent) nanny, May Pocock from Aberdeen, a succession of grim temporary minders had charge of us. We spent much of our time confined to barracks. My brother was shipped off to boarding-school at seven or eight years old, leaving me lonely and bewildered.

The kitchen became my refuge. Below stairs was warm and friendly with the scent of hot ovens and baking. The cook was merrily fat. Her white aprons smelt of rice-starch and blue bag. The kitchen was full of bustle and boil. No-one paid any attention to me, or even told me not to eat with my mouth open, talk with my mouth full, or scrubbed my face with a flannel as wet and rough as a shark's tongue.

There was a large oilcloth-covered table in the middle of the room, and it was here that all culinary activities began and ended. Sitting at it was like being in the first row of the stalls at some endless, enchanting pantomime. Sometimes, if Cook was in a good temper – and at times she had a fearful rage on her – I was allowed to take my place behind the footlights. She would swaddle me in an enormous white apron to protect my clean smocked frock, and then, wonder of wonders, she would let me roll dough and cut out biscuits, choosing my favourite scallop-edged cutter from the heavy round tin in which they were stored in magic circles, like Russian dolls.

The butter biscuits for the drawing-room tea had to be perfect: the audience must not suspect a child's hand or, I was told, Cook would get the sack. So it was an adult task, a dangerous responsibility, and I was proud of my skill. After the upstairs biscuits had all been neatly cut out and arranged on the baking sheets, I was allowed the trimmings to make jam tarts and currant-eyed gingerbread men for the nursery.

In the kitchen, I felt useful. In the drawing-room, I felt I was a nuisance. Below stairs, too, there were no shiny French-polished

Butter Biscuits

These are the first biscuits I learnt to make – rationing was still in force after the war, and they were a real treat. They're easy, delicious and store well. Serve them with a glass of sweet wine instead of a dessert.

──────────── MAKES 20–30 BISCUITS ────────────

8 oz/250 g flour
4 oz/100 g ground almonds
or hazelnuts
A short length of vanilla pod

or 2–3 drops vanilla essence
6 oz/175 g butter
4 oz/100 g caster sugar
1 large egg

1. Sieve the flour into the almonds. Add the contents of the piece of vanilla pod, if you have it – lovely sticky little black seeds with a heavenly scent.

2. Using a wooden spoon, beat the butter with the caster sugar until the mixture is light and fluffy. Keep going – this takes longer than you think. Beat in the egg (plus vanilla essence, if using). Work in the flour and nut mixture until you have a ball of soft dough.

3. Cover with a clean cloth, and leave the dough to rest for an hour to firm up.

4. Heat the oven to 425°F/220°C/mark 7.

5. Roll the dough out to twice the thickness of a pound coin. Using a biscuit cutter, cut out rounds and transfer to a lightly buttered baking sheet dusted with flour.

6. Bake for 15–20 minutes until they are well risen and tipped with gold. Transfer carefully to a baking rack to cool and crisp. Store in a tin.

surfaces or little mats to protect against the rings left behind by damp saucers or dripping glasses. No-one scolded me when I put my mug of hot milk down on the table. This was the closest thing I knew to heaven, and I have been happy in the kitchen – anyone's kitchen – ever since.

When I fell in love, which I did with great frequency in my hooligan youth, I would cook beautiful suppers for the object of my desire. Other girls had themselves taken out to dinner. I would have none of it. A truffle in the hand is worth two in the trattoria. I think the young men of my fancy, brought up to the puritan rigours of public schools, found all this nurture a little alarming. Their mothers may have warned them that girls who cook have marriage in mind. Luckily the man of my dreams, my husband-to-be, had been brought up in the midst of women – a mother and four sisters – and found female nurturing not only perfectly normal but essential to his happiness.

My first family kitchen, after Nicholas's bachelor flat became too small to hold us, was a prefab slapped on the rear of a Battersea workman's cottage. The kitchen had a hatch which gave access to the dining-room which did double duty as the day nursery: a physical bridge across the two sides of the green-baize door. I fully intended to be cook-hostess. I knew that with a little forward planning and a well-primed hostess trolley I would be passing perfectly risen soufflés through to my glittering dinner-party guests. Then I would take my place at the gleaming dinner table and join in the sparkling exchanges – frock unspotted, make-up uncracked. Aproned genius on one side, stylish sophisticate on the other, I meant to be that rare and wonderful being, all things to all people.

I had studied Mrs Beeton. I believed in Constance Spry. I can only say, it's lies, all lies. There is no such animal as the cook-hostess. There is cook. And there is hostess. And never the twain shall meet.

Let's take the hostess first. The hostess has *someone else* to cook for her. A chef and a butler, maybe. Or, at a pinch, a cordon-bleu cook and a waitress in a black frock and a white pinny who comes in on the night. There's no need to envy her: as my wealthy Great-Aunt Elsie explained when she had trouble replacing the second footman – when you have servants, you have servant problems. Guests have

Cheese Soufflé

Soufflés are not nearly so difficult as they are made out to be – and a cheese soufflé is the easiest. This was the second dish I learnt to make, after butter biscuits.

─────────────── SERVES 2–4 ───────────────

2 oz/50 g butter
2 oz/50 g flour
½ pint/300 ml hot milk
4 oz/100 g hard cheese, grated
(Parmesan or pecorino,
or Cheddar)

1 teaspoon paprika
½ teaspoon cayenne
3 eggs
Salt
Freshly milled pepper
½ teaspoon grated nutmeg

1. Make a white sauce first. Melt the butter in a small pan. Stir in the flour and fry gently until the mixture is still pale but sandy. Whisk in the milk slowly, beating till you have a thick sauce. Simmer for 5 minutes.

2. Preheat the oven to 400°F/200°C/mark 6.

3. Stir the grated cheese (save a little to sprinkle over the top) into the sauce with the paprika. Season with salt, pepper and nutmeg.

4. Separate the eggs. Beat the whites until they hold soft peaks – don't overbeat, or they go grainy and fall back. Should this happen, either beat another lot of whites and use the yolks to make an egg custard, or give up the struggle and make a puffy omelette with the mixture. By now the sauce will be cool enough to stir in the yolks. Then fold in the whites, turning well to tire the mixture. Taste and adjust the seasoning.

5. Butter a 6 in. soufflé dish and spoon in the mixture. Run a knife round the rim so that the soufflé can rise easily. Sprinkle the top with the reserved grated cheese.

6. Bake the soufflé for 25–30 minutes until it is well risen and has a crisp brown hat. Serve immediately. A soufflé waits for no man.

to clock into dinner at eight o'clock sharp because the kitchen must be cleared by ten. I can only sympathize: if I was delivering my services for money, there would be a great many things at which I would draw the line. And ten o'clock would certainly be one of them.

Now for the cook. If, in those balmy early days when babies go to bed at six, you choose this role (it's one on which I can speak with authority), you must fight off all attempts to foist gracious living on you. Start as you mean to go on. Move the party into your own territory. Set up the candlesticks on the kitchen table and dig your heels into the cooking hearth.

I have always sacrificed everything to a roomy kitchen, even if it means losing the living-room. You need enough space for people as well as fitments, so I keep the matching cupboards to a minimum. I like to bump up the work surfaces – you can never, ever, have too many tabletops. At a pinch, I sling a drawing-board across the kitchen sink to give me an extra chopping board.

When the children were small, my kitchen did double duty as the nursery. A kitchen is waterproof enough to accommodate flour-and-water play, spongeable enough to shrug off finger-painting. Above all, you can be there to supervise and assist as required, and still keep an eye on the pot simmering on the stove.

Later on, when school kept everyone occupied for half the year, I had space, if not to go out to work in an office – my secretarial skills were not much in demand in the Andalusian cork-oak forest where we had taken up residence – but to do something of my own. I returned to supplementing the family income as a natural history painter. At first, logically enough, I set up my drawing-board in my own private space in a small secondary bedroom.

The arrangement didn't last a week. Maybe the family thought I was lonely, maybe they and their friends thought I was starved of conversation. Whatever the reason my space rapidly became standing room only; the audience was packed shoulder to shoulder around me. I decided to move back to the kitchen, and to hell with the odd splash of gravy on the night-heron and a dribble of wine on the delicately rendered wild orchids.

In the kitchen, apart from the drawing-board and a toy-chest, I find two items of equipment indispensable: a large table and a small sharp knife. The knife is replaced when it gets blunt – I'm hopeless at whetstoning and stropping. But the table has travelled round the world with me. It was made for me twenty-five years ago in the workshop of a Spanish shipwright who repaired the sturdy wooden fishing boats which patrol the seas between the Pillars of Hercules. Anyway, I like to tip the shopping out on to it and admire the fruits of my gatherings.

In addition to the essentials, every cook should be allowed frivolities, the ornaments of her traveller's tales. I have a wooden cream jug (battered and cracked) for storing those things which serve no useful purpose except as grist to memory's mill; a yard-long wooden spoon which I once used for stirring jam in a copper cauldron over a fire in a Hungarian plum orchard; a miniature steel cow's udder for dripping egg yolk into boiling syrup to make Spanish egg-threads; an implement like an oversize garlic press essential to the making of Swabian noodles; snail tongs from wanderings in Provence; a paella pan wide enough to feed thirteen hungry Andalusian peasants; a pine-twig whisk for stirring Slovakian corn porridge.

I have few mechanical kitchen aids. I can't be doing with Magimix, microwave or freezer. But there's one piece of machinery without which I am lost: a large, sturdy Kenwood mixer as old as my marriage, and give me a dishwasher, and I'm yours for life. When I was soon to be married, my mother asked me what I would like for a wedding present. By then, I had some notion of what life was likely to hold in store.

I did not hesitate. 'Something I can use and something I can sell.'

A trinket is for now, but a dishwasher is for ever. The exquisite Cartier cigarette case didn't last beyond the second pregnancy. The dishwasher was still there to greet my silver wedding. Anyone who has ever faced a hangover and a sinkful of congealed gravy will know just what I mean. Ah me, in the morning – the bliss of a squeaky-clean plate, the joy of a sparkling glass, the delight of a polished fork.

The cook can have no secrets once she lets her guests into her kitchen: you have to accept that the invited audience will witness your funny little culinary ways. We all have our trade secrets – but it's surprising how little people notice if you just go quietly about your business. A few of mine are: a pinch of raw curry in the salad dressing to give it a taste of walnut oil; a drop of gin in the mayonnaise; I use cold tea to colour the gravy; I recycle saucepans to suit the menu without scrubbing them out in between.

Some people select their guests for beauty, wit or fame. Not I. I choose mine for their skill with the balloon whisk, accepting carrot-scrapers and garlic-choppers with gratitude: you meet a better class of person in the kitchen. I set all volunteers to work, and try not to criticize their methods or aesthetic decisions. A job, once delegated, is no longer mine to control.

Kitchen entertaining is specifically designed to avoid the four-course dinner sent up – as the Victorians had it – 'à la russe': that is, handed round by a servant with clean plates and new eating utensils for each course. This was a Victorian innovation designed to demonstrate how many second footmen you could afford to employ. Great-Aunt Elsie, you should be with us now. The system is perfectly suitable for restaurants and hostesses, but quite unsuitable for cooks.

I have always chosen to serve meals in the pre-Victorian manner – as in any self-respecting farmhouse kitchen – putting most of the dishes on the table at the same time, with the hors d'œuvre laid out ready to welcome the diners to table. This is followed by a main dish which has to be eaten with your fingers, like lemon and garlic chicken. The number and variety of dishes can be increased at will, as in a Chinese banquet, to accommodate more guests. Hot food replaces the cold as the dishes empty, the washing-up is kept to the minimum, and good fellowship replaces display as the guest of honour.

In my kitchen, the first and second 'remove', as the pre-russe Victorians had it, is help yourself onto the same plate, with supplementary space on side-plates. There is absolutely no dictatorial behaviour over whether you like to sop up the hollandaise sauce with the potatoes or the poached salmon. And I provide a large empty bowl in the middle of the table for debris – pips, stalks and bones. Once the hot food is safely on the table (for preference served in its cooking dish so that it does not cool down too fast), I can settle down to an hour or two of pleasantly uninterrupted social intercourse – which is, after all, the main purpose of breaking bread with friends.

Lemon and Garlic Chicken

This is the fast cook's hostessing: we have minimum washing-up, no fiddling about with garnish or sauces – everything on the table, serve yourself. And absolutely no artistic arrangements on the plate.

————————— SERVES 4 —————————

1 chicken (2½–3½ lb and free-range)
1 lemon, chopped up
1 small onion, halved
1 bay-leaf
6 tablespoons olive oil
4–5 garlic cloves, skinned and chopped

1 heaped tablespoon thyme (lemon thyme is nicest, and worth growing your own)
1 teaspoon powdered cumin
Salt and pepper
New potatoes

————————— TO ACCOMPANY —————————

Green salad – look for interesting leaves to go with the lettuce – spinach, dandelion, flat-leaf parsley, big-leaf basil

1. Tuck the chopped-up lemon, the onion and bay-leaf inside the chicken and put it upside-down in a roasting tin. Trickle on the oil and sprinkle the chicken with the garlic, thyme and seasonings.
2. Roast the chicken for 60–90 minutes at 350°F/180°C/mark 6 – basting and turning it right way up after 40 minutes. Give the bird a good roasting, it should be succulent rather than juicy.
3. Boil the new potatoes until tender, and put them round the chicken for the last 10 minutes of the cooking. By the time it's ready, the chicken should be falling apart. Divide it into joints, and pile it up on a plate with the potatoes.
4. Use the juices to dress the salad.

Come the end of the first session, I clear the table of all but the side-plates, and put out a bowl of green salad. This is to amuse the appetite or clear the palate, whatever pleases – or some might like to have it with the cheese. Individual quirks are no business of mine, and I have never thrown anyone out for eating with their fingers.

The third and fourth courses – in whatever order chosen – can share the same plate. A strawberry tart or a nut cake are my two standard treats. As for the cheese, the most you will get at my table is one soft and one hard – but they will be the best I can afford – and a basket of digestives, rye biscuits and oatcakes. If I haven't made a dessert, I'll offer a plate of good chocolate biscuits. Or sometimes, if my purse will run to it, a sweet wine with dry almond biscuits for dipping. I like a bowl of fruit on the side: nothing exotic – cherries in season, or Cox's Orange Pippins. I can be persuaded to make coffee, but I much prefer infusions sweetened with a honey whose flavours match or complement the herb – lime tea with lime-blossom honey, camomile with spring-flower or, after a heavy winter meal, mint sweetened with pine-tree honey.

I do have a bottom line: I never let anyone stack plates. It's undoubtedly a hangover from boarding-school dinners – maybe because I was always at the end of one of the long dining tables, and had to camouflage everyone else's congealed leftovers. Now I have freedom of choice, I remove the plates discreetly one by one. We cooks are all allowed these little foibles.

It is when you're entertaining informally in the kitchen that children have an opportunity to cut their social teeth. As soon as someone is old enough to wield knife and fork and has acquired elementary table manners, he or she was expected to share the same menu as the adults. Mediterranean parents expect and get no less. The reward is an independent trencherperson who can be relied upon to do its parents credit in public places.

I never thought my children would enjoy everything I put on their plates the first time round. If they didn't like it, the deal was there should be no complaining. They simply slipped the stuff into a certain drawer in the kitchen table which I would discreetly empty when necessary. Through such small accommodations family life survives.

When something luxurious came our way I would share it out among all of us. These efforts to lead my offspring on to the sunlit uplands of gastronomic maturity gave me something of a reputation. On one celebrated occasion an adult offered the small Francesca a lick of Beluga – rather as one might offer a pit bull-terrier a nut cutlet – in the confident expectation of rejection. She accepted with alacrity.

'I don't really like caviare,' she explained. 'But Mum says I have to *learn* to like it.'

I made no apology. An educated palate is like any of the social graces – it has to be earned. My own experience in foreign places had taught me that if someone else ate something with enjoyment, it was probably perfectly palatable once you knew how to peel it, crack it, scoop it or suck it. I expected no less of my own children.

They swiftly learnt that there was much pleasure to be had from sharing a table with the adults who thronged their lives. But shared experiences comes much later, when everyone has long dispersed. Then, at moments of great happiness or deep trouble, you can come together again, knowing that whatever else goes right or wrong, the simple act of breaking bread together will provide what's needed at that moment.

Whether for comfort or celebration, what matters most is the sharing of memories – and there is no memory more powerful than that shared round the kitchen table.

CHAPTER FIVE

On being under five

*'The institution of the family is to be commended for precisely
the same reasons that the institution of the nation, or the
institution of the city, are to be commended.'*

G.K. Chesterton★

THE FIFTH BIRTHDAY IS THE LIMIT OF BABYHOOD, THE TRUE
watershed in the childhood of the young human – before then
all is permitted, all is possible. Anarchy rules.

At first sight, at that magical moment of birth, I did not rate the
material over-promising. Compared, say, to the young zebra or
newborn hartebeest, up and about and functioning like a small adult
within a matter of minutes, the newborn human is a dead loss.

★From *Heretics*.

Nothing, I soon discovered, could be further from the truth. The newborn infant may have a fuzzy grasp of reality, yet all the while the wires are humming. The view from the cradle is purely practical. Unfamiliar objects have to be submitted to all the senses – tongue, eyes, nose, ears, hands. First-hand experience – unsifted, unprocessed – is piling up in a corner of the empty attic of the infant mind, ready to be dragged out and examined at leisure. Equipped with nothing but a passionate curiosity, the developing human is a new-experience junkie for whom no doorknob can be left unpulled, no bottle left screwed-up.

Even with children as close in age as mine were, sharing the same environment as well as the same cocktail of genes, I quickly found each baby was as individual as the adults they were to become. Caspar, the first-born, was always the one who had to break new ground – decisive, funny, firm in his likes and dislikes, content if his needs were catered for, and blue with fury if they weren't: I greeted many a pale dawn with him in my arms. Fran was tranquil by night, but as curious as a cat by day, never satisfied unless she had her fingers jammed in some unexplored drawer; possessed of an extraordinary capacity for winning intersibling arguments by fair means or foul. Poppy, like Cas, was capable of twenty-four-hour action: a dreamer, egalitarian, an idealist, vigorously determined – once she had fixed on a notion, she would follow it through to the end. As the youngest by two whole years, Honey, always several paces behind everyone else, was joyous, combative, competitive, fiercely ambitious, by day and by night a bundle of irrepressible energy. Looking back I wonder how it was possible that these characteristics could have been apparent in babyhood, but they were.

Each of the babies set its own development timetable. Each advance followed another in strict rotation – one step at a time, like the first man on the moon. This could be walking or talking or pushing teeth or some invisible intellectual development at which I couldn't even guess. The uncertainty made for anxiety in the mother-and-baby clinic. Someone else's was sure to be doing everything mine wasn't – lisping 'Dadda' at every passing trouser, while mine sat mute, blowing bubbles.

But with four children to bring up, I scarcely had time to make comparisons. I simply assumed that, unless a medical expert told me otherwise, each infant was as normal as the next. Plough follows fallow. Nature has only the daily dinner to convert into energy – and if hair is the priority, hair is what she hands out. You eats your porridge, you takes your choice.

Newborn babies do little more than sleep, eat and excrete. For these activities, they need priming at roughly four-hourly intervals. This means they can manage a prodigious amount of sleeping. A tranquil infant snoozes away day and night; a restless infant can keep you up all night every night for a month. This has nothing to do with whether or not the child is breast-feeding. I know. I had both kinds, and I never discovered what made the difference. The only consolation is that whatever they're doing, they grow out of it.

Babies, even tiny ones, cannot live by bread alone. They need intellectual stimulus, the sound of voices and the patterns of movement. Brought up in the mainstream of family life, an infant does more or less what it should do naturally – picking up new tricks, like young starlings, by observation.

In the second month the pace hots up. Focusing on moving objects and a bit of gurgling is on the agenda. Bubble-blowing is a major pleasure. By this time, all my babies liked to whack into the orange juice and the rose-hip syrup between feeds. Fruit juice may be good for a baby, but it curdles a mother's milk. Curdled milk brings on the indigestion – like new wine frothing up in old bottles. In the baby clinic you can tell who's at this particular stage by the faint scent of fresh cheese which hangs about the shoulders.

Indigestion is the cause of many a hiccup in the mother-baby relationship, even after the breast-feeding is over and done with. It takes more time and patience to bring up a baby's wind than it ever does to feed it. I've tried every alternative: Gripe Water, gentle pressure against the shoulder while rubbing the back of the ribcage, firm pressure on the tummy while bouncing the sufferer up and down on the knee.

The remedy of last resort is the bottle – alcoholic rather than the one with the teat on the end. My own choice was an eye-dropperful of kümmel. I accept that when my children are found under the arches with a meths bottle for company, the debris and the responsibility will surely be laid at my door. Those who want to do it the hard way might like to try a nip of plain water – not iced but good and cold from the tap – dropped into the infant digestive system immediately after the feed. Hot air rises.

By the third month a baby likes to be dandled so that it can work out with its feet – a pounding, punching movement with clenched toes. This is great fun for a baby, but it turns your thighs black and blue. More raised eyebrows in the mother-and-baby clinic.

Around four months a baby likes to pull itself up to a sitting position by hanging on to any proferred fingers. Some kind of connection is made between fingers and objects – and what you do with them when you have them in your grasp, whether rattles, spoons or the cat's tail. Eye and hand co-ordination is a pretty hit-and-miss affair. Watch any two babies trying to pass each other a rattle and you'll see what I mean.

Infants of this age like toys for banging. They aren't interested in soft toys. Tweetie-pie cuddly teddies, so endearing to adults and older children, are boring for babies. I mean, let's face it, you can't really chew one, hit anyone with it, or use it to make a din, so what's the use? A wooden spoon, an enamel mug and a tin plate make much more interesting playthings – all easily to hand in the kitchen – useful for the first go at tomato soup.

Teeth were the next hurdle. These put in a first appearance any time between four and ten months, depending on the sequence each baby had chosen for its personal blueprint. Teething comes second only to indigestion as a cause of sleepless nights. In my family, with four babies so close in age, someone, or some two, was always teething. The front teeth seemed to pop through top and bottom without much trouble. It was always the sharp little incisors – vampire teeth – which gave the problems.

A little rash and a lot of gum-grinding was the first sign that something might be coming up. I was too mean to buy the necessary industrial quantities of rusks, so I made my own supplies of hard-baked stale bread. When things got really bad, a drop of whisky rubbed on the sore gum usually did the trick. Or if it didn't it acted as a perfectly effective general anaesthetic.

At the sign of the first milk teeth, we moved onto the bottle-feeds – smartly. From then on, we were less of an embarrassment in public places.

Walking was the next step, and my four solved their mobility problems each in its own sweet way. Most popular was snake-hipping across the kitchen floor and into the rubbish bin. That led to

Quick Tomato Soup

This is the household's emergency supper when there's nothing else in the house.

——————————— SERVES 2 AND THE BABY ———————————

1 lb/500 g ripe tomatoes,
scalded and skinned (or tinned)
1 slice of onion
¾ pint/450 ml milk

1 teaspoon sugar
1 tablespoon plain flour
1 tablespoon butter
Salt and pepper

1. Put all the ingredients into the liquidizer and process to a purée – it will look curdled, but don't worry.

2. Tip it all into a saucepan, bring to the boil, turn down the heat and let it simmer for 5–10 minutes. Taste and season.

3. Grown-ups can have it with hot croûtons and cubes of fried bacon. Babies like it with breadcrumbs crumbled in.

mountaineering out of the cot and bottom-bumping down the stairs, and finally to full-scale, take-it-or-leave-it *crawling*.

That epochal achievement created a period of domestic disruption. It's amazing how fast a crawler can move. Take Harrods (I'm afraid my grandmother had bequeathed me her expensive tastes without the wherewithal to indulge them). Picture me at sale time, Cas fully mobile, Fran in the pushchair, Poppy on my hip. I set her down for a minute while I find the money to pay for twelve pairs of socks, the family's spring quota. The next moment she is two rooms downwind – in the china department pulling down a stack of Spode. Crash.

I can still remember that magic moment when each crawling infant turned into toddler, and the child on my hip could be put down on the ground without nosediving straight into all the least salubrious, rubbish-garnished corners of the universe. It was liberation – up to a point. If you turn your back on a moving infant for an instant, you can be sure it will work its way along the skirting-board until it finds an electric outlet, a pair of steel knitting-needles and plugs itself in. As a precaution, I plotted the shortest distance to the nearest casualty department.

Toddler or crawler, no child likes bedtime. It's scary in the dark. I used to leave on a night-light – either low-wattage or one of those plugs which give a pale glow – in one corner of the room. People *do* grow out of fear of the dark, but if they're not allowed night-lights there's a risk they'll never come to terms with the monster which crouches in the shadows. My husband, a soldier with the special services and now into his second half-century, still likes a landing light left on at night.

Bath-time was sheer joy. Even the tiniest babies love warm water – I imagine the medium is still familiar from the womb. I always tried to allow plenty of time: half an hour is not too long for the full performance. Unplug the telephone first – you need all your wits about you. The only thing which puts a baby off its bath is a fear that it's not being held securely enough, or an experience of water that is far too hot or too cold. Babies have long memories for unpleasant experiences.

All four of my children would splash happily (or quarrelsomely) in the same bath. They treated it like a paddling pool: I would drop in a quota of plastic mugs, bowls and wooden spoons and leave them to discover their uses for themselves.

A baby who has had plenty of opportunity to splash around in the bath has already learnt that water is a friendly element. I like salt water best for teaching a child – there's more buoyancy in brine. An enthusiastic swimmer myself, I discovered that you don't have to wait till a baby turns into a toddler before you teach it to swim. And as a mother, secure in the knowledge that your baby can float, you worry less about duck ponds.

By the seaside, when the water was warm enough (I'm not one of your North Sea addicts myself) I would take the new learner in the water in my arms, held against me tightly like a baby koala. When we were both used to the temperature, and I felt the baby was comfortable enough to be adventurous, I'd pass it to another adult and encourage it to kick off in my direction for a pace – or two, or three, or four. Buoyancy is a matter of confidence – after the eldest had learnt the trick, teaching the others was a pushover. Literally, mostly. This is the great strength of production-line births: four can learn as easily as one.

The next excitement was potty-training. There's no natural reason why this should happen at all. From the infant viewpoint, contentedly filling its nice clean nappy in the clear expectation that this will be changed on demand, there's absolutely no reason to alter the *status quo*. From the parental viewpoint, you can be assured that whatever you do, it'll lead to the psychiatrist's couch. Continence is not something which comes easily to the young human. It must be learnt.

Potty-training would try the patience of a saint, let alone a common-or-garden mother. I'll come clean. I had access to a saint in Nanny Pocock. Her method was as simple as are all such miracles. She would take the tiniest infant – she didn't consider a month too young – and sit it on a small plastic pot accommodated in her ample lap. Then she would turn on the wash-basin tap. There the pair of them would sit, for as long as it took, listening with rapt attention to the rippling stream, until, like a small tributary joining the mighty river, the infant would do its stuff.

Potty-training is not the same as continence – not needing a nappy at night. The first is the product of will. The second is an accident of birth. Some children have naturally good control of the bladder. Others don't. A mechanical problem is best treated mechanically – there's no blame attached at all. The solution was easy enough: the last adult to bed was responsible for taking the child to do the necessary – in our family, with a novelist-husband who did not have an office-clock to punch, this was usually Nicholas, and never before the early hours. Sooner rather than later the midnight trips were no longer required. No-one likes to wake up soggy.

After the first year, innovation comes thick and fast. Happiness is a dry nappy and the freedom to lurch from one outcrop of furniture to the next without let or hindrance. Add to this someone to pick you up and cuddle you when you fall over, a mouthful of teeth for chewing up the landscape, an iron digestion, a vocabulary adequate to the imposition of will-power on your besotted dependents – and you have infant heaven.

The next four years – until the State takes over the provision of entertainment for a good proportion of the day – need careful planning, particularly if you are used to a level of conversation which rises above knee-height. I found sitting in a city playground while the offspring hurled themselves off the bits of scaffolding provided by a caring council about as interesting as a wet Sunday afternoon on the Brighton promenade. Later, when the victims themselves were able to express a comparative opinion, they were in complete agreement.

Chores and children are best tackled together – even small things like mixing up the muesli. The more children you have, the more the chores preoccupy you. It's less exhausting to do them in tandem than in sequence. I mean, if you were a baby, would you want to be forever posting square bricks into round holes while the adult in your life hoovered round you? It's much more fun posting sardine cans into supermarket trolleys. And even more fun, we found, trundling around a Mediterranean market where the stallholders offer you delicious things to eat.

As with all good things, this has its drawbacks: the cheek-pinching which accompanies the gift is a trial to the most stoic of non-Mediterranean infants. Geographically speaking, the line which divides those who take their infants everywhere and those who leave their children anywhere, is the northerly limit of the black truffle: the 47th parallel. Perhaps this is because small babies are more welcome when there's plenty of sunshine and wide open spaces for a playground.

Muesli

Here's the right way to start the day.

——————— MAKES ABOUT 2½ LB/ 1.5 KG ———————

1½ lb/750 g rolled (porridge) oats
4 oz/100 g shelled hazelnuts or almonds, toasted and roughly chopped
4 oz/100 g sultanas or raisins

2 oz/50 g dried apple rings or apricots, chopped
2 oz/50 g dried figs or dates, chopped
2 oz/50 g muscovado sugar

1. Spread the oats in a baking tray and set them in a low oven to toast until lightly golden – they're ready when they smell toasty and no longer taste floury.
2. Mix all the ingredients together. Store in an airtight tin. Eat by the handful in a hurry, or slowly with milk, cream, yoghurt, fresh berries, sliced banana, grated apple – in any combination.

In northern lands, where children are tucked away from the mainstream of adult life, people forget they were once babies themselves.

Mothers, no less than babies, cannot live by bread alone. I, too, needed the intellectual stimulus of my peers. It's not only cheaper but easier to take the baby to the party than to get hold of a baby-sitter. Here, I found discretion was the better part of valour. When accepting an invitation, it was wiser not to let on I intended to bring my baby with me. Presented with a *fait accompli*, even the most baby-hating host had to display good manners. There was always a risk we wouldn't be invited again – but then, better an invitation in the hand than two in the bush.

Some billets were better than others. Caspar snuggled down in Ken and Kathleen Tynan's bed on the first night of the all-nude, all-dancing revue, *Oh, Calcutta!* Only he can say whether this had any effect on his embryo libido. Francesca spent many an evening tucked into her godmother Annie Ross's arms, drinking her milk out of Billie Holiday's mug, while Annie sang to her. Naturally, she dropped the mug and that was the end of that. The poet Christopher Logue, not noted for his love of small children, used to read to his god-daughter, Poppy, when we dined with him and once wrote her a wonderful poem. Honey, ever the tail-ender, had to make do with the odds and ends as I trundled her around, but she didn't do badly either. For all of us it may not quite have been Good Queen Bess's progress round the four-posters of her realm, but near enough.

I never subscribed to the view that children should be seen and not heard. In summer, we trawled the great outdoors. In winter there was the warm kitchen – a natural playground with a wealth of danger to be negotiated. Danger appeals to children. No infant worth its salt enjoys a safe life, and mine were no exception. Never is life more exhilarating than in the kitchen, what with chillies to be tasted and bowls to be licked clean.

It seemed to me that if you take no risks, you never learn. For the amusement of visiting toddlers, I kept a jar of dangerous toys: large beads from broken necklaces, nappy pins, foreign coins, small plastic toys from cereal packets, all the sort of things which caring mothers scoop out of the way of frantic junior fingers. The babies absolutely loved it, and it kept their mothers on their toes.

I rather wish I'd been even more adventurous. Babies are natural clowns who give of their best for an appreciative audience – and I don't mean the goochy-goo sentimentality which affects certain spectators not involved in the daily round of baby-rearing.

That least sentimental of women, the great biologist Dr Miriam Rothschild, agreed with me. She told me that when her own children were little, she used to encourage small unaccompanied visitors to pretend they were dogs. She said she preferred dogs to people anyway, and the children found the dog experience liberating. Her programme included spending all day on all fours without any clothes on if the day was warm enough, eating meals from a bowl on the floor, communicating dog-fashion – barking, howling, yapping, growling, sniffing each others' rear ends and lifting legs against the table legs and trees. Baskets and cushions were provided for those who wished to curl up for a snooze. She said the children were happy as puppies all day, and learnt a great deal about canine pleasures into the bargain. They did not, said Dr Rothschild, usually tell their parents why they had had such fun.

A baby is the philosopher's dream: a purely existential being. Lacking self-awareness, all it has to do is *be*. The first time Cas spotted another baby, he had no notion that it belonged to the same species as he did. He simply thought the creature hilariously funny: he reeled with helpless laughter as it threw its food around and bumped into the furniture. As far as a baby is concerned, all the world's a playground, and heaven and earth have nothing to do but dance attendance on one member of the human race.

I have never learnt so much or so fast as when my children were small. Cas and Fran, Poppy and Honey taught me how to see the world anew – to question the movement of the heavens, the purpose of the universe, the nature of God, the function of man. When we are little, we have no natural limitations. All our ambitions have yet to be formulated, let alone realized – all doors are open. The world will teach us our place soon enough, tell us that we cannot achieve the goals we have set ourselves; that we are too old or too young, too stupid or too clever, too beautiful or too plain. But for now – all is possible. The sun need never set. The ocean will never run dry.

Some people never grow out of that marvellous strength and innocence – and they're the ones who change the world.

CHAPTER SIX

Playschool

*'A man ought to read just as inclination leads him; for what he
reads as a task will do him little good.'*

Dr Samuel Johnson (1709–1784)*

I'M NOT ONE TO SET MUCH STORE BY EARLY SCHOOLING, BELIEVING
that five or even six years old is quite soon enough for any child to
suffer daily deprivation of life in the nest.

If education is begun at home, where there's no real division
between learning and playing, the acquisition of knowledge becomes
part of ordinary experience. With four children at home, keeping my
children out of school until the last legal moment was probably an
easier decision for me than for most. There was a time when all the
junior members of our family were under seven and still at home. It

*From *Boswell's Life of Johnson*.

55

wasn't really planned like that. It was just that I was in no hurry to post my tender saplings into the sawmill of formal education, and the Inner London Educational Authority inadvertently gave us one extra year of grace before the long arm finally felt the family collar.

As I mentioned before, we had a house to live in. When our second daughter, Poppy, was born, we moved from Nicholas's bachelor flat at the smart end of town over the river and into then-unfashionable Battersea. I may not have been a flame-haired heiress, but I had just enough to throw the price of a modest freehold dwelling into the family kitty. This was lucky for all of us, since Nicholas had by now embarked on the uncertainties of establishing a publishing company.

We had space at last. There were three bedrooms and a bathroom on the upper floors, a living-room with space for working on the first floor. On the ground floor was a lean-to kitchen, a hall which accommodated the pram, and a nursery which did duty as a dining-room. The arrangement of the living space reflected my priorities. Most glorious of all, a staircase linked the three floors.

Anyone who has ever lived in a city flat with small children will understand the luxury of something on which exercise can be taken in wet weather. We never had a nursery gate at the top of the stairs – that would have been a red rag to four little bulls. First-timers had to negotiate the staircase backwards. The two younger children, of course, fell down it immediately – without an instant's hesitation. After that they became more respectful, and treated their staircase as a vertically extended play-pen. Both of them learnt to crawl by hauling themselves up it and bottom-bumped all the way down. The elder two appreciated the other virtues of a staircase. You can hide at the top of it. You can slip away at the foot of it. You can store things all the way up it. You can chuck things down it.

The staircase also allowed both adults and children to escape each other's company. As the four grew older, it was clear each needed to establish an individual identity. This is an issue which doesn't concern an only child, nor does it arise in a family where the births are widely spaced. But with us, to be different from the others, it was never enough for the difference to be acknowledged within the group alone. You need public recognition – to climb out of that limbo where everyone knows whose child you are but no-one can remember your name.

The easiest way to do it is in the way you dress – not by conforming, but by breaking the rules. The girls particularly felt the need to declare their difference from their siblings: they would rather have gone naked to a party than dressed alike. Perhaps because I, too, enjoy a little sartorial anarchy – I'm always the one in the extravagantly embarrassing hat at the wedding – from an early age the girls claimed the freedom to present themselves as they pleased, within the limitations of the available wardrobe. Much was second-hand, giving me a practical as well as a financial reason for patching jeans and altering other people's hand-me-downs.

If the simplest way to express personality is visually – through the image you present to the outside world – once the children realized they could use clothing to advertise belonging or declare separateness, it was easier to explore the ways in which they could learn from each other. This kind of intellectual knock-on is one of the great unsung pleasures of a large family born within a short time span.

If you feed knowledge into one end of the line, it permeates up or down the system. But here is danger as well as gain. As soon as a child shows a particular aptitude or weakness in one particular department, each can all too easily be typecast for life. 'Poppy's the artist, Cas is the mathematical one, Fran's the dancer, Honey can't spell.' A mythology develops. Once established it can stick like glue: the doors to equal opportunity bang shut. Artificial limits are imposed not only on one child's development, but on brothers or sisters, or even best friends as well.

While physical developments can be observed quite easily, intellectual shifts are harder to spot. Nevertheless, every day, every month, every year we are different. All four of my children changed their interests throughout their school days, but because these shifts often coincided with a move to a new educational establishment, they didn't meet with the usual opposition from their teachers.

In these early days, we were not idle: far from it. We had an education to gather. As a babe in arms, each of the children in turn had already made the simple connection between the book and the rhythms of the voice – everyone, however small, loved the bedtime story.

Now I determined that the elementary educational tools, including the three 'r's' and a second language, should be picked up before anyone reached school age. We were already accustomed to spending the summer holidays in Spain, and the children acquired the rudiments of the language with ease. At first we set aside two hours in the day for playschool, and worked it up as suited us. Education, we were agreed, was a mutual arrangement between pupil and teacher.

We started with mathematics. To the infant mind, untrammelled by preconceived notions and fear of failure, this is a naturally sympathetic subject. As an exact science, governed by precise rules, the concept is easier to grasp than reading and writing. Cas and I worked out our own system – nothing sophisticated, naturally, and certainly nothing of which the inspector of schools would approve. The principle was simple enough, involving the consumption of a great many of a certain proprietory brand of sugar-coated chocolate beans. One colour was designated a single unit, another symbolized ten, a third counted for a hundred – I'm sure you get the picture. What you could count, you ate. The basic skills can be tested every time someone needs to know what time it is – a home-made clock face with moveable hands provides the necessary equipment.

Numeracy skills can be put into practice by weighing out ingredients in the kitchen, shopping in the supermarket, counting out the small change in the launderette. The tasks certainly take longer when someone has to add everything up on their fingers – but then, as I reasoned, we had nothing much else to do of a rainy Tuesday afternoon.

Anyone old enough to remember those heady days before the arrival of the computer and day-long telly – that universal electronic nanny – will recall that parents were accustomed to read their children a bedtime story. Children learn most quickly by example. It's all very old-fashioned stuff, but rewarding in that the realization soon dawns on a child that reading stories is something you can do for yourself. Cas was the first to master the art, and once he had learnt, he was proud to take turns with me reading to the others. The two eldest girls, seeing their brother had a grand new skill, nagged him and me to teach them too.

Only Honey, the youngest by more than two years, had to work hard for her literacy and that was because, as will become clear in the following chapters, she had to learn three languages – Spanish, French and English – almost simultaneously. Languages are most easily learnt in the old-fashioned way by rote, chanting as loudly as possible the days of the week, numbers and so on. Shouting is important: the sound somehow echoes in the brain, and it sticks.

Anyone teaching a child to read in English has to tackle the problem of English spelling, which is undeniably eccentric, unpredictable and only too rarely phonetic. If you were Spanish, you would just set down exactly what you heard, not a vowel more, not a consonant less. If you were French, you would have grammar to tell you what agreed with what. Germans have even more precise rules to follow. But English spelling lacks all discipline. We don't much bother with grammar – we used to get all that when Latin, the language of the church, was on the school curriculum. Once this was dropped as an obligatory subject, we never replaced it – and more's the pity.

Children seem to assimilate knowledge slowly, nibbling round the edges of the less digestible information rather than gobbling it all down like a chocolate bar. Take sex education, for instance. Small people have a limited attention span for those things with which they do not feel directly involved. I found mine only needed small dollops of information – short answers to short questions fulfilled the need to understand *why* rather than *how*. This is a long way from a demand for all the mechanical details. And I never left it to outside 'experts', these being personal matters not to be entrusted to strangers, however well-meaning.

Anyone else's language, we found, can be learnt in the same way as you learnt your own – by building up a small vocabulary which refers directly to everyday family life. Comics and children's books written in the new language were the best learning tools. Textbooks, even if they do not belong to the school of my-postilion's-been-struck-by-lightning, are mostly about other people's everyday lives. Small children are only interested in those things that immediately concern them – preferably what they can eat, squeeze or catch. Mothers have a head start in gaining an infant's attention – all children like their mother to concentrate on them alone, particularly if, as in our family, there was considerable competition. Even so, and with the best teacher in the world, the infant attention span is limited to about the time it takes to consume a triple-blob ice-cream without the stuff melting the cone.

We took a swipe at history with the broadest of brushes. At this early stage, there's no need to get into the historical reasons for the fall of Rome, and even less to worry about what was happening in China. It is enough to know that here be Greeks draped in sheets, here Romans in togas, here a Celt in tunic and leggings; there is a medieval knight in his thundering armour; and there an Elizabethan sailor in doublet and hose; and so on until we get to 1900. Anything after that can be considered journalism: possibly more accurately recorded, but lacking the benefit of hindsight.

As for extracurricular activities, beggars can't be choosers, particularly on a snow-bound February afternoon with nothing to play with but the last of the week's housekeeping money. Of those burdens which are the inevitable lot of the mother with a young family, there are three which I can recommend as capable of being turned to good account – all as inevitable as death and taxes.

The first is housework, the second (naturally) is cooking, and third (few guess this one) is the family quarrel – that full and frank exchange of views which serves roughly the same purpose as a cat sharpening its claws on the furniture. I admit none of these has the universal appeal of a day on the beach in a tropical paradise, but they serve to pass the time.

Take housework for instance – and as far as I'm concerned you're absolutely welcome to it. We all have our little weaknesses. Mine is a hearty dislike of the mop and the bucket. I take no pride in a well-scrubbed floor. Pushing a vacuum cleaner round the furniture is my idea of purgatory. Anyone who will wash my floors earns my undying gratitude and if necessary every penny I can garner. The scent of beeswax polish reminds me not that Wednesday is polishing day, but that I should be out of doors, counting bees on the lavender.

The offspring rumbled me early: I never had any success in persuading them that housework is an enjoyable group activity. Shopping can be fun. Cake-making's a real pleasure. Washing-up has its devotees. Even ironing is just about tolerable if someone's prepared to read to me while I do it, or the radio or the television is on to take up the intellectual slack. But housework is hell. I have long looked for ways to shift responsibility. As the children grew older, I declared areas of guaranteed non-intervention, rooms where a mother's writ did not run.

Bedrooms are personal to those who inhabit them. Nor would I intervene in quarrels between siblings who shared accommodation –

they had to come to their own arrangement. A shut bedroom door is no business of mine. I am indifferent whether beds are made or left unmade according to the temperament of the sleeper – although anyone who left their bedroom door open risked the whirlwind.

Common parts – bathrooms, kitchens, halls and living-rooms – were another matter. In the absence of adult help with the cleaning, I resorted to the least honourable course and paid whichever child was willing on an hourly basis. It went against the grain, but I did it. I blame the urban environment. There's so much payment for goods and services that we have reduced everything, the smallest kindness, to a financial transaction.

Cooking was another matter. As might be expected in a household like mine, from the earliest years, the preparation of meals was a group activity. Up to a point, many hands make light work. Most kitchen tasks are repetitive – there's no special skill in scraping carrots, peeling potatoes, rubbing-in fat into flour for pastry, kneading bread.

Accidents can happen, of course – and we had our share of sliced fingers, scalded wrists and chilli rubbed into the eyes. The kitchen is a high-risk zone, so I kept emergency first aid on the shelf by the cooker – Elastoplast, burn cream, an eyebath for a boiled-water-and-salt rinse.

Proximity was no guarantee that the adventurous infant wouldn't get itself into some kind of trouble. When anyone was at the crawling, fingers-into-everything stage, I did as much of the cooking as possible in the oven. And then, as soon as the crawler had the necessary vocabulary to understand the nature of danger, I would explain exactly where this lay, and the consequences of putting the information to the test: fire burns, boiling water scalds, knife cuts.

You're never too young to help in the kitchen. Children love the theatricality of cooking a meal, particularly if a visiting child or an extra adult is in the audience. Best of all, they love a party. We would plan ours for weeks, and then I would withdraw from the fray, sit in the corner on a stool with a book, remonstrate when necessary and keep an eye out for trouble.

Sometimes it was as much as I could do to keep from diving in – the temptation with small children is always to do it yourself. And when we played host to outside children, I discovered an unexpected bonus – the most conservative of trencherpersons will eat unfamiliar things if they have had a hand in preparing them.

After a bout of 'I don't like it – what is it?' during one particularly damp London summer, the older children were allotted one day a week on which to cook *everyone's* supper. Modest shopping requests could be submitted in advance. If you were rude about someone else's efforts, you could be sure they would pay you back in kind. Each child developed its own speciality. Cas chose a sophisticated cauliflower cheese. Fran delivered well-browned bangers and buttery mash. Poppy – later to earn her living at one stage as a chef in a fashionable London restaurant – turned in a delectable spaghetti with tomato sauce. When Honey joined the team, she took charge of everybody's favourite baked potatoes.

The last in my trio of in-house amusements is the most contentious. Most people wouldn't consider the quarrel a source of entertainment – but they would be wrong. The battlefield of family life is no more than a communal jousting ground – a healthy exercise offering a chance to get a lot of anxiety out of the way. You can always explain away anything which popped out in the heat of the moment. But nothing festers like those things which are left stoppered up.

Nevertheless the home skirmish differs from all others in that there is no withdrawal. It's a useful training exercise for the negotiations of adulthood – you learn where to draw the line. Problems have to be resolved, or the household constantly trips up on them. The trick is to learn to resolve them quickly. From minor nit-picking to major confrontations, quarrels have to be settled there and then.

In the general day-to-day rough-and-tumble of inter-generation squabbles, I never believed in making the punishment fit the crime. I went for the global solution: Might is Right. This is not to say I belong to the flogging brigade; far from it. I remember all too vividly being beaten as a child – not frequently, but enough to remember each occasion. And I particularly resented it when punishment was meted out several days after the transgression – an exercise which did no-one any good, being not only humiliating but thoroughly confusing.

With my own children, I always reacted immediately, never in judicious retribution. Those who tried my tolerance beyond en-durance learnt retreat was the better part of valour, and I would be

Cauliflower Cheese

This is a good dish to start a cooking career. The preparation involves three basic skills: boiling vegetables, making a white sauce, and using the grill.

────────────────── SERVES 4 ──────────────────

1 large cauliflower
3 tablespoons butter
3 level tablespoons flour
1 pint/600 ml milk

4 tablespoons grated cheese
1 teaspoon strong mustard
½ teaspoon grated nutmeg
Salt and pepper

────────────────── TO FINISH ──────────────────

More grated cheese

1. Trim the cauliflower of any yellowing leaves, and cut the stalk close to the curds. Cut a deep cross into the thick stalk, and put the cauliflower, stalk-side down, in a saucepan with enough salted water to come halfway up the florets (the top will cook in the steam).
2. Bring it to the boil, turn it down to a fast simmer, lid tightly and cook for about 20 minutes, until the cauliflower is soft. Drain it well, leaving it in the colander to drip dry.
3. Meanwhile make the cheese sauce. Melt the butter in a small saucepan, sprinkle in the flour and let it fry a little, but not enough to brown. Whisk in the milk gradually, letting each dollop heat up and amalgamate before you slurp in any more. Then let the sauce simmer gently for 5 minutes, stirring while the flour cooks. Beat in the cheese, mustard and nutmeg. Taste and add salt and pepper.
4. Drop the cauliflower stalk-side down into a hot gratin dish, and spread out the florets like an exploded bomb.
5. Pour the white sauce over everything.
6. Finish with more grated cheese and slip the dish under the grill. It's ready when it's brown and bubbling.

Bangers and mash

This is a very easy supper: cheap and just right for all the family. The better the bangers, the better the meal, so go for the butcher's own make, with the highest possible ratio of meat to rusk. If in doubt, make your own skinless ones with minced pork and breadcrumbs, thoroughly pounded together with seasonings.

_____ SERVES 4 _____

2–3 pork sausages per person
(or 4–6 chipolatas)
1 tablespoon cooking oil or
dripping

3 lb/1.5 kg old potatoes
2 oz/50 g butter
¼ pint/150 ml hot milk
Salt and pepper

1. Separate the sausages and prick them once or twice with a fork.
2. Heat the oil or dripping in a frying pan and lay in the sausages. Fry them gently but steadily, turning regularly, until they are well browned on all sides.
3. Meanwhile, peel the potatoes and cut them into quarters, depending on how large they are. Each potato piece should be about the size of small egg.
4. Bring a pan of salted water to the boil. Put in the potatoes. Bring them back to the boil, turn down the heat a little, lid and leave them to boil steadily for 20 minutes.
5. Test with a knife. When they are quite soft, tip them immediately into a colander to drain.
6. Return the potatoes to the pan and set them over the heat for a moment to dry. Mash them with a potato masher.
7. Beat in the butter, then the hot milk. Reheat, taste and add salt and pepper.
8. The potatoes and the sausages will be done at the same time. Serve on hot plates, with mustard.

Spaghetti and tomato sauce

This is an extremely easy recipe. If you prefer, make it ahead, spread it in a gratin dish, sprinkle with grated cheese, and reheat it in the oven.

─────────── SERVES 4 ───────────

4 handfuls spaghetti
2 tablespoons olive oil
1 garlic clove, peeled and
chopped

1 tin plum tomatoes
½ teaspoon thyme
Salt and pepper
Grated cheese

1. Warm the oil in a frying pan. Put in the chopped garlic and let it fry for a moment without taking colour.
2. Add the tomatoes and the thyme. Bubble the mixture up, turn down the heat, and let it stew gently, uncovered, until you have a nice thick sauce. Taste and add salt and pepper.
3. Bring a large pan of salted water to the boil. Put in the bundle of spaghetti, pressing down from the top until all the sticks are submerged. Cook for 8–10 minutes, until tender.
4. Drain and toss with a little extra oil.
5. Tip the spaghetti into a bowl with the tomato sauce. Mix it all together.
6. Serve on hot plates, with the cheese handed separately. Eat it with a spoon and fork.

Baked potatoes with ham

This produces results for the trainee cook without any undue risk to life and limb. You can vary the filling as you please – grated cheese or chopped onion and tomato is nice.

─────────── SERVES 4 ───────────

4 large baking potatoes　　　　*Butter*
2 slices ham, chopped small　　*Salt*

1. Turn the oven on to 350°F/180°C/mark 4.
2. Scrub the potatoes until they're quite clean. Dry them, prick them with a fork 2 or 3 times and sprinkle them with salt.
3. Put the potatoes in the oven and bake them for 1–1¼ hours, until they are soft right through when you test them with a knife.
4. Cut a cross in the middle of each hot potato, and stuff in the chopped ham and a knob of butter.

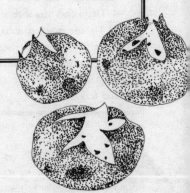

obliged to chase the whole bunch round the house until I caught up with the tail-ender. On these occasions – and I could usually bring moral rather than physical authority to bear – the children learnt to head for their bedrooms and dive under their eiderdowns, by which time not only my energy but the worst of my fury was spent. At least the exercise made *me* feel better, making peace much easier to declare.

One of the more onerous duties of motherhood is adjudication of intersibling disputes. Few of us have the wisdom and still less the leisure of Solomon. Most intersibling arguments – those which do not descend to the physical – are a matter of presentation and reputation. Those known for a quick temper only have to *look* cross to win the day. As in a court of law, representation moves the dispute into neutral territory. I would take on the role of advocate for the intimidated.

Physical fights – hair-pulling, shin-kicking and other outright punch-ups – require physical solutions. It's no good thinking you can do anything with will-power alone. Separating the disputees geographically merely puts off the moment of reckoning. My solution was to lock the warriors up in the *same* room, and let no-one emerge until they came to some arrangement. With any luck this doesn't take long, not least because the antagonists, as in any war-zone, find a joint purpose in defeating authority, the common enemy.

When dealing with general household disasters such as who dropped the teapot or fed the goldfish to the cat, I am no Sherlock Holmes. I cannot deduce the truth from the trace of a hair in the soup or even the shape of the tea-leaf dregs.

The four tumbled this shortcoming from the moment they learned to lisp 'Not me, mum.' When in hot water, they hung together like unstirred macaroni.

'Who dunnit?' met with Mafia-style *omertà*. It was useless to line up and question the suspects.

I countered with Victim-of-the-Week. Looking back on it, the concept was an idea of such blinding simplicity, such clarity, such unarguability, that Dr Goebbels himself would have been proud of me. One week in each month was allotted to each child. During that week it alone was held responsible for the misde-meanours of all four.

'Fine, whose week is it?' was the total intellectual input required. I didn't need to question, interrogate, adjudicate, retire or reach a verdict. I just needed the name. I could then punish with perfect economy of effort.

Francesca might have filled the car-door locks with superglue, Poppy might have turned the donkey loose in the forest, Honey might have spiked her father's port decanter with laxatives – and it was Caspar, innocent of all the transgressions, who would catch it in the neck.

Of *course* it's not fair. *Life* is not fair. The beauty of it is that it is manifestly *unfair* – minimalizing the guilt as well as the blame. Better still, the method has its own built-in fail-safe: the victim knows that if they behave badly in someone else's week, sure as eggs is eggs one of the others will raise Cain in theirs.

By this simple expedient, a major drain on parental energies was unblocked, freeing Solomon to pay attention to the important things in life – beating up a few *profiteroles au chocolat*, or even carrying out an in-depth investigation into the sex life of the tadpole.

The system works best when there are three or more participants. With two it just turns into an unseemly tit for tat. Parents of an only child might consider including themselves in the rota: it might produce interesting results.

CHAPTER SEVEN

The great urban outdoors

'Struggle little by little against idleness.'

The Reverend Sydney Smith★

IF YOU LIVE IN A CITY WITH SMALL CHILDREN, IT'S PLEASANT TO FIND that society occasionally has the interests of the family at heart.

As every mother with baby carriage knows, in the parks and open spaces of all cities can be found designated play areas equipped with municipal swings and climbing-frames. These are plastered with warnings that the city fathers will not be held responsible for any injuries to the young and vulnerable of any nature whatsover, including those sustained by malfunctioning equipment.

Whatever the mechanical risks, it doesn't take a degree in sociology to work out that those places earmarked by a caring

★Advice to a young lady in low spirits (*c.* 1830).

Liver and Bacon with Onions

Toss this up when you get home from the playground. It's not only delicious, but good for growing children. A high proportion of onion to meat makes all the difference to the flavour.

——————————— SERVES 3 AND THE BABY ———————————

1 lb/500 g lamb's or pig's liver, trimmed and sliced into thin fillets
6–8 tablespoons oil
1 lb/500 g onions, skinned and finely sliced

4 oz/100 g bacon bits, chopped
Flour
½ pint/300 ml water
Salt and pepper

1. Remove any visible tubes from the liver. Cut it into bite-sized strips, sprinkle with pepper and put aside.

2. Heat the oil in a wide, heavy pan. Add the onions and let them cook very slowly for 25–30 minutes, until they are quite soft and lightly caramelized. Push them to one side. Throw in the bacon and the strips of liver, lightly sprinkle with flour and sauté the pieces briefly (no more than a couple of minutes).

3. Add the water and allow it to bubble up. Season with salt and pepper, cover, turn down the heat and let it simmer for as long as it takes to tenderize the liver, about 20–40 minutes. If you can afford calf's liver, it will need no more than a few minutes sautéing, and should be left pink.

Either way, it's lovely with baked potatoes, or with mashed swede and potatoes beaten up with milk and butter (I never *did* like the flavour of margarine in mashed potato).

For the baby – whizz it up with a little potato.

council for the children to play in, might also act as a magnet for those people who most emphatically should not be playing with the children. There's no help for it – you either have to join a supervised playgroup or do the job yourself. And there is only a certain amount of time that a sentient being wishes to spend watching the collected apples of her eye swinging from the galavanized steel branches of an urban would-be jungle before her mind starts wandering to thoughts of the all-important evening meal.

These are problems at which fortunate families can throw money. There are plenty of amusements which can be bought. In our household, as has probably become clear, the purse-strings tightened with the arrival of each child.

In this task – the art of getting the most out of the household budget – I found myself an unlikely mentor. On the next street but one to Nicholas's bachelor flat lived Tessa Kennedy – now an internationally successful interior designer, but then married to the late Dominic Elwes, my grandmother's godson. Nicholas and Dominic had business together – and as neighbours, we wives fell into each other's company.

Dominic, a legendary raconteur – a modern court jester – had a penchant for the gaming-tables and a habit of getting into financial scrapes, and Tessa's fortune was never enough to cover them both. Luckily his wife was possessed of that quality essential for any young mother – formidable survival skills. With three boys already at knee-height while mine were still in the pram, Tessa had developed a dealer's eye for a household bargain.

The daughter of a Yugoslav shipping fortune, with the blood of the rug merchants still hot in her veins, Tessa was fearless – the first person I knew who shared a similar background to my own, who would cheerfully riffle through jumble and second-hand clothes, beating down the barrow boys until she had carried off her bargain.

As young women with husbands whose primary concern was not the stuffing of the family coffers, we shared the problems of the new poor. Two can do as a gang what one cannot do alone. Each supermarket was a challenge, each street-market a jousting ground. Trailing our accumulated children in our wake, we negotiated delicately for the end-of-the-day leftovers. We formed a two-person co-operative whenever one of us hit pay-day, bulk-buying catering-quantities of household necessities and dividing the spoils.

As an apprenticeship, it was unbeatable. By the time Poppy was born and we moved to Battersea, I was a fully paid-up member of the shopping brigade.

There was nowhere we would not go – the whole city had become our gathering ground. Four is a perfectly manageable number to cluster around a moving baby carriage: the newest infant snoozes inside, the toddler is strapped securely into the baby seat and the other two hang onto each side of the handle. Any more and the equation breaks down. But with four anchored to the pram and one to push, we trawled the shop-fronts and department stores to our hearts' content.

If free entertainment is available in the gaps between the thundering rivers of steel, it's not only the heavy traffic which has to be negotiated. In other cultures, children accompany their parents to the market-place, the unofficial information exchange and social club of the Mediterranean housewife. Not so in the city. British shopkeepers do not naturally see the child as a future consumer, nor yet as the big spender of tomorrow.

To put it politely, they would much rather you left the children at home, with the child-minder, in a playgroup – anywhere but in the market-place. To the devil with civic responsibility. Self-service stores actually lay traps: magpie fingers have to be prised out of the help-yourself chocolate bars at the checkout. In department stores they train the store detectives to trail small people round the aisles in case they might pocket a cut-price item from the basket on the floor. We were made of sterner stuff. We held our ground – shop one, shop all.

Whoever was learning to write made out the basic list – and it's remarkable how much reading, writing and arithmetic there is in a shopping list. You can start with the staple household countdown: flour, tea, cereal, butter, salt, sugar, lavatory paper, soap powder, floor cleaner. If someone is learning to add, they can make quantity decisions along the lines of how many tins of cat food the cat gets through in a week (and if your cat is anything like mine, that is exactly twice the recommended dose). Or if it is a matter of potatoes, how many pounds a family of four, or six, or three, will consume in the same period. Comparative pricing keeps the mathematicians on their toes: working out whether this brand is cheaper than that, how much you save if you buy the family size – taking into account how much of it is likely to stick to the sides or split in the transferring from large bottle to small. All sophisticated stuff.

Certain supermarkets are more suitable as family entertainment zones than others. Best, we found, is one which has wide alley-ways: there's less chance the knee-high child will rugby tackle a pensioner in its search for the last can of beans on the bottom shelf.

I found it sensible to take a few elementary precautions before venturing out on shopping-as-entertainment. The spending of the little you have is all the better for some forward planning.

The first precaution was a good breakfast: porridge for preference (in the Scots manner of course – in a wooden bowl, with salt and treacle, and the milk in separate bowl for dipping). As a natural supermarket grazer myself, I know what the sight of all that design-targeted packaging does to the infant gastric juices. It's far harder to prise the choco-hoops away from the clutching fingers of a hungry child than to coax them back from one who is already full of nourishing oats.

The second is to allow twice as much time as any normal human being. You're not a normal human being. You are a one-person entertainment centre taking up temporary residence in a super-market. Time is the only commodity the mother with children has in plenty. Squander away – there'll be more tomorrow.

The third is a contingency plan in case the mother-ship loses contact with its landing craft. Something along the lines of: 'See you at the last checkout counter from the exit, when both the clock's hands are pointing to the top.' I always took two trolleys – one for me and one for the junior shoppers.

Inside the supermarket, it's hot. There's a reason for the popularity of the Mediterranean diet, and it's not health – it's central heating. Heat makes people irritable and thirsty – each of which has its attendant problems. The first step was to remove everyone's excess outer garments and stow them. The second was to withdraw from the fray, cruise gently across the aisles (rather than up and down), and leave the list-makers to do the collecting. I deferred the decision to return those items which were seductive but unnecessary until I reached the checkout counter. Then I stacked one trolley with the goods I really needed, and another with those to be returned to the shelves. The purse-holder's decision was final. (There's no representation without taxation.)

Then I held my position at the checkout counter. The law of natural disaster rules. Whatever the precautions, someone was sure to get lost. In a crowded place, I stood still with my hand in the air and waited for the lost one to find me. There's an element of blackmail about this. Children are easily embarrassed by parental eccentricity – no child wants its mother drawing attention to herself, particularly if she's wearing Tibetan moon boots and a floppy velvet hat with a feather in it.

Then there's eating out. Throughout our early years in London, 'No children or pets' dogged our every social outing. Holiday hotels and boarding-houses proudly advertise their unwillingness to accommodate anyone under double figures. You couldn't take children into pubs and places where they serve alcoholic refreshment. On holiday, the choice was the teashop, the motorway café or the lay-by with a tin-opener. In London, any place of recreation provided by a caring management was likely to be a dismal lino-floored ghetto somewhere by the conveniences.

In this barren desert, we found one oasis. In those days London had one Chinese restaurant which served dim sum. Once we had discovered it – the long-since vanished Young's in Cambridge Circus – it became our regular Sunday treat. Chinese food is communally shared, pretty to look at, and neatly chopped up, which suits inexperienced wielders of table-furniture. Dim sum, chosen from the heated trolley, was cheap – noodles and vegetables are not the most expensive of ingredients – and as long as everyone drank tea and no-one wandered off into the à la carte, the bill would come to no more than a roast-meat lunch at home.

Sunday lunch was followed by culture – a trip to an art gallery. It's a matter of association – if cultural activities can be linked to a full belly, the habit sticks. In London, the National Gallery was conveniently to hand after Sunday Chinese – there are some wonderful Dutch pictures to be gathered in by the back entrance. After a Sunday picnic in the park, the Tate offered rich trawlings.

Provided they were not required to involve themselves for longer than a pre-arranged half-hour, I found my children excellent companions on such forays. At first, imagining they would only like pictures with plenty of action, I headed straight for the Victorians – Richard Dadd and Samuel Palmer, and the Pre-Raphaelites, the Barbara Cartlands of the artistic fraternity.

The four soon proved me wrong. Lacking sophistication, unlimited by preconceptions, they did not judge, they simply used their eyes. I galloped along behind them, intrigued by what they might reveal. The innocent eye brings startling insights: a small child's response to an abstract can be every bit as vigorous as it is to the representational.

As soon as we acquired our Battersea house, we tried our hand at gardening. The aspiring urban horticulturalist, unless the owner of a small estate in Hampstead Garden Suburb, must run the gamut of cat droppings and broken glass. I quickly threw in the towel and concentrated on the kitchen window-sill – with a bit of overspill onto the concrete patch outside the back door.

The first step for any new gardener is to draw up a plan. This can be a communal activity. I allowed one trough or three flowerpots per person – not exactly the Royal Botanical Gardens, but there's nothing like a little forward planning to increase the pleasure. The nicest pots are classic red earthenware – plastic is cheaper but not so satisfying. If times were hard, we used empty baked-bean tins. I checked the cans for jagged edges, gave them a lick of paint, punched a few holes in the base for drainage, dropped in a few stones to provide a soakaway, and filled up with potting compost.

Now we were ready to decide what to plant. I learnt to discourage the trainee horticulturist from attempting to grow difficult plants from seed, like chrysanthemums or cabbage roses. In winter, bulbs were the best bet – all you need to do is buy them, plant them and not overwater them. In summer, annuals grew the quickest – small children have a short attention span. Nasturtiums and marigolds were particularly rewarding: you can eat the flowers, buds, young leaves and seeds of the nasturtium; marigold petals are sold in Eastern markets as Mexican saffron, and were used in Elizabethan cookery to colour rice and prettify a salad.

The more ambitious (and gastronomically adventurous) planted lettuces and salad leaves – rocket, American land cress, parsley, corn salad, Italian *misticanza* mixtures – which gave quick edible results

Marinated Chicken for Backyard Barbecues

A good marination can make the dullest of urban chickens into something worth eating. Make sure the chicken pieces are not too thick – chop them small, through the bone, with a hammer.

———————————————— SERVES 6 ————————————————

1 chicken, jointed into about 20 pieces, back and all.

———————————————— MARINADE ————————————————

2 tablespoons oil
1 whole lemon, chopped small
2 garlic cloves, skinned and chopped
2 tablespoons paprika

2 tablespoons chopped marjoram or oregano
1 teaspoon salt
1 teaspoon pepper

1. Rub the chicken pieces thoroughly with the marinade ingredients. Leave overnight in the fridge in a covered dish to take up the spicing.
2. Let the chicken come up to room temperature before handing it over to the barbecue cooks for grilling.
3. Test the thicker pieces to see if they are ready by prodding down to the bone with a sharp instrument – when the juices run clear but not pink, it's done. Finger-licking gorgeous.

and could be cropped regularly to add to bought salads and all marinades. Supermarket herbs – the ones in little pots – were cheap and could be successfully replanted in bigger pots. If someone remembered to keep them watered, they went on cropping for a full season.

There's something very satisfying about being able to control the means of food production, however modest. We are all hunter-gatherers at heart.

CHAPTER EIGHT

On the move

*'The grand object of travelling is to see the shores of the
Mediterranean.'*

Samuel Johnson★

WHILE THE FIRST SEVEN YEARS OF OUR FAMILY LIFE WERE BASED IN
London through the winter, spring and autumn, we fell into the
habit of spending the summers in southern Spain.

I already felt perfectly at home in Andalusia – as the stepdaughter
of a diplomat on the hispanic circuit, I had spoken Spanish from
childhood. After a year or two in the hills behind Malaga, I rented a
small white-washed box of a house on the outskirts of a little fishing
settlement further to the west, an outpost of Spain's most southerly

★Quoted by James Boswell in his *Life*.

port of Algeciras – the gateway to Africa, an old warhorse of a
trading port, with an oil terminal and industrial installations bringing
new prosperity.

For the first few years, Nicholas's commitments in London meant
that he could join us only intermittently, but the living was cheap
and easy in the Mediterranean sun and I was grateful for the chance
to recover from my difficult pregnancies. Most years I managed to
persuade Venetia, my best girlfriend and long-time kitchen companion, to keep me company through the summers. Always one to
follow the sun, Venetia was on the rebound from a love affair in
Mexico – an encounter which had equipped her with fluent Spanish
and a huge repertoire of wonderful Mexican recipes. The ports of
Andalusia were the first to receive the New World's bounty, and the
raw materials available in the *andaluz* countryside were perfectly
compatible with her methods of culinary attack.

Possessed of a healthy appetite for the good things of life, Venetia
was never one for sentimentality as far as infants were concerned – or
adults either, for that matter. She had a robust view of the capacities
of the junior contingent, treating them as perfectly normal adults
who happened to be on the small side. This insouciant tolerance
extended to what they ate – if frittered sea anemones was the *plat du
jour*, sea anemones was what they got, and no complaints.

We had no transport, but we did have a part-time babysitter in the
form of an elderly maid of all work, an unlovable old black-clad
scold blessed with the unlikely name of Esperanza – Hope.
Esperanza lived in the village with her family, and she and her
multitude of unseen dependents ate us out of house and home. She
was a terrible housekeeper – her only virtue being that she could be
persuaded to do a bit of child-minding while we walked the three
miles to do the weekly shop in Algeciras market. The price of this
service was a week's supply of condensed milk and locally tinned
sardines, which she much preferred to the fresh ones the village boys
caught on the shore.

In those days, Algeciras was a busy fishing port, but above all it
served as a clearing-house for the smuggling trade which flourished
in the frontier territory between Africa and Europe. Dark-skinned
Moroccans, red-faced Russians, the raffish French from Casablanca,
went about their business in the harbour-front cafés. Few tourists

found anything to interest them in the town – unless it was the elderly grand hotel, the Reina Cristina. Built by an Englishman as a stage on the road to Ronda for the gentlemen of Gibraltar's garrison, the hotel had a reputation for comfort and respectability.

If we finished our shopping ahead of time, Venetia and I would brave the braided doorman at the hotel, deposit our loaded baskets outside the pink-stuccoed entrance, and take our ease on the grand terrace shaded with palm trees. Here, for the price of a *fino* sherry and a sunny smile for the barman, were unlimited supplies of olives, salted almonds and company. A clearing-house for all the extramural activities in the area, both expatriate and Spanish, it provided us with a weekly fix of social intercourse. We *did* have friends in the neighbourhood, but with neither vehicle nor telephone, we were hardly on the beaten track. Here many a bullfight ticket could be scrounged, there were lifts to be cadged, maybe an outing on somebody's boat. It was worth every penny of the overpriced glass of sherry.

That we might not be entirely the kind of passing trade the hotel's pinstriped management relished was put to the test one morning when our shopping included several kilos of live snails for which Venetia had exciting plans. Disaster in the shape of a mass snail break-out might have been averted had we not fallen into conversation with a local torero – a hero of Spain's national sport, and something of a social lion. The chance encounter, promising transport and corrida tickets, meant that we took rather longer than usual to savour our refreshments. By the time we emerged the entire squadron of gastropods was on the march up the pink stucco – inadvertently liberated from summer hibernation by a shower of rain. Abandoning our intended supper to the untender mercies of the enraged doorman, we beat a hasty retreat.

Back home, our main entertainment of the day was the evening meal. It was a shared adventure and the children found themselves with a whole new culinary vocabulary to assimilate. Venetia, with the authority only an outsider can wield, never questioned that they would enjoy her spicy dishes of lemon-marinated raw fish, re-fried beans with fierce little chilli sauces, green peppers stuffed with goat's cheese, avocado salads scented with coriander and lime.

I would balance these exotic treats with the staple beans-and-bones stews of the country people – made to recipes gleaned from

Mexican Refrito

This is the classic Mexican hashed beans – a *refrito*. If you use dried beans, soak them overnight and then boil them with bay-leaves and some peppercorns, a tablespoon of oil and a chopped tomato, for an hour or so until soft (only top up with *boiling* water).

SERVES 3–4

4–5 tablespoons oil
1 garlic clove, peeled and chopped
1 teaspoon powdered cumin
½ teaspoon chilli powder or cayenne pepper (use more if you like it hot)

1 lb/500 g cooked, drained black beans, *frijoles*
3–4 tablespoons grated Cheddar cheese
1 egg each (more if you're hungry)
Salt and pepper

CHOPPED SALAD

1 tomato, chopped
¼ onion, chopped
¼ cucumber, chopped
1 small garlic clove, finely chopped

1 tablespoon chopped mint or coriander
1 tablespoon lemon juice or vinegar

1. Heat the oil in a heavy frying pan and stir in the garlic, cumin and chilli powder. Tip in the drained beans and mash them into the hot oil. Fry gently until the beans form a crust, rather like making bubble and squeak. Stir in the grated cheese and re-fry until another crust forms.

2. Fry the eggs in the oil which remains in the frying pan after you have removed the beans – add more if you need it, of course.

3. Combine all the ingredients for the chopped salad.

4. Serve the re-fried beans topped with a fried egg, flanked with a spoonful of the salad, plus a handful of tortilla chips (re-fried Indian chapatis left over from the take-away are the perfect substitute) or potato chips or crisply fried bread. A helping of guacamole (see p. 83) adds extra pleasure.

Rajas Poblanas

This is Venetia's favourite Mexican dish. The price is roaring indigestion – but well worth it.

─────────────── SERVES 4 ───────────────

1 lb/500 g thin-fleshed green peppers
8 oz/250 g good strong goat's cheese or Cheddar, grated

About 1 pint/600 ml cream – single or double
Salt and pepper

1. Make a slit in the side of each green pepper and stuff it with grated cheese. Arrange in a shallow gratin dish. Cover with cream. Season.
2. Smack the dish into the hottest possible oven for 20 minutes, until the cream bubbles and browns a little.

Easy Guacamole

Guacamole, Venetia explains, should be a well-chopped salad – not a squishy green gunge.

──────────── SERVES 4 ────────────

2 ripe avocados, skinned, de-stoned and chopped
1 garlic clove, skinned and finely chopped
1–2 tomatoes, chopped small
1 onion, chopped small
½ green pepper, de-seeded and chopped small

1 small green chilli, de-seeded and chopped small
Juice of 1 lime or lemon
1 tablespoon chopped fresh coriander (at a pinch, parsley and ground coriander seeds can substitute)
Salt

1. Mix everything together in a bowl. Don't squash it too much.
2. Pile it up in a dish. Serve it with tortillas or crisps or bread for dipping. Lovely with a Mexican *refrito* (see p. 81).

P.S. If you are not serving the guacamole immediately, bury one of the stones in the middle. Mexican folklore has it that this stops the avocado going brown – and who am I to argue?

the market stallholders who sold me the raw materials. We ate lentils, chickpeas and haricot beans slow-stewed in a rich broth made with whatever came to hand – a length of bone from the salt-cured wind-dried ham which is Andalusia's Christmas treat, an old hen whose services as a layer were no longer needed, a bit of oxtail going cheap after a bullfight.

The villagers, also dependent on the single journey of the daily bus, had their own ways of laying in supplies. We bought bread from the baker's van which set up shop by the beach each morning. We negotiated for the fish caught by the boys from the shore – a silvery bucketful which might include anything from eels to anchovies. Sometimes there might be real treats – a haul of clams or razor-shells or weed-crusted, spiky spider crabs. We begged eggs from anyone who kept hens and had a few to spare; we had crisp lettuces, sweet-fleshed red-skinned onions, fat white garlic, peppers, tomatoes and aubergines from the smallholdings flanking the little river which formed the fishermen's estuary.

On market-day we brought back strange fruits the children had never tasted before – creamy-fleshed custard apples, persimmons and scarlet-pipped pomegranates, grenadines and water melons, bananas on the stalk, fat ripe figs, *nisperos* – little apricot-coloured fruit with shiny brown pips and delicately juicy flesh.

Entertainments and excursions were limited to the distance a woman and a loaded pushchair can cover between sun-up and sun-down. Our days were spent on the beach or in the hills, following the course of a mountain stream, exploring the old whaling station hidden round the headland. Never having learnt to drive, Venetia was a prodigious walker. Of an evening, in the slow scarlet twilight when the babies were safely tucked up in bed, we would climb up the hill behind the house.

Here, as nowhere else, we were at the crossroads of the ancient world. In front of us lay Africa, the glittering lights of Tangier cocooned in the blue mountains of the Rif which mark the northern limit of the Sahara's dunes. Behind us, the great plains of Iberia, most southerly of Europe's ramparts.

More than anything else, it was the romance of that view which gave me the notion that it was a place where, as a family, we might flourish. Our decision to build a house in a clearing in a cork-oak forest in the hills behind the little port of Tarifa was more by accident than design. Never intended at the start for more than summer living, it seemed to grow of its own accord until it was huge – more of a vast Moorish tent than a house: leaky when it rained, draughty when the fierce wind blew from the east, and chilly all through the winter.

Yet the setting was one of the most glorious on earth, over-looking the Pillars of Hercules, in the land the Moors called the gateway to paradise. Inevitably, as any builder of a house always discovers, the costs of construction proved far higher than we had bargained for. In the end finishing it took all we had. It finally gobbled up our small house in Battersea, leaving us in rented accommodation while the two eldest children, finally scooped up by a disapproving state, attended London schools.

By the time Poppy was due to join Cas and Fran at St Peter's Primary, it was clear we had a space problem. The six of us were bouncing off the walls of an attic flat which had never been designed to house more than a Victorian butler and a couple of tidy house-maids. When we finally decided something had to be done, the scales were already weighted in favour of foreign parts.

Instinctively I felt all that mattered was that there should be space for the children to grow. In Spain we could have all the space we needed. The rooms were tall, light and airy, and there was the entire forest for a playground. The decision to choose rural Andalusia for the four to spend their childhood years was almost as unconsidered as the decision to build the house itself. With the benefit of hindsight, I have no doubt that the advantages far outweighed the drawbacks.

The children were already – according to their ages – capable of communicating in Spanish. Better still, I knew from my own experience that as a family we would be accepted as we might not have been as mere tourists. Children are not only welcome in a Latin culture – they are seen as a treasure, a reason for celebration. In any Mediterranean bar, there will be a dozen children racing around the tables, being treated to a fizzy drink and going about their business under the benevolent eye of the adults. Everyone takes pleasure in their antics. And when babies are tired, they simply curl up in a lap or a corner and drop off to sleep while the adults sip their wine, play dominoes, gossip.

I knew it would not be easy for the children when we finally went back to the land of their birth. There would be educational trip-wires to be negotiated. Yet, in spite of dire warnings from the professionals that my children would be disadvantaged, personal experience had taught me otherwise. My own primary education had been at the Anglo-Uruguayan school in Montevideo, which taught its largely Spanish-speaking pupils in English for half the day, and in Spanish for the remainder. When, at the age of eleven, I was despatched to an English boarding-school in the Malvern Hills, I had a good grasp of the principles of maths, a firm grip on Spanish, reasonable French and slightly foreign English.

There was nothing the matter with my capacity to take in new information – but I was undeniably a foreigner. For my own children, that was a lesson I knew must be taken into account. We had to have books – and the books had to give some contact with what was, eventually, to be home. I made an arrangement with London's most indulgent bookshop, Heywood Hill in Curzon Street, and throughout our years in foreign climes, like the expatriate ladies of the Raj, we had a regular order of books shipped out surface mail. It took a month or two, but it was well worth the wait and the cost of postage.

The parcels were greeted like manna from heaven – the brown paper eagerly ripped open, the books captured and dragged off to lairs. Those books which had long words and no pictures were read aloud, turn and turn about, slow or fast, hesitant or confident as dictated by each reader's developing skills.

The only rival evening entertainment was the small screen. Spanish television, still in its infancy of black-and-white mono-channel, offered re-runs of *The Avengers* spiked with Clement Freud's dog-food advertisement dubbed in the same quick-fire Madrid tenor as Patrick McNee. The magic box had its uses as an educational tool at the beginning, when the children spoke practically no Spanish. They had seen the programmes in their mother tongue, so it was easy enough for them to follow the action – picking up the shape of the sounds naturally as the film rolled on.

We had to find a local school. There were three possiblities. The nearest was the village school. Ten miles away, in the town, there were the two conventional establishments of the nuns and monks.

The third, in Catholic Spain a great innovation, was a new, small, fee-paying establishment set up to cater to the children of the burghers of newly prosperous Algeciras – lucky recipient, in the wake of the closure of the Gibraltar frontier, of a large tranche of the dictator's development funds.

Fortunately we had an in-house expert in our general factotum, Ana. Born and bred in a poor suburb of Algeciras, Ana was the younger sister of my mentor and guide to the local indigenous community, Maria, the housekeeper, with her husband and children, of a nearby rarely occupied villa.

At eighteen, Ana was a sturdy country girl, darkly pretty, quick-witted and firm-viewed, although she was scarcely able to print her own name. But she could add up the price of a week's shopping in the shake of a donkey's tail without recourse to pencil and paper. She adored babies and had already had a hand in the upbringing of her younger sister and twin brothers. She enjoyed housework, but hated the kitchen and all its works. I liked markets and cooking. It was the perfect division of labour.

Ana considered the educational options on our behalf. Under no circumstances were the daughters to be sent to the nuns, because the Sisters of Mercy pinched you in the same place every time so the bruise only showed once. And it hurt. The monks, she knew from her brother, were no better. Nor did the guardians of morality, she added bitterly, consider it part of their brief that their charges should be taught to read and write. The powers of the church agreed with the state that if you educate the poor, your reward will be godless communists. And Andalusia, it was well-known, was a hotbed of communists.

The nearest village school accommodated all ages in the same classroom and was mainly concerned with basic literacy and numeracy – the lack of which was increasingly a social disability. However, she concluded, there were a good few of the local peasant community's children in there too, including her cousins, and my young foreigners would receive a crash course in the life of the countryside, if nothing else. And later, she explained, there was an alternative: a new school not far from the dirt-road settlement on the outskirts of Algeciras in which her family lived, and she had heard that it was very modern. Modernity, she continued with satisfaction, was much to be desired in so backward a country as Andalusia.

We compromised. The village school was to have our custom for the first three months. Then everyone would move down to the big city to join the sons and daughters of Franco's brand-new middle-class at Los Pinos, the secular learning academy, accessible because of modest fees, in which Ana declared her confidence.

I had four English children. I was about to see them transformed into four little Spaniards.

CHAPTER NINE

Travellers' tales

'Pay, pack and follow.'

Colonel Fawcett*

IT WAS IN 1969 – THE LAST YEAR OF THAT TUMULTUOUS DECADE –
when our house in the Andalusian cork-oak forest was finally
completed. And when, three years afterwards, we cut loose from
our London life and took up permanent residence in the valley
overlooking Africa, there was plenty of travelling to be done.

We were always a family of wanderers, never happier than when
out on the open road. Right at the beginning of family life, noticing
that motorized transport seemed to have a hypnotic effect on the

---

*The explorer's instructions to his long-suffering wife, on leaving for the jungles of
Brazil.

most wideawake infant, I fell into the habit of using the family vehicle as a peripatetic cradle. Cas was the most determinedly nocturnal – a natural all-night swinger, bright-eyed and bushy-tailed at three in the morning, sleepy as a kitten by breakfast. Many was the morning we greeted the sunrise together.

There was little anyone could tell my son and me about the first-light glories of Tower Bridge. It was a partial solution to that perennial problem which faces the urban mother – a howling infant who keeps the neighbours awake all night. Whatever racket we might make, at least we were now making it somewhere else.

We were a migratory family by choice as well as by accident. Each summer, as I've written, following the ancient pattern of seasonal transhumance, we packed our household effects on the available transport and took to the high road, serenaded by The Seekers on the tape machine. There's a glorious freedom in taking your children everywhere – at its simplest it means there's no need to worry about what might be happening to them elsewhere – the triumphs and disasters happen in full view.

Children make the best travelling companions. If properly trained, they'll go anywhere, do anything, eat anything. They learn to read maps and menus easily, a skill which can elicit – at least in Latin countries – the admiration and co-operation of the adult natives, particularly useful when dealing with policemen or motor mechanics.

When everyone was still under five and on the ten-per-cent ticket, we travelled to Spain and back by air. We took full advantage of any special treatment provided by airlines for children. With due warning, we would be ushered on the plane ahead of the crowd, provided with our own private minder, and generally treated like the explosive package we might easily turn out to be.

As a travelling companion, a baby is the best value: high in sympathy-generation, and, at least when quiet, low on maintenance. There's only one major snag: it's one of the mysteries of the infant digestive system that babes in arms share with pigeons and seagulls a capacity to evacuate their bowels in mid-flight. There were always at least two changes of nappy to be negotiated in the air – and with bulky, expensive disposable nappies newly available, this was the only time I took advantage of the alternative to the standard terry-towelling (I rather liked the sight and smell of freshly laundered nappies).

I found that small babies are only difficult at take-off and landing, when the change in pressure blocks ears – so I would give a suckle or a bottle at either end of the flight. Once in the air, each baby conformed to its usual behaviour pattern – yelling or snoozing, as nature dictated. Francesca, as befits the eldest daughter, was the only one of the four whose behaviour was impeccable in the air – a natural-born flier, wings were her birthright.

My secret weapon was the travel bag – a sealed paper carrier bag containing carefully selected small inexpensive treasures, a kind of portable Christmas stocking. It was part of the agreement that the bags were not to be opened until the plane was airborne, but speculation on the contents was encouraged. Then the journey could be spent playing with the new toys and games – all the more entertaining since there were three other people's bags to be explored as well as your own.

Toddlers see an aircraft cabin as a giant play-pen. Knowing that the children could not come to any lasting harm, I relaxed and let them wander. Francesca loved other people's babies, volunteering her services as a surrogate mother. Honey was adept at adopting alternative adults, perhaps because her little round spectacles gave her the air of a small wise owl. Once she discovered the use of two feet, she would stagger down the aisles, ricochetting off the armrests like a drunken sailor, peering hopefully into friendly faces. Poppy would hold intense conversations with businessmen in smart suits, offering to share a half-sucked sweet stuck to the tip of a cheerful pink thumb. Cas, firm and responsible, was usually in charge of fielding his sisters' worst excesses. I saw the children's antics as the acquisition of people-skills – all good practice for the social intercourse of adult life.

When the cost of air-tickets escalated beyond our purse, we took to the roads. Travelling continuously for eight hours a day, the journey took us five days to cover the fifteen hundred miles which separate London from the southernmost tip of Europe. A certain etiquette governs behaviour in cars. For instance, we learnt that it was unwise to bring up contentious matters on the road – and that includes the shortest way between any two points. The reason is purely physical: you can't leave a moving vehicle. A row can turn a perfectly ordinary family saloon into a fighting-cock pit. If we felt a quarrel coming on, it was up to the driver to stop the caravanseria and pitch camp until the bone of contention had been satisfactorily chewed.

Honey was usually the centre of any car-born whirlwind, mainly because, as the youngest, she fell victim to Might is Right, and always scored the least desirable position in the vehicle. From there she had to do battle for all privileges – the view, the vantage point for 'I Spy', the last tangerine. We carried a large cotton pillowcase to pop over her when tempers reached boiling-point, rather like jamming the Dormouse back in the teapot during the Mad Hatter's Tea Party.

When they were very small, the children would curl up in sleeping-bags in a heap in the back of the family vehicle. For a brief and wonderful time we had one of the earliest Range Rovers. It was a splendid machine: solid and fast, with the take-off speed and the appetite for fuel of a jumbo jet. It had wrap-around eight-track stereo and was painted pillar-box scarlet. The only drawback – petrol was still very cheap – was the amount of attention it attracted as we streaked down the motorways. We were regularly stopped by traffic and frontier police anxious to discuss the merits of this four-wheel innovation. Sadly our high-luxury transport didn't last long. Before twelve months were out, the family fortunes hit a bumpy patch, and the vehicle had to be returned to the HP company. I really missed it.

We replaced it with a Mini Moke – the smallest vehicle on the road, but the only possible alternative. After it had been painted the family scarlet, it was endowed with much of its predecessor's charm. Square and sturdy, it looked like a travelling pram, with an oil-cloth roof which came up and down on metal struts; a souped-up engine which delivered an astonishing punch; and (replacing the Range Rover's quadrophonic sound) a plug-in removable tape recorder. Soon the passengers established their bridgeheads and managed to find somewhere to curl up in the back. All possessions were stowed in the hollow sides, and it was business as usual on the long run south.

In those early years, when I was often travelling alone with the children, I packed an illegal hand-pistol in the glove compartment. Pearl-handled and silver-barrelled, it had once graced the windows of Asprey's as part of a display of Ian Fleming's James Bond novels, bound in gold-tooled calf leather. It was a gift from Francesca's godfather, Bruce Donn, a buccaneering entrepreneur whose business took him into dangerous places. I never used it, and I kept the magazine separate in case of accidents, but as a frontierswoman I felt myself properly equipped. Nicholas finally found it, or rather I admitted to its possession, one day on arrival at the customs' post at Dover.

'Do we have anything to declare?' he asked me confidently, as we drew into the nothing-to-declare lane. 'Only my pistol – and I've been carrying that for years,' I replied cheerfully.

Anarchy came naturally to me and I had seen no reason to mention it before. As an ex-soldier and far more law-abiding than me, he threw up his hands in horror and turned it in to the authorities, where no doubt it languishes to this day, the centrepiece of some black museum display.

We travelled in four-hour stretches, stopping only briefly to fuel car and people, but when we reached the day's destination or a high spot on the route, we did it *properly*. There was absolutely no cultural corner-cutting: in Paris we did the Louvre and the Orangerie and the Musée de Cluny; in Chartres we did the cathedral; in Avila we walked the walls; in Madrid we visited the Prado. All the same, I knew well enough that culture is best taken in small doses – and should immediately be followed by a treat. Half an hour is the most a child can manage in a museum.

We grew very adept at identifying treats. Chartres is blessed not only with the most glorious cathedral in Christendom, but with a wonderful ice-cream parlour in the cathedral close. Albi not only has the Toulouse-Lautrec museum, but also an excellent patisserie on the other side of the square. In Paris, after a glimpse of the *Mona Lisa*, we had our first taste of oysters in the rue de Rivoli.

The journey was mapped out carefully in advance, and then the plan adhered to. Caspar, as the chief map reader, was in charge of the route, and his decision was final. It was also Cas's duty, as the eldest, to keep the travel diary, a stiff-backed, lined exercise book in which we recorded all useful information acquired along the well-beaten track to the south. Gastronomy was always the family priority: we noted the best markets and the days on which they were held, with listings of seasonal specialities; the locations of those vast French hypermarkets which sell everything from Roquefort to paintboxes to camping stools; those modestly priced restaurants where we had enjoyed the prix-fixe menu; truckers' pull-ins on the long run through Spain where we could be sure of a good hot bean stew and a warm welcome for the children; those food shops – *traiteurs, patissiers* and *chocolatiers* – whose specialities were worth a detour. We listed the rural bakeries where we could find the best bread, the most delicious cakes and the most succulent confectionery. We marked the sites of municipal swimming-pools where we could take a quick respite from the heat of summer. Most important and practical of all, the log recorded the public lavatories which had been visited and found acceptable.

The travel diary, too, included information on natural history: locations of nature reserves (we carried binoculars and bird and botany identification manuals as well as travel guides). We noted sightings of rare birds – azure-winged magpies in a certain clump of trees between Zafra and Valladolid, red kites hunting grasshoppers in a valley below Segovia. We listed the sites of particularly exuberant wild flower meadows where we might spread a picnic, and took note of the road verges where orchids might be found in spring. It's a wonder we ever made it to the next town let alone the thousand or so miles.

As a migratory tribe, we budgeted for one night indoors, so that everyone could have a break and a proper bath, and listed affordable motels whose proprietors would let us pile into one room. For the rest of the time, we became expert campers. Not caravaners, but good old-fashioned pitchers of tented accommodation – packed away each morning, and set up again each night. Eventually, as the group outgrew the Mini Moke, a Volkswagen camper-van, bought cheap and umpteenth-hand from outside Australia House in London, became our second home. We stripped the inside down to its bones, lined it with plywood, installed a collapsible table and comfortable benches with foam cushions covered with Harris tweed – all very Habitat, as became the spirit of the time.

Now all we needed were the tents. As in a palace, so in a tent – you can never be overhoused. For comfort and tranquillity, we learnt to allow twice the recommended area under canvas. Between six of us, we had accommodation for ten adults – one six-man pavilion and a pair of two-man ridge-tents. The main space in the big tent served as the communal living-room, equipped with a gas-lantern, table, chairs and stools. A zip-closed inner compartment provided a bedroom for the adults. Pitched to form two other sides of a square were the two satellite tents shared by the four children. It was the camping equivalent of the Taj Mahal.

When we first acquired the tents, we practised putting them up and dismantling them before we left home. Francesca, the profes-sional packer of the family, made a checklist of all the necessary bits and bobs, including tent-pegs and mallet, and ticked everything off each time we struck camp. With a little experience under our belts, it took seven minutes exactly to get the tents up, with one person at each corner and Honey hammering in the pegs. As the cook, I was not expected to take part, being in a reserved occupation – as they had it in wartime – essential to the well-being of the workers.

We found it best to stick to official camp-sites – they were safe, cheap and had communal washrooms and sometimes even swimming-pools. We had a guide which listed and graded them, but as migrant campers rather than holiday residents, we scored low on the list of desirable clients and had to take what we could get. We learnt to avoid seaside camp-sites, all too often there was no room at the inn. Inland sites were much more accommodating to one-night stands.

Best of all were the municipal camp-sites, facilities provided by local councils in both France and Spain. These were cheap, clean and conveniently sited either in the middle of villages or on the outskirts of big towns so that we could shop for the evening meal without having to drive anywhere. Nicholas was the acknowledged connoisseur of camp-site conveniences. He would co-opt one of the daughters as a scout to make sure the coast was clear, and vanish with the newspaper into the ladies' lavatories. He maintained the risk was well worth taking: the continental gents was always a hell-hole – one of those pits with two places to put the feet and absolutely no reading facilities. To his daughters' delight, he was regularly flushed out by some irate matron and sent packing with a flea in his ear. He met his mechanical match one afternoon when, discovering a brand-new convenience with automatic flushing, he pushed the wrong button and emerged soaked from head to foot.

Certain other lessons were learnt the hard way – the most important of these is to pick high ground in preference to low in the summer when the ground is hard. It's logical, really. If it rains in the night – and there's nothing so wet as a summer rainstorm – the water will bounce off the hill, and a tent at the bottom will soon be slopping around in a sea of mud. We had to up-stakes at three in the morning once when we were washed off a dusty hillside near Madrid.

On the road everyone loses everything all the time. It's the most frustrating part of travelling. So each person had their own stuff-bag made in plain cotton with a band of colour stitched round to distinguish ownership. This doubled as pillow and travel bag. A single large laundry bag served for everyone. A hanger-bag – a large multi-pocketed bag sewn onto a clothes hanger – held extras of all basic essentials. If something vital went missing, we replaced it immediately and without recriminations at the next supermarket.

There were too many of us to make full-scale restaurant meals anything but a special-occasion treat. The midday meal was always light – a picnic, market-food, whatever was on offer: bread from the bakery with the longest queue, cheese and chorizo and tomato and onion, fruit.

The evening meal was a different matter. At night we ate like kings. We took nothing edible with us on our journeys – no emergency rations of cornflakes and long-life milk – instead we went native, shopping locally and every day. In France, made-up dishes could be bought in the *traiteur* – the cooked-food shop – offering an instant guide to the region's specialities. If our budget wouldn't stretch to the ready-prepared, we scoured the local markets, sure to be overwhelmed with advice as to the best way of preparing and serving whatever was in season. The evening food-foray became the highlight of the day's journeying, a reward for long hours of patience on the road and a chance for the children to practise their languages on the natives.

Our cooking facilities were limited to a two-ring camp stove and a charcoal barbecue – no baking or oven cooking, and dishes couldn't be browned under the grill (the only lack I felt keenly). Speed was the only requirement – as the Spanish say, 'Hunger is the best sauce'. With a little ingenuity, we could manage most things except those slow-cooked bean stews which were the staple daily dinner at home.

This alone expanded our culinary repertoire: the essence of a feast is unfamiliar food – something you don't eat every day.

Everyone lent a hand with the preparations, and every morning, to pass the early hours of travelling, the previous evening's experience would be thoroughly discussed and noted in the travel diary. Particular meals quickly became identified with particular places at particular times of year – and as we grew more experienced, we plotted our route accordingly.

In summer the living was easy – every market was piled high with summer fruits and fresh-picked vegetables. In autumn, we took care that our route south led through Bordeaux, where we could be sure to find cèpes – most prized of the autumn crop of wild fungi – to be cooked *à la Bordelaise*, in oil with garlic and parsley. If we travelled in spring, we headed for Burgos, where we ate roast milk-piglet – crisp-skinned, sticky-juiced, tender as a ripe fig – and finished the meal with fresh curds and honey.

Yet of all these exotic pleasures, we all agreed that the most memorable of our peripatetic meals was the simplest. Like all the best things, we had not even planned it. We were expecting little of that particular evening – on our way back to Tarifa after a summer spent in Britain, nervous at the notion of the start of a new school ahead. The ferry had been delayed by rough weather, and we arrived at Dieppe too late for the shops.

Gloomily, we headed south through the autumn fields of Normandy. It was the end of the season, and we soon discovered that the only camp-site on the route had already been closed down for the winter. Never mind, said the owner, we might be able to persuade the neighbouring farmer to let us pitch camp in his apple orchard.

The farmer took pity on the travelling circus which had turned up at his gates, and gathered us in. We were indeed welcome to camp among his apple trees – better still, his brother was the village butcher. That day he had sent his autumn pigs for slaughter – fat as butter on the orchard gleanings – and we were given some of his famous saucisse for grilling over the fire. Since there was an autumn chill in the air, he threw in a bottle of his own home-distilled applejack, and for the children a big jug of the newly pressed juice – and permission to help themselves to the freckled golden fruit.

Sausages with Cream and Calvados

The sausage must be of the best – all meat, as made in France. One of the delights of this delectable dish is guessing which chunk is apple and which is potato. The cream of Normandy is thick, yellow and slightly soured.

--------- SERVES 6 ---------

2 lb/1 kg all-pork sausages or Cumberland sausage
– the best you can find
A knob of butter
6 largish potatoes, peeled and chunked
6 eating apples, cored and thickly sliced

1 small glass calvados (or any white brandy)
½ pint/300 ml thick yellow cream
1 tablespoon French mustard
A pinch of nutmeg and allspice
Salt and pepper

1. Prick the sausages and set them to fry gently in the butter in a wide frying pan, loosely lidded.

2. Meanwhile, put the potatoes to boil in plenty of salted water. Drain them as soon as they are just soft.

3. When the juice from the sausages runs clear, turn up the heat so that they brown. Remove and keep warm.

4. Fry the drained potatoes in the sausage juices and butter until they crisp a little. Remove and keep warm.

5. Fry the apple slices – a few minutes only, as they just need to caramelize on the outside, and should remain quite firm.

6. Splash in the calvados and let it bubble up, scraping in all the brown bits. When it no longer smells of alcohol, stir in the cream and mustard. Spice, season and sauce everything with the creamy gravy. Gorgeous. Lick your fingers so as not to miss anything.

The sky was already indigo-dark, the moon had risen, and the stars were brilliant by the time our little gypsy encampment was ready and the pans were on the stove. We set up our table under the laden branches. I can taste that meal still: the succulent hoops of nutmeg-spiced saucisse slowly fried in butter; the apples – crisp-fleshed, vanilla-scented – sliced and browned; the creamy mass of potatoes sauced with applejack and golden cream.

A pair of pale-winged owls hunted moths in the firelight, and the air was sweet with the scent of ripe fruit. Afterwards, warm and content, we crawled into our tents and slept the sleep of the angels.

CHAPTER TEN

Andalusia: Life among the cork oaks

'Of Paradise I cannot speak properly, for I have not been there.'

Sir John Mandeville★

AFTER WE MOVED TO SPAIN, WE DIDN'T ENTIRELY CUT OUR TIES WITH home. We kept our London flat – as statutory tenants on a fixed rent, we could just about afford to do so. Our plan was to return to Britain each summer, renting the flat out to university students for the rest of the year and letting the house in Andalusia while we were in England – our travels were always against the tourist flow.

In those first Spanish years before Nicholas became a full-time writer, he was still anchored to his work in London. So, as we entered our new life, it meant that for much of the time, and

★In his *Book of Travels*, a remarkable thirteenth-century literary tall tale.

certainly as far as day-to-day organization of life was concerned, we were to all intents and purposes a one-parent family. Nicholas visited us as and when he could. The rest was up to me.

Not for the first time, our priorities were at odds with conventional arrangements. Certainly we lived in a large house – positively palatial by local standards. Indeed we had the hard-working Ana to keep us clean and in order. And, for lack of a permanent man about the place, we had José – a distant cousin of Ana's who lived further down the valley – to hew wood for the fires so necessary against the valley's chill winter rains, and to prod the garden into productivity. Yet in spite of – or more accurately because of – all this magnificence, we no longer owned a vehicle.

The neighbourhood didn't think any the worse of us. In Andalusia, it's accepted that purse-strings are tighter at certain times than at others. Nevertheless, until the next publisher's advance or whatever the good Lord might deliver, it seemed sensible to acquire at least some means of transport for the daily school run.

It was José who came up with the donkey as a solution. Lacking green fingers – his efforts as a gardener were about as effective as Agent Orange – José was always a man for animal husbandry. In addition, Bernardo the donkey came well-recommended, his character vouched for by Manolo the dustman, who, as the holder of a powerful well-remunerated post, also doubled up as the neighbourhood's banker. In spite of this recommendation, we soon discovered Bernardo was not a natural-born worker. A clock-puncher, if ever there was one. Brought out of semi-retirement at Manolo's *cortijo*, a small farm a mile or two up the valley, he was an amiable idler rather than a beast of burden.

He was also expensive. Not in the provision of fodder – that, as José and Manolo were in complete agreement, was a matter of supreme smallness since he would naturally forage for himself. No, the expense was to come in suiting-up Bernardo to a standard the neighbours would consider appropriate to his lofty status as our transport – not just any transport, but the transport of well-to-do foreigners.

In short, there are plain old donkeys, and there are donkeys of category. What we had on our hands, until something was done about it, was most emphatically the former.

'Believe me, *señora*, category is all,' José explained thoughtfully as he examined Bernardo through narrowed eyes. 'There is no shame in a donkey. Our Lord himself chose the sainted animal as his transport into Jerusalem. A person of the highest birth, even one as clearly a lady of category such as yourself, can take a well-dressed donkey anywhere. A well-dressed donkey can hold his head high in the company of a pure-bred Arab stallion. Look at Don Quixote and Sancho Panza. A properly equipped ass can visit places where only a horse, and a thoroughbred horse at that, might be welcome.'

'By the blood of God, it's no more than the truth!' Manolo agreed.

José explained what must be done. A visit must be paid to the sainted donkey saddler in Tarifa. Obediently we all climbed on the bus with José, juddering down the potholed coastal road to be deposited – along with a crate of live hens and a piglet – at the entrance to the little port. Tarifa was a stronghold of the Spanish navy – the powers-that-be held that the danger of invasion came from the North African coast. They'd done it once before – and then it had taken seven centuries to persuade them to go home. Moorish fortifications still defended the harbour which marked the southernmost tip of Europe, and access to the town was through a Moorish keyhole arch.

The saddler's shop was located in a labyrinth of streets which backed onto the quay. Occupying a narrow passage between two fishermen's houses, it was no more than a roof tacked onto outside walls. The shadowy interior, scented with hay and hemp, was a hive of activity, with sewing-machines whirring, sacks being shifted and stuffed, children racing about in the dust.

This busy emporium was presided over by Luis, a merchant of substance, as important to the life of the town as Manolo was to the countryside. Luis not only equipped donkeys but also mended sails – a perfectly compatible activity, since donkey saddlery is made of canvas. In addition, as a supplier to the charcoal burners who used donkeys to transport their crop – a secondary product of the cork-oak forests – he controlled the trade in charcoal. Charcoal was then an important commodity in Andalusia – fuel for the braziers which were used for cooking a *puchero* on the doorstep in summer, and as central heating in winter. Luis also traded in bull-leather, providing the cattle-ranching *señoritos* with the beautifully stitched leather chaps – *zahones* – which protect a horseman's legs from the thorns of the thicketed mountainside.

As an arbiter of donkey-taste, Luis the saddler was without peer. But by the time Bernardo was fully equipped he cost almost as much as a second-hand Seat 600, the alternative form of transport we could not quite afford. At the end of the day's shopping, we had acquired a scarlet, yellow and emerald wool-embroidered bridle with cross-stitched blinkers; a headstall decorated with a handsome woolly tassel to bob up and down on his forehead; a girth-strap of finely plaited cotton webbing; and for a saddle, a straw-stuffed antimacassar made of striped mattress-ticking with a thick hemp underblanket. All this came with elegant palm-fibre panniers, just in case he might be required for harvesting, or carrying goods to and from market.

We climbed back on the bus and dragged all the magnificence home. Thereafter the toilette of Bernardo was a ritual worthy of any Edwardian dandy. Proust would have been proud of him.

José and Manolo – eagerly sought and brought up to the house for a second opinion – were in complete agreement that Bernardo was now a donkey of a very high category indeed.

'He will need his toenails clipping regularly – you would be surprised how fast they grow,' advised Manolo. 'It would not be proper to shoe him, even if he is a donkey of category, and grand enough to be a mule.'

'In addition, there is the gastronomic consideration,' José added as a clincher. 'You must bear in mind that the donkey has not only the distinction of a useful life, but makes a succulent end. He will provide, after his demise, the best and leanest *chorizo* the heart could desire. When I was a child in the war, my mother used to spice her donkey-sausage with a little chilli and plenty of marjoram: they were a rare treat.' He slapped Bernardo's rump appreciatively. 'Truly a sainted animal.'

I shall not give a donkey-*chorizo* recipe – although I *could*. Indeed, there were moments during that first month, when chorizo was about all I reckoned he was good for.

As a beast of burden, rather than an ass-about-town, Bernardo was far from co-operative. Curiously enough, unlike engine-driven modes of transport, he was better going up than down. Human will-power prevailed uphill, but downhill he came into his wilful own. He would plant his feet firmly on the road, point his long ears

Puchero

This is a one-pot meal, the classic *andaluz* midday dish. Sometimes I served the broth first, more often it was all dished up together in a deep soup-plate and eaten with a fork and spoon.

1 lb/500 g chickpeas
2–3 thick-cut rashers of salted pork belly or unsmoked bacon, cubed
1 whole garlic head
2 dried red peppers (pimentos) (optional)
or 1 tablespoon paprika
½ small chicken, jointed (an old boiler has the best flavour, but a young one will do)
1 short length of ham bone or bacon knuckle
2 small chorizos or paprika sausage (optional)
1 carrot, scraped and chopped

2–3 sticks unblanched celery, rinsed and chopped
4 tablespoons olive oil
A few black peppercorns
1–2 links black pudding (morcilla) (optional)
2 large potatoes, peeled and sliced
2 beef tomatoes, skinned if you prefer, roughly chopped
1 lb/500 g greens (spinach, chard, cabbage, turnip tops) shredded
Salt
Approx. 4 pints/12.5 l water (excluding soaking water)

TO FINISH

1–2 tablespoons olive oil

2 tablespoons chopped parsley

1. Put the chickpeas to soak in fresh water for at least 5 hours, or overnight. You can keep a supply of pre-soaked chickpeas in the freezer – handy if you're in a hurry.

2. Remove the rind from the pork belly or bacon. Cut the rind into squares. Cube the meat.

3. Do not skin the garlic or separate the cloves, but hold the whole thing in a flame to char the papery covering and roast the cloves a little. De-seed the red peppers if you are using them, and tear them into small pieces.

4. Drain the chickpeas and put them in a heavy saucepan with the chicken (if using a boiling fowl), the ham bone, the salt pork or bacon, chorizo if using, carrot, celery, the singed garlic head, the dried red peppers or paprika, olive oil and peppercorns – no salt. Bring all to the boil, and then turn down to a fast simmer – chickpeas must be kept on the bubble. Lid loosely. You may need to add extra *boiling* water during the course of the cooking. Cook for as long as necessary to soften the chickpeas – they are variable in the length of time they need – from 1½ hours to 3 hours.

5. After the first hour, add the joints of the young roasting chicken (if using), without allowing the broth to come off the boil. When the chickpeas are tender, add the optional black pudding, potatoes and chopped tomatoes.

6. When the potatoes are nearly soft, stir in the greens, turn up the heat to return the broth to the boil, and simmer for another 5 minutes or so, until the vegetables are tender.

7. To finish, taste and add salt (the ham or bacon will have contributed to the saltiness), and stir in the extra olive oil and the parsley. Bubble up and serve with a salad of roughly chunked tomatoes, cucumber and mild onion and plenty of good bread.

forward and his head down, and whoever or whatever was on top came sliding down onto the sticky hot tarmac below. Being bested by a donkey is not very dignified – and as a mode of transport, give me a no. 19 bus any day. Although I suppose, looking back on it, it's certainly character forming. Not many big-city children have been donkey-borne to learn their letters.

The school in Pelayo – with its single classroom accommodating pupils drawn from the surrounding countryside – gave Caspar, Francesca and Poppy their educational baptism of fire. Honey was scarcely more than a toddler, but she came along for the ride. Although the little village was only a couple of miles down the road, sometimes it could take us, if Bernardo was not in the best of moods, an hour to get there. Fortunately the school timetable was loosely fixed, and our frequently late arrival was greeted with tolerance. As foreigners, we were considered to have conferred a certain cachet, in spite of our gone-native method of transport.

For the children, total cultural immersion included not only a language of which they had only the rudiments, but the swift acquisition of rural skills. That first week, nervous as any mother might be, I would enquire delicately each day as to what had been happening in the schoolroom, to be met with giggles and the minimum of information. At the end of the first week all was revealed by Cas.

The first lessons of that autumn term – perhaps in deference to the new arrivals – were taught in the small patch of garden which adjoined the school. On Monday, Cas explained, the class had learnt how to dig the ground for cultivation. On Tuesday they had learnt how to plant lettuces. On Wednesday the children were shown how to set traps for the rabbits which would surely follow the lettuces. On Thursday, a couple of furry marauders were caught. On Friday, the pupils learnt how to skin the rabbits, scrape and salt and peg out the skins to make a waistcoat.

Also on Friday, Cas concluded triumphantly, it was to be rabbit – *conejo en salsa* – for lunch, relieving all parents of the need to supply provisions. Only an *andaluz* housewife can stretch two rabbits to feed twenty schoolchildren. Here were the lessons of a lifetime crammed into five days – the Creator himself couldn't have done better.

The first week set the standard for the three months the children attended Pelayo. From Monday to Friday it was donkey-transport and rural lessons. But on Saturday we were free as birds – liberated from responsibilities, we took ourselves to market, borrowing the kindly neighbour's Land Rover and rattling down the bumpy road to Algeciras, where anything and everything was to be had.

We never ate breakfast at home on Saturday. We began our shopping by selecting a fresh roll hot from the baker – a particular roll shaped and baked for this very purpose – to be taken straight to the delicatessen kiosk and filled with a slice of salt-cured ham or salami or salty cheese. Everyone had a preference, a luxury affordable because the quantity was so small.

Street food is the migrating family's best friend. There is no better way to find out how the other half lives than to dive straight into the market-place and share what's on offer. Tailor-made for sharing – a little taste of something unfamiliar but clearly enjoyed by a whole streetful of other people is more likely to gain approval from the most conservative children than a piled-up plateful in a restaurant. And mine, as you might imagine, by now were far from conservative.

We had other entertainments, not least the attentions of a clan of gypsies who had settled down on the outskirts of the town. The gypsies of Andalusia are well-established communities, sedentary rather than travelling people, with a visible presence particularly around the seaports. The gypsies of Algeciras kept themselves to themselves and were rarely seen about the town, except when they came to market.

Like us, they always came on the busiest day of the week, but they came not to buy but to sell. The gypsies' traditional wares were wild-gathered delicacies – mushrooms, asparagus sprue, thistle rosettes – all that was available on the hillsides, free food which we later learnt to gather for ourselves. The gypsies also came to beg, a highly skilled business conducted by forceful matrons with borrowed babies on the hip, their demands for alms reinforced by the threat of the evil eye.

We quickly acquired a guardian gypsy-child, Puri – short for Purification of the Virgin Mary – a young girl only a few months older than Francesca, a ragged little beauty with the high cheek-bones, translucent golden skin and the shimmering straight black hair of a true daughter of the Romanies. Although looking at the two of them together, Francesca – an equally graceful dark-haired

Conejo en Salsa (Rabbit in Tomato Sauce)

The secret of feeding a lot of people on very little is to make plenty of sauce and heap everything onto a mountain of chips. The more mouths to feed, the more chips you fry, and you can bump up the vegetable content if your guests look particularly hungry. If it really looks a bit on the mean side, fry eggs and dump them on top of everything. Supply plenty of good bread to mop the chins. With olives to nibble, a crisp salad and maybe a dish of fried green peppers on the side, no-one will go hungry.

SERVES 8–10
---

2 wild rabbits or 1 tame rabbit
1–2 tablespoons seasoned flour
8 tablespoons olive oil
1 slice fatty bacon or salt-cured ham, diced
2 garlic cloves, peeled and chopped
1 large onion, peeled and finely sliced
2 carrots, scraped and chopped

1 stick celery (in Spain, this is unblanched and stronger flavoured)
1 red pepper, de-seeded and sliced lengthways
½ teaspoon peppercorns, crushed
1 bay-leaf
1 lb/500 g tomatoes, scalded, skinned and chopped
½ bottle dry sherry or white wine
Salt and sugar

TO SERVE

Lots of chips

1. Joint the little wild rabbits into bite-sized pieces. If nothing is wasted, you will get 15 little joints from one rabbit: 2 hind-legs make 4 joints, the forelegs 2 more, the saddle is chopped across into 6 (and don't forget to include the head, liver and kidneys). Dust the pieces with seasoned flour – easiest if you tip everything into a plastic bag and shake it around.

2. Heat the oil in a heavy casserole and fry the meat over a high heat until it takes on a little colour. Push the rabbit to one side and add the bacon or ham, garlic, onion, carrot, celery and sliced red pepper. Fry gently until the vegetables soften and brown a little.

3. Add the tomatoes, sprinkle in the crushed peppercorns, tuck in the bay-leaf, pour in the sherry or wine and bubble up. Bring everything to the boil. Sprinkle in a teaspoon of salt and a pinch of sugar.

4. Lid tightly and leave to simmer very gently either on the top of the stove or in a low oven, 300°F/150°C/mark 2 for 1½–2 hours until the meat is very tender. Check every now and then and add a little water if it looks like drying out. Remove the lid and turn up the heat at the end to concentrate the juices.

5. Serve the rabbit stew heaped up on a mound of thick-cut chips twice-fried in olive oil (for really crisp tasty chips, salt them first rather than after the cooking). The sauce soaks into the chips, and you don't really notice if you only get a little taste of the rabbit – particularly with all those bones to suck.

child with her skin tanned from the sun – could easily have passed for Puri's twin.

Purification adopted us as her private source of income in return for taking responsibility for our welfare in the market. She would always know when we had arrived – not a cat moved in Algeciras on market-day but the gypsies knew it – and on payment of a tiny but regular stipend would protect us from the attentions of her kith and kin, run errands, and field any of the four children who went astray.

'In Rosario's shop, señorita,' she would grin cheerfully in reply to my frustrated request for information on the whereabouts of Poppy – whose creative requirements led her into the dark little shops in the old part of town in search of those small essentials for sewing, modelling or painting. 'Shall I fetch her, señorita?'

As for Cas, Puri quickly had the measure of him. As is the way with boys, he would get bored of the market and disappear for a game of table football in the bars of the upper part of the town. 'The Bar Central', or 'The Bar Taurino', would be the swift reply when I had lost touch with him for an hour or so.

We bought from the gypsies those things which only they could supply: wild fruits like prickly pears – cactus fruit, skilfully peeled by the vendors to avoid the needle-sharp thorns; paper cones crammed with the fruit of the strawberry tree, *Arbutus unedo* – the rosy berries as seductive to the eye as they are dull to the palate. From the gypsies, too, we learnt how to strip back the green covering of a stick of raw sugar cane and suck at the sweet juices secreted in the pith. In the fish market we watched out for the dark-eyed, brown-skinned fisherboy – scarcely older than Cas – who sold sea urchins, deftly snipping open the spiky ball to reveal five little orange roes, each a delectable sip of sea fruit – handing them over to be squeezed with lemon and scooped out with a thumbnail.

I would let the children roam the town while I marketed – secure in the knowledge that children come to no harm in Andalusia. The stallholders as well as Puri would keep an eye on them, while I added to my housewifely skills in the market-place – learning how to test the freshness of just-landed shrimps by dipping a finger into the brine and tasting it for salt, how to select the fattest plaits of garlic and ripest strings of peppers essential to an Andalusian stew. The stallholders were soon accustomed to me, and would encourage me to try new things.

After the vegetable baskets were filled and left with the stallholder who had our regular custom – loyalty was rewarded with assistance in loading up the vehicle later – it was time for the mid-morning snack. For us it was always *churros*, airy loops of frittered flour-and-water batter (the crispest include potato in the mix) – bought hot from the fryer and strung on green reeds so that the buyer did not burn his or her fingers. In the north of Spain, *churros* come ready-sugared, but in the south, in Andalusia, they are left savoury, to be carried to the nearest pavement café and enjoyed dunked in milky coffee or thick chocolate, spiced, Moorish-style, with cinnamon. Later in the day, the fritter-man turned his business over to frying potato crisps for those slaking their thirst in the cafés and bars. The fun of market-food is not only the chance to try something new at an affordable price, but to see it cooked in front of you.

South of the olive-tree line, people live as much of their lives as possible in the open air. In a warm climate, it's natural that the community's social life is conducted in public – offering everyone, ourselves included, a chance to join in the fun. The evening promenade, the *paseo*, when the whole population takes the air in the village square, has its morning equivalent in the market, with gossip and greetings exchanged throughout every commercial transaction. In the market-place there was the added bonus of instruction in necessary skills such as how to shell dried sunflower seeds by cracking them between the front teeth and spitting out the husk while retaining the kernel.

By midday the market was already packing up, Puri was despatched to warn the wandering children – and I and any adult companion I had dragooned into accompanying me settled down for refreshment. A tiny cup of fiercely strong coffee or a glass of Moorish mint tea for the grown-ups; lemon juice sweetened with sugar lumps and diluted with fizzy water for any of the four who were not occupied in racing round the town. Here, comfortably ensconced, I could continue my gastronomic education, learning by observation such essential culinary skills as how to pick the flesh from a spider crab, how to slice up a grilled octopus tentacle into bite-sized slivers, how to hold a grilled sardine by the tail and nibble the flesh neatly off the spine.

Afterwards, before we made our way home in the rattling Land Rover with our crammed baskets, we would nip into the cake shop for a quick sugar-fix. If you buy one cake only, it is assumed that you'll want to eat it on the spot. Your chocolate éclair or honey-trickled pastry or soft custard-filled meringue is snuggled in a square of tissue-napkin, and a glass of cold water pushed across the counter so that you can refresh your palate – a courtesy acquired from the Moorish occupation.

The eastern habit of taking a meal on the move, with visits to different establishments to sample each course, lives on in the peripatetic Spanish habit of taking *tapas* – surely, for all of Seville's claims to the ritual, a legacy of Andalusia's Moorish colonizers. The Moors left their mark, too, in a taste for ice-cooled nut-milks and honey-and-almond sweetmeats. Almonds – toasted and salted or crusted with crystalized honey, sold by weight in a screw of sugar paper – were our grandest, most luxurious treat.

If a nation's character and history is to be read in the market-place, Algeciras remained staunchly Moorish in its gastronomic tastes. The gathering of country and town, merchants and sailors, has always provided a forum for the exchange of ideas – so perhaps it is not surprising that the market-snack is the first culinary bridgehead to be captured as a result of immigration, or colonial involvement, or simply in response to the tastes of migrant workers.

In the spice-merchant's sacks could be seen the evidence of ancient trade routes, traces of conquest, the indelible evidence of colonial adventuring. It was Phoenician traders who first brought the saffron which perfumes the rice dishes of Andalusia; the powdery scents of cumin and turmeric, cloves and cinnamon spoke of the centuries of Moorish occupation; precious phials of vanilla pods told us of the long Atlantic voyage to discover the New World. Golden oil and the straw-pale wines of Jerez, the product of olive groves and vines planted by the Romans, were evidence of that earlier colonization. Roman wine provided yeast to leaven Andalusian bread. Two thousand years later, nowhere can the legacy of Rome be more clearly seen than in the daily dinner.

Bread is truly the staff of life in Andalusia. Until recent times, each little hamlet milled and baked its own, and the fame of individual bakers spread far and wide. In rural households such as those of our neighbours in the valley, every meal was based on bread, eaten fresh or stored and soaked to make a gazpacho – not

Fifteen-Minute Soup

This is the first resort of the *andaluz* housewife confronted by a lot of hungry people who want something hot to eat *now*. The quality of the broth dictates the excellence of the result. A splash of white wine or sherry at the beginning of the cooking helps the flavour if the stock is less than perfect – all the alcohol evaporates in the simmering.

SERVES 4

2 pints/1.25 l chicken, meat or vegetable broth (home-made is best, but a good stock cube will do)
About 4 tablespoons finely chopped lean bacon, gammon or ham

2 heaped tablespoons cooked rice or a handful of soup noodles (the very thin ones)
2–4 hard-boiled eggs, peeled and chopped
Mint and parsley

1. Bring the stock to the boil.
2. Stir in the gammon or ham and the rice or noodles.
3. Bring the soup back to the boil, and cook for a few minutes (long enough to soften the noodles if you are using them).
4. Stir in the chopped hard-boiled egg, mint and parsley. Serve in hot bowls, with fresh bread or thick-sliced toast.

the delicate tomato-based chilled soup of urban chefs, but a thick bread porridge flavoured with a rub of garlic, a splash of vinegar and a trickle of oil. The alternative was fifteen-minute soup, based on broth from the *puchero*.

In the bakeries of that time could most clearly be seen the rapid transition from an agricultural to an industrial economy. The shape of the bread dictates its purpose: town bread is baked in tins for ease of slicing – it can be taken straight home and replaced daily, so longevity is not of any great moment. But a countryman's bread has a rounded shape, kneaded by hand to suit the requirements of the customer: a rounded or bolster-shaped loaf will not easily break; it can be transported without injury in a donkey-basket; small loaves can be taken in the pocket to the field; large ones have fuller volume and lack hard edges so that the crumb stays soft for longer.

The baker in Pelayo – whose sons also attended the school – came to market on Saturday to sell his country bread from the back of his van: he found a ready market among those who had only recently moved to the town to find work and were already nostalgic for the life, hard as it might have been, that they had left behind. Those who were going on long journeys – ourselves included – could order seven-kilo loaves which came, as his bread always did, blessed with the sign of the cross.

Already things were changing. Among the emerging middle-classes – the old dictator's legacy to his countrymen – sliced and wrapped bread was a sign of affluence. Steam-baked in industrial bakeries, Pan Bimbo – an inadvertently accurate description of a characterless fluff – was full of recycled vitamins and processed bran. It was considered 'modern', that most desirable of epithets in a country which suspected itself of backward leanings.

The Saturday trip to market was as vital to our understanding of the people among whom we had chosen to settle as anything learnt in the schoolroom. By the time, three months later, the children decided they were ready to tackle the more sophisticated education available in Algeciras, they were already at home in Andalusia. Modern life beckoned.

CHAPTER ELEVEN

School days in Algeciras

'No business before breakfast, Glum!' says the King.
'Breakfast first, business next.'

William Makepeace Thackeray (1811–1863)*

LOS PINOS, A SPRAWLING MODERN BUILDING IN ALGECIRAS'S MOST
prosperous suburb, was as modern as anyone could possibly wish. It
was, in effect, the educational equivalent of Pan Bimbo. And, like
Pan Bimbo, it satisfied all nutritional requirements without providing much in the way of a meal.

Fortunately for our standing in this affluent community, the
family fortunes had recovered sufficiently to permit the replacement
of Bernardo with transport more in keeping with our status. I joined

*From *The Rose and The Ring*.

115

the car pool and began to take the provision of lunch-boxes seriously. The children were absorbed into the crowd of impeccably turned-out children in the neatly manicured playground.

Although fees were modest, the school's up-to-the-minute outlook required the regular replacement of textbooks at considerable expense, providing a fascinating insight into the rewriting of history books, geography manuals and science handbooks at a time when Spain was in the process of rapid adaptation and change. Modernity in the classroom was supplemented with modernity in assessment. Psychiatrists were employed to monitor the children's progress. Computers were installed to assess the results of questionnaires. School reports were monuments to impenetrable computer-speak which left the teachers as bewildered as the pupils.

Nevertheless, the three eldest (Honey was not yet a candidate for anything but the adjoining infant school, *Pulgarcitos* – Little Fleas) settled down quickly to their new educational rhythm, perhaps more easily because, unlike children who are sent away to boarding-school, they knew they would come home every evening. During the day, they worked at their lessons according to their inclinations, formed new friendships and shared their friends with each other.

Since there was no uniform, the two elder girls began to worry about sartorial conformity. In Los Pinos fashionability was all. Dependent as they were on a mother who was a dyed-in-the-wool maker and mender, fashionable they most certainly weren't – at least by the standards of smart middle-class Algeciras. Ana saw to it that they were clean, darned and mended – and we would sometimes acquire the latest dungarees from America or the *dernier cri* in bell-bottom cottons from the King's Road. None of this cut much ice in Los Pinos. Cas faced other demands among the boys. Thoughtful and aware even at the age of ten, he was fiercely democratic – not a popular position in Franco's Spain – and he sometimes found himself obliged to defend his politics with his fists. Honey would walk over to join her siblings for the two-hour break for lunch, taken at the house of one of their schoolmates.

All this, to put it mildly, might seem something of a challenge. The four of them, perhaps because they were a formidable gang in their own right and had always done everything together, rose to meet it. I suppose I have never thought it was *what* was learnt which was important – believing instead that the ability to learn was all that mattered. Intellect no less than physical muscles can only develop if pushed constantly to the limit – and that we were certainly doing, all of us. Once you've acquired this essential equipment, you can do anything; without it, you can do nothing. Knowledge is different – it can be gathered at any time from the cradle to the grave.

We had time on our hands as well. More than half the year is holidays – school's out for seven months out of the twelve. Since I had trained as an artist before my marriage, painting was one area in which I felt confident enough to supplement the school's teaching. All children like to make pictures. It's caveman stuff – a form of self-expression which comes as naturally as walking and talking. We are only discouraged when our parents and teachers demand too much of our skills – all too swiftly separating sheep from goats.

I don't believe artistic skills are inborn – they are acquired, a vocabulary of communication, like any other. As an artist you need to practise – all the time, whenever and wherever you can – and with small children at the knee, the first opportunity I had to earn a little extra money was with the brush. I have never been the kind of artist who paints from the imagination. I need to see my subject in the round to make the transference to the page. Wherever I go, I pack a sketch-book instead of a camera.

Sometimes I'd have company when one of the children would come out and join me. In the Doñana Nature Reserve, where I cut my artistic teeth on the heronry, Cas, the keenest bird-watcher, would spot birds for me:

'Spoonbill down to the second branch on the left. Stork's moved two nests up. Cattle egret coming in to land. Irritated eagle overhead.'

You can never tell. Anything can happen on a painting outing – it should never be planned. I just carried my equipment on any expedition, and settled down if the opportunity presented itself. As a concession to family life I carried spares. Someone was sure to join me for half an hour and make use of the extra equipment. Young artists have the stamina of a feather duster and the attention span of a gnat. You need patience. Those who lack patience can go wild-gathering.

On the way to school, the children had already learnt from their fellow pupils which roadside plants were considered edible. Favourites were the sorrel-sour stalks of Bermuda buttercup. *Oxalis pescaprae,* and *huevos de buey* – 'ox-eggs' – plump round seed-heads gathered from the drooping sepals of *Cerinthe major.*

Spring brought wild asparagus. Our gathering-patches were high in the scrub on the hillside, marked throughout the rest of the year by a tangle of prickly fronds – city dwellers will recognize them as the feathery green fern the florist tucks in with the wedding carnation. We collected big dark-gilled field mushrooms in the autumn, a crop for which we competed with the professional gatherers – the *gitanos.*

Each year when the forest fires raged, the gypsies were accused of burning the hillside so that the asparagus would shoot more strongly and the mushrooms be more abundant. Peripatetic people, it was felt, did not care about the destruction of fixed property. Nevertheless, everyone knew that the roots of the scrub-maquis could easily hold hot embers underground for months – waiting to be fanned into life by some natural accident. Whatever the cause, brush fires were a continual hazard – and each summer they raged over miles of the tinder-dry hillsides. And sure enough, the next year, the wild crops which sprang up through the charcoal would be doubly luxuriant.

In late June we would go out into ochre-dry fields which fringed the seashore, in company with a good part of the population of Spain's southern littoral, to crop the little snails, no bigger than a thumbnail, which aestivated on the tall dry thistles. The thistles themselves are a wild crop, the ancestor of the artichoke, gathered as young tender rosettes at the beginning of spring, stripped of their sharp infant thorns, and stirred into the beanpot as the first green vegetable of spring. In the colder months there were shellfish to be gathered from the shore and quickly steamed open in sherry.

Through our interest in the edible, we learnt to recognize and appreciate the daily lives of the insects, reptiles, birds and mammals who shared our forest. In addition, we had had the unplanned good fortune to set up home right on the avian equivalent of the flight path into Heathrow – the main bird-migration path between Europe and Africa.

In the autumn we could track the bigger birds – hawks and buzzards, eagles, storks, cranes, kites – stacked over us in formation, circling patiently, waiting for the thermals to give them enough height to carry them across the Pillars of Hercules. Beneath them, carried across on a following wind, were the goldfinches and

Shellfish Cooked in Sherry

We bought a wide variety of shellfish in the markets of Tarifa and Algeciras. Bivalves such as mussels, clams, oysters and scallops are good for as long as they can hold water in their shells, which they can do for a surprisingly long time – weeks rather than days.

──────────────── SERVES 4–6 ────────────────

4 pints/2.5 l fresh live shellfish
– clams, mussels, etc.
2 tablespoons olive oil
2 garlic cloves, peeled and sliced

4 tablespoons chopped parsley
1 generous wineglass dry
sherry or white wine

1. Rinse the shellfish, checking over and discarding any which are broken or gape open.

2. Put the oil to heat in your widest frying pan (a wok is fine). When the oil is lightly hazed with blue smoke, toss in the garlic and fry for a moment. Add the parsley, quickly followed by the shellfish. Pour in the wine or sherry. Turn up the heat.

3. Cover with a lid, shaking the pan to redistribute the shells so that they all have a chance to cook. If you have no lid, keep moving the shells with a metal drainer. It will take 3–4 minutes for all the shells to open. Do not cook them any longer but serve them immediately. They should not be reheated, and are delicious even when cold.

bee-eaters, swallows and other small birds whose survival depends on the arduous annual voyage from winter to summer residence. In the spring they would be on the other end of the see-saw, swooping low over the valley at the end of the long run across from Africa. Sometimes the birds would give up in despair, flopping exhausted onto the windswept shoulders of the *sierras*, and we might, on one of our donkey-borne Sunday outings, come across a conference of honey-buzzards regrouping in a ravine, or a gathering of storks cropping grasshoppers and slow-worms in a sun-bleached, upland valley.

Once, returning from a spring visit to make sure the bee-eaters had returned to their nesting grounds in a sandy bank round the other side of our mountain ridge, we saw what looked like a flock of brown sheep on the hillside.

Honey – as the youngest, she had the least say in such decisions – was deputed to make her way up the hill to see if they were indeed brown sheep. And if so, why they were brown. She had to go up very close. When she saw what they were, she trundled back down the hill as fast as her legs could carry her. They were not brown sheep at all, she breathlessly explained, but a flock of griffon vultures, about 150 of them, holding an open-air conference on the hillside, too gorged on a carcass – a young bull destined for a nobler fate in the ring – to take to the air.

When we returned to London in the summers, the parks offered our only opportunity for 'glamour' bird-watching. Nevertheless such captive creatures as the ducks and geese on the lake in St James's Park are a good training ground for spotting in the wild. We would see if we could spot the jokers in the pack – the wild birds, unpinioned travellers on their way north or south, who will suddenly abandon their fellows and surge off over the tall buildings.

The British Trust for Ornithology supplied each of us with our own little booklet listing all the birds of the world, with spaces to tick when and where they have been seen. But the real pleasure of bird-watching lies in knowing habitat and identifying song, and quietly observing the local avifauna as it went about its business. For this a local list of birds was useful, a pair of binoculars essential. Cas saved up his pocket money for a second-hand pair – army surplus and heavy as dumb-bells. The exercise probably did more to develop a fine pair of biceps than his afternoon sessions on the judo mat.

We lived a communal life in our house in the cork-oak forest. There was no dining-room, just a huge and airy all-purpose living space with towering windows and a tiled floor. One end was heated by a big log fire, and accommodated two sofas and a scattering of easy chairs. At the other end, conveniently near the kitchen, was an enormous dining table which doubled up as a work area for anyone who needed it – children with homework, adults with projects, artists with paints, pets with problems.

The frames of the dining chairs were made of scaffolding tubes upholstered by Luis the saddle-maker in bull-ranch leather – so cumbersome and heavy that no-one could move at all once they were seated. The room itself was designed along the lines of an airport hangar and just as draughty: the architect's previous commission had been the saloon of a transatlantic liner.

In the summer we moved the dining table out onto the central patio, among the geranium pots, but in winter we followed the Spanish tradition of the *mesa camella*. The usual form of this primitive but practical spot-heating is a small round wooden table with a shelf beneath, in the centre of which is a large hole into which fits a shallow metal dish containing red-hot charcoal. A floor-length blanket is thrown over the whole thing, and then tucked round the sitters' laps. The arrangement permits everything below the waist to be bathed in a delicious subterranean warmth. Very sensual: many an Andalusian maiden, in stricter days, did her courting surreptitiously under such a table in full view of her chaperones.

My double-length table needed two braziers with their free-standing supports, one at each end. Two heavy woollen rugs trapped the warmth below, a clean white sheet covered the top, and everyone could enjoy the coldest evening without a shiver. Sometimes the matting beneath would singe a little, scenting the room with a whiff of roasting maize husks, but it never actually caught fire. No doubt no-one would ever manage to get *that* to pass the fire-safety regulations.

As my children grew, and their appetites with them, they started bringing unexpected guests home for any meal that took their fancy. So the store cupboard as well as the table was constantly over-stretched. As the nearest corner shop was some ten miles down the hill, I became adept at producing the loaves-and-fishes to feed the 5,000 and could turn in a gazpacho at the drop of a sombrero.

Gazpacho

Ana's gazpacho, Andalusia's traditional all-purpose meal, was basically bread soaked with water. For flavouring (rather as one might eat porridge with sugar and milk) there was olive oil, vinegar, and garlic – plus maybe a little chopped hard-boiled egg and diced *jamón serrano*, and a sprinkling of whatever the vegetable patch might offer. In winter, the dish was taken hot. In the summer it was eaten cold. The bread, garlic, vinegar, and water are either pounded in a mortar, or merely infused together. Here is our (modern) family version of this ancient bread porridge.

―――――――――――― SERVES 6 ――――――――――――

2 slices day-old bread (crusts off)
2 pints/1.2 l cold water
2 tablespoons wine vinegar
2 cloves garlic
1 small cucumber or half a large one, peeled
2 lb/1 kg ripe tomatoes

2 green peppers
1 large Spanish onion
½ pint/300 ml tinned tomato juice
4 tablespoons olive oil
Salt and sugar

―――――――――――― OPTIONAL EXTRAS ――――――――――――

Chopped hard-boiled egg

Croûtons fried in olive oil

1. Put the bread to soak in a few tablespoons of the water and all the vinegar and the garlic for 10 minutes, while you prepare the vegetables.

2. Dice the cucumber, chop the tomatoes roughly (they may be peeled if you wish – in which case, scald them in boiling water to loosen the skins first). Take the seeds out of the green peppers and chop the flesh roughly. Peel the onion and chop it up. Put aside a quarter of the chopped vegetables in individual dishes, to be handed separately, diced small, as a garnish.

3. Either liquidize the soaked bread and garlic, the rest of the chopped vegetables, and the olive oil in a blender, or pound them in a mortar. (If you need to keep the gazpacho, omit the onion from the soup – it ferments rather easily.) Add the tomato juice and then the rest of the water until you have the consistency you like. Adjust the seasoning with salt add a little sugar. Put the soup in a cold larder or the fridge for an hour at least. Serve as iced a possible (but not with ice-cubes in it – ice-cubes always seem to taste odd and will dilute the soup overmuch).

4. Hand round small bowls of the extra diced vegetables for each person to sprinkle on his own serving – as in the everyday peasant version. This final garnishing is an integral part of the modern dish.

P.S. Chopped hard-boiled eggs and little *hot* bread croûtons fried in olive oil can be included as a special treat.

It was in Andalusia that I first learnt from my neighbours, who took pride in prudent housekeeping, how to stock a store cupboard rather than depend on running out to the shops.

A rural lifestyle dictated the choice of fuel-foods – mainly pulse vegetables, home-grown, podded and dried. For snacks, the children were encouraged to raid the larder whenever they felt hungry – dried fruit and nuts were cheap and easily available, and far better for growing children than sweets and biscuits. So in winter, when fresh fruit was more expensive and the choice less wide, I would take care to set out a bowl of raisins, dried figs, prunes and hazelnuts for nibbling after school. And in Andalusia, where no commercial breakfast cereals were available, I made our own supplies of muesli.

As a young family regularly on the move, we took no stores with us – relying instead on what was available locally. This adaptability helped us greatly when we were settling into new territory. Perhaps by shopping and cooking the food of the country, we *smelled* right to our neighbours – and they could accept our presence more easily. Many factors dictate our response to strangers – and scent is surely one of them. It's no accident that we greet visitors with an offer of drink or food (and feel a little offended if it isn't accepted), or that we choose to discuss commerce over a shared meal.

Eating the same food as our neighbours, we were more easily able to share their lives. It sounds simple, but it worked for us.

CHAPTER TWELVE

Eagle owls and other pets

'Make your room gay.'

Reverend Sydney Smith (1771–1845)*

IT SEEMED PERFECTLY NATURAL, LIVING AS WE DID, THAT WE
should share our lives with whatever creatures cared to adopt us
– ownership would have been far too limiting a description for the
random companions we acquired.

As soon as we set up house in the forest, the four children decided
that teddy bears and fluffy toys were no substitute for the real thing.
Here were many lessons to be learnt – the first that nature, not being
given to sentimentality, does not make her creatures convenient. Few
of them are cuddly, many of them need round-the-clock home

*Advice to a young lady in low spirits (c. 1830).

comforts, and, given half a chance, they reproduce themselves with inconvenient regularity. Sex, birth and death – all those matters which humanity finds so difficult to tackle – can be observed at first hand whenever two or more warm-blooded mammals are gathered together.

Our household pets fell into one of three categories, at least in initial intent: the decorative, the edible, and those required to work for a living.

Cats belonged to the last category. The household moggie was expected to keep the rodents out of the larder. Our first feline hunter was acquired by Honey, as a direct consequence of the inordinate length of time it takes a fisherman's wife to prepare a proper paella.

Let me explain. Sunday is paella day in Andalusia – considered an outdoor dish to be prepared in a rural setting by the father of a family for the enjoyment, and admiration, of his womenfolk, children and friends. We followed the custom of the country, taking the raw ingredients and the twin-handled iron pan up into the hills to cook our own over a brush fire. But in summer, as a special treat, we would drive round the coast to a certain beach where we could persuade the fisherman's wife to cook the dish for us. As with any culinary masterpiece, the making of the fisherman's wife's paella could not be hurried. Neither customers nor cook had a telephone, so advance warning was out of the question. Even the selection of the raw ingredients could not begin until we arrived.

Sometimes her husband's morning catch had yielded a handful of squid, a few prawns, a monkfish or two – all of which she considered appropriate. Sometimes one of her children might have brought back a bucket of spiny rockfish or a handful of the little jumping shrimps which would give the right flavour to the rice. If not, a rabbit or a chicken had to be killed and prepared for the pot. Then there were the vegetables to be fetched from the *huerta,* the garden patch behind her lean-to kitchen.

The fisherman's wife was a perfectionist: whether the ingredients had to be gathered or came easily to hand, she did not think it proper to serve the dish until the afternoon shadows were lengthening. We, her audience, were meanwhile free to take our ease. The wind is always strong on Tarifa beach – a cool breeze whips up an appetite, and by the time she was ready, we were always starving.

That day our regular beachcombing expedition produced live booty – a rickety black-and-white kitten with turned-over claws. As a love-object she was clearly a disaster: skinny as a broomstick, and with more fleas than a hedgehog. Bad-tempered, the runt of a semi-wild litter, she did not trust a human as far as she could spit.

Honey thought otherwise. The bedraggled little creature was all that her heart had ever desired. For both girl and kitten, it was love at first sight. I reasoned with them both. The little cat would surely miss her home, and a rickety kitten with no visible claws was hardly the obvious candidate for the role of resident rodent-controller. Love conquered all objections. By the time the paella was ready, Jane – Honey hoped the little creature might one day find her Tarzan – had joined the family. The first square meal of her gypsy existence was quite rightly provided by the debris of the paella whose tardiness had saved her from certain starvation.

Back home, Jane took up residence in a battered cardboard box under the ramp which led to the kitchen door. We could find no cure for the rickets, but the condition did not seem to interfere with her daily life – or her appeal to the opposite sex. Scarcely out of kittenhood, Jane found her Tarzan, a marmalade tom, and a litter of kittens was soon in search of a home. The local methods of feline birth control were somewhat rough and ready – any kittens who could not be found accommodation were drowned.

After this unsentimental episode, Honey took Jane to the vet to be neutered. There's a price for everything – even a stray moggy. With her feline mind relieved of the mating urge, Jane proved me no judge of character by swiftly establishing herself as a demon ratter. She lived out her allotted span on the fat of the land – finally coming to a watery end in the flooded cellar, on the prowl as usual.

In *feria*-time we acquired a transient population of small birds – won as prizes at the fairground's shooting-gallery. A bird in the hand seems a curious reward for a marksman – or markswoman, since it was Francesca who won most of them. Her brother was not absolutely convinced that her success was entirely due to her skill. There was no doubt she had an eye for a moving target, but he felt it was more likely that the circus urchin who set up the tin ducks had fixed the odds in her favour.

We did not limit our affections to warm-blooded creatures. The stream down the valley below the house teemed with terrapins, small fresh-water turtles. Amiable little creatures, slow-witted, they loved

Beach Paella

This is an approximation of the paella the fisherman's wife cooked for us on the day Honey acquired her stray kitten, Jane. There are as many recipes for paella as there are days in the year: the paella is an opportunist dish, a peasant recipe – depending on season and gathering. There must be rice and there must be saffron, but beyond this the only requirement is that the rice and the ingredients which flavour it are cooked together (never assembled later) in the shallow twin-handled iron pan which is still made to a design familiar to the Romans. The pan itself dictates the cooking method and the amount of people who can be fed from it. Paella pans come in sizes for uneven numbers, 3, 5, 7 etc. – to allow for seconds. Alternatively you can use a wide frying pan or flat-bottomed wok. The best heat source is a bed of coals such as a barbecue.

—————————————— SERVES 6 ——————————————

1 lb/500 g round rice
(Spanish round rice, Italian
Arborio or Carolina pudding
rice)
8 oz/250 g raw squid
8 oz/250 g raw shrimps
1 wild rabbit or half a chicken,
raw, chopped into bite-sized
pieces
6 tablespoons olive oil
2 garlic cloves, skinned and
chopped

1 red pepper, de-seeded and
roughly chopped
8 oz/250 g green beans,
top-and-tailed and chopped
1 lb/500 g tomatoes, skinned
and chopped (or tinned)
12 strands saffron infused in
an eggcup of boiling water
1 pint/600 ml water
Salt

1. Pick over the rice. Empty out the squids' innards, discard the soft intestines and eyes, and slice the rest neatly into rings and tentacles. Pick over the shrimps and the meat.

2. Heat the oil in the pan until lightly hazed with blue. Put in the garlic and let it perfume the oil for a moment. Add the squid, shrimp, chopped red pepper and beans, sprinkle with salt, and let the whole lot fry for 3–4 minutes.

3. Sprinkle in the rice in a single layer and turn the grains until they are well-coated with aromatic juices. Fry for a moment until the grains turn opaque.

4. Add the tomatoes, the saffron with its water (put it in the whizzer first for a denser colour), followed by the water – you need 3 times the volume of liquid to the volume of rice. Let it bubble for 15 minutes – the heat under the pan should be as even as possible, so you should not need to stir it to stop it from sticking. Add more water if it looks like drying out. If your heat source is not well spread (a charcoal barbecue fire is ideal), add a little extra water and finish it, after the initial frying, in a medium-hot oven.

5. Remove from the heat and leave to rest and swell, loosely covered with a cloth or newspaper, for 10 minutes. The rice should be juicy but firm, not tender and dry as in Indian or Chinese rice.

This is strictly an outdoor middle-of-the-day dish. It is traditional to dig into the portion in front of you, without ladling it out onto plates. In the vine-shadowed arbour where we ate our paella, a big plate of grilled sardines and a salad of cos lettuce and slices of mild Spanish onion always preceded the rice.

nothing better than sunbathing on the rocks. It was Cas who discovered that by removing his sneakers and creeping up on them very quietly as they snoozed, they were quite easy to catch. He immediately roped in the sisters for a raiding party. Fran and Pops were posted downstream, and Honey was in charge of the holding-basket. The captives were emigrated up the hill in the hope that they would take up residence around the natural spring which rose at the back of our garden. For a few days, the terrapins humoured their captors, settling down with tranquil patience in their new home. Then they vanished, making their way downstream again to their oleander-shaded pool. It became a weekly ritual. A new raiding party would be organized, the terrapins would be gathered up and placed in the spring, only to return to their pool. A little disorientating for the terrapins perhaps, but at least no-one made them into soup.

One might have thought a reptile – even one with portability-value such as a terrapin – had its limitations as a companion on life's rocky road. It's not a creature with which an intimate relationship can easily be built. But Caspar was already hooked – enchanted by all things reptilian. He acquired a large glass tank at the second-hand market, and set it up in a corner of his bedroom. Patiently he began to capture tenants: a pair of handsome yellow and black salamanders; a trio of silvery slow-worms – like fat four-legged snakes; a viridian-scaled grass snake; a little squadron of amber-eyed geckos with tiny suction pads on their splayed feet. In the warmth of the house, the creatures developed a prodigious appetite for insects. The secret was to keep them cool, then they would slumber contentedly through the night. A bowl of ice in the tank worked wonders. Otherwise life was one long search for grasshoppers, blue-bottles, anything which might be manna to the voracious jaws. With ownership, Cas swiftly learnt, comes responsibility.

Animals seem to know instinctively when any human is likely to be a soft touch. Bernardo the donkey, with the shrewdness of his kind, picked Francesca. As soon as she poked her nose out of the door in the morning, ready for school, he would bray at her for a bucket of water, or to explain to her that his rope had worked itself round a tree. He could recognize her footsteps and never even lifted his head from grazing for any other member of the household.

His affections were not misplaced. After the first year, when he provided our only means of transport, Francesca decreed that fourteen years' hard labour had given Bernardo the right to his leisure. From then on, he earned his keep as an ambulatory lawnmower – a useful by-product of his labours being regular supplies of manure for my vegetable patch. Sometimes his rope would snap, and he would wander off into the surrounding thickets to hide out in the hills for a few days. Since his coat was exactly the same colour as the rocks, we could never find him until he had decided he wanted company. He rarely went very far, and when he was ready to return, he replied only to the call of his chosen beloved – his throaty bray telling her that he was now willing, nay anxious, to come home.

The valley's human inhabitants took note of our tender hearts, and we rapidly acquired a reputation as a first-aid post for nature's casualties.

Bubo bubo, to give the eagle owl its scientific name (which, being easy, we did), was our first in-patient. The nearest thing to a flying tiger, she stood fully three foot high on her feather-sheathed talons. She arrived in a basket, angry, bedraggled and earthbound. A long-time resident of the crags above our house, the bane of the local goatherds who held her responsible for kid-slaughter, she had somehow managed to crack a wing-bone.

We gathered round the basket in which she'd been gingerly delivered to us. Bubo, weak as she was from lack of food, still looked as if she could give as good as she got. Nicholas donned thick leather gardening gloves and held her firmly while we examined the damage. Between us all, we managed to set the bone and bound it up as best we could. Poppy's neat fingers were as nimble as any surgeon's with the needle and thread, and we had high hopes of success. For want of more conventional housing, Bubo was accommodated in a cavernous walk-in cupboard in the guest bedroom, confined to a limited space so that the wing might have a chance to heal. Her appetite returned immediately – she was an excellent trencherwoman, capable of consuming a whole rabbit a day.

As befits a grand duchess – the country people's name for the bird – Bubo soon began to take charge of the household. She had firm notions on who was permitted to approach her. She tolerated the males of the house, but couldn't stand the females. She would let her favoured flirts feed her titbits – raising her hooked beak to permit

Nicholas or Cas to stroke the downy feathers under her chin. Her standard greeting for strange females was a theatrical threat display, inflating her brushed-velvet marmalade feathers and rocking from one huge taloned foot to the other like a sumo wrestler sizing up an adversary.

All this was punctuated by a flurry of beak-snapping and hissing – a similar effect might be achieved by slamming a heavy door and following through with a squirt from a fire extinguisher. Her best feature was her enormous orange eyes with powder-blue lids. Like all of her species, she was equipped with an extra eyelid, a vertical veil which she could draw across like a peeping neighbour closing a net curtain. Coquettish as a chorus girl, she would wink each in turn at visitors.

Uncertain how effectively the wing had healed, we moved her into a half-finished annexe, stretching netting across the unglazed window so that she could keep an eye on the wild. While we were debating whether she would be able to hunt, she took her own decision. Her liberator was a rival predator – a mongoose, who tore a hole in her cage in order to get at the remains of the rabbit she had enjoyed for lunch. The valley supported a large population of these elusive mammals – and a hank of mottled fur caught in the chicken-wire told its own tale. Bubo had made her way to freedom through the gap the mongoose had made. Later we had reports she was back to her old kid-snatching tricks – a situation viewed with some disapproval by the goatherd.

Bubo's place in our affections was taken by a scops owl, an elegant lemon-eyed little creature with needle-sharp talons and tweed-patterned feathers. She was a hand-reared orphan, a temporary visitor while her minder, a schoolfriend, was on holiday. Caspar, into whose care she had been given, was kept busy trapping slow-worms and lizards for her (certainly not the residents in his vivarium): she literally ate him out of house and home. Even the sisters were persuaded to catch grasshoppers and crickets to post into the bottomless well of her digestive system. All debris – carapaces, bones and skin – was ejected in a neat tear-shaped pellet. In the wild, she was a resident of the cork-oak forest, so her silvery feathers were exquisitely patterned to mimic the shimmering runnels of cork-bark.

Although a cheerful little balloon by night, by day she slept in full camouflage, drawing herself up into a thin branch-like tube and closing her eyes to wary slits. Unfamiliar visitors or too importunate observers would be treated to her personal threat display, a diminutive version of Bubo's. She, too, puffed up her feathers and rocked from side to side, emitting a fierce little whistle like the air escaping from a punctured tyre, clicking her tiny beak like a tap-dancer's heel-and-toe.

The migration path above our valley yielded other weary avian travellers. A honey buzzard which claimed territorial rights over the patio. Honey took charge of her namesake, setting out his supper of bread and milk every evening on her return from school. He quickly learnt to recognize her, and greeted her arrival with plaintive little mews, like a lost kitten.

Our first tragedy was a short-toed eagle, a handsome fellow with saffron-yellow feet and round mournful eyes which gave him the look of an exhausted owl. We never managed to diagnose his malady. It seemed at first that the army of tiny parasites which infested his feathers were what ailed him. Cas and Nicholas did their best to treat him with cat-flea powder, but it was soon clear that the multiplication of his natural fauna was a symptom and not the cause. By this time, he had become a focus of the household's attention, and his untimely passing triggered much discussion of the nature of mortality and the existence of the soul.

The demise of a pet is often a modern child's only chance to experience death at first hand, and the children gave the bird a solemn burial, interring him in a cardboard box with a view of his intended destination.

CHAPTER THIRTEEN

Of rabbits, pigs and other home comforts

'We are not angels and we have bodies. To want to become
angels while we are still on earth is ridiculous.'

St Theresa of Avila, (1515–82)*

AS WITH MOST EVENTS IN OUR FAMILY'S LIFE, THE ARRIVAL OF PILA
the Flemish Giant was a matter of chance rather than choice.

A veritable colossus among rabbits, he arrived on our doorstep
one morning unceremoniously bundled up in a sack. A label
proclaimed him a gift to Cas from a neighbouring landowner.
We soon discovered the reason for his generosity – Pila was a
true maverick, a creator of mayhem in the harem, a tiger in rabbit's
clothing.

*From *The Interior Castle.*

Pila pined for his ladies. Clearly, one rabbit is no good without another – and the landowner was persuaded to add a female to make the pair. Once accustomed to the fine rabbit run which José provided for him, Pila proved himself a prodigious sire – a real Lancelot of the burrow. His first female, a gentle little soul, set the breeding pattern: never less than eight at a time. Once his colony was established, Pila embarked on a rumbustiously licentious sex life, breeding merrily with his daughters and using his razor-sharp front teeth to emasculate all his sons. Scarcely an ideal role model for his owner, particularly at that delicate moment when a young man's thoughts might be turning from slugs and snails to sugar and spice.

The local dogs – a scrofulous bunch of goatherding yappers – treated him with respect, and did not repeat the mistake of considering him an ambulatory snack. He could give a sharp nip, but his preferred defensive weapon was his back legs: under attack he simply turned his back on the enemy and thumped. After a merry three years distributing his genes with impunity, he finally met his match in a passing eagle. The debris of what must have been an epic battle told its own sad tale – the morning after the encounter there was feather and fur all over the garden. By then our patriarch had achieved the closest any of us will get to immortality: a race of giant wild rabbits peculiar to our valley.

We ate the rabbits, naturally. And just as naturally, I had to learn to do the necessary. In Andalusia, killing poultry and rabbits was considered women's work. The baker's wife was the expert – and I was thought pretty limp stuff when I was obliged to call on her assistance with the despatch of a Christmas goose. 'You hold her here, señora, and I twist the neck here – just so.' Snap.

I had joined the ranks of the women of the valley – I never looked back.

Our colony of hybrid doves was not initially destined for the pot. The first arrivals were purely decorative. Their rightful owner was Kentucky Norah, a merry widow who had abandoned the ancestral hearth fire to set up home down our valley with a smooth-talking bounder from Morocco. Soon after their arrival, the marriage was contracted in front of the Tarifa notary.

Kentucky Nora undertook to endow her new husband with her not-inconsiderable worldly goods. He presented her with that ancient symbol of fertility, a pair of mating doves – snowy-plumaged

Andalusian Rabbit with Garlic

Rub the inside of the cavity with a cut lemon, and joint the rabbit neatly.

— SERVES 2–4 (DEPENDING ON THE SIZE OF THE RABBIT) —

1 rabbit, jointed into bite-sized pieces
1 tablespoon seasoned flour
4 tablespoons olive oil
8 garlic cloves, whole and unskinned

1 teaspoon thyme
A few sprigs rosemary
1 glass dry sherry or white wine
Salt and freshly milled black pepper

1. Toss the rabbit joints in seasoned flour.
2. Warm the oil in a deep frying pan, and when heated through add the rabbit and garlic and let everything fry gently until it's deliciously brown. Add the herbs and the sherry and bubble up. Turn down the heat and let it cook gently, loosely covered, until the rabbit is tender – you may need a little more liquid.
Allow 30–40 minutes.
3. Serve piled in a dish and eat it with your fingers, with chunks of bread to wipe up the juices.

fantails. It was his avowed intention, when Allah permitted, to provide his bride with a love-nest in the Rif Mountains visible from their balcony.

Unfortunately, the ink was scarcely dry on the marriage lines when an earlier commitment arrived on Kentucky Norah's white-washed doorstep. The prior claimant, a formidable dark-skinned matron accompanied by two sulky teenage daughters, announced her intention of settling down in the matrimonial home. Far from scolding her husband, she was delighted by his thoughtfulness in providing her with a deputy and maid-of-all-work. Called to account by the junior wife, the bigamist explained that under the laws of Mohammed he was entitled to as many wives as took his fancy, within reason and the limits of his purse, now comfortably swollen by Norah's dowry.

Norah stuck it out for the full cycle of one moon. All might yet have been well had it not been that the doves which had promised so much future fertility, remained curiously infertile. Norah sum-moned the neighbourhood chicken-sexer. He confirmed her worst suspicions: the feathered duo were both males. This was the last straw: Norah abandoned both the joint bank account and the fantails, and ran for the blue hills of home. Before she left, she transferred responsibility for the wedding birds to our household.

The fantails, liberated by Poppy from the confines of their cage, took up residence in the windowed eaves. Perhaps the science of chicken-sexing is not exact, or perhaps freedom loosened their inhibitions – but the birds went forth and multiplied exceedingly. Once a month, regular as clockwork, another nestful fledged and took to the rafters. There was only one answer – pigeon pie.

On the night of the new moon I set my ladder in place. I meant to creep up on the birds under the cover of darkness, hoping that all heads were safely tucked under wings. The birds waited until they could see the whites of my eyes – and shuffled over to the neighbouring eaves.

I racked my brains. Fair is fair and fowl is fowl – but shotguns were out of the question. Anyway, I knew perfectly well that if I let the local huntsmen loose, they'd shatter every pane of glass in the house. It was not until a somewhat merry evening in the local *tapas* bar, where marinated pigeon was on the menu, that the solution

Drunken Pigeons

Don't forget to remove the grain-crop at the neck end –
you can feel it through the skin.

―――――――――――――― SERVES 4 ――――――――――――――

*4 pigeons, plucked, cleaned
and wiped
2 tablespoons brandy
8 tablespoons olive oil
2 onions, peeled and chopped
16 garlic cloves (not skinned)*

*2 glasses dry sherry or white
wine
2 bay-leaves
A few juniper berries
Salt and pepper*

1. Pour the brandy over the pigeons and light it. This singes the skin
a little and burns off any tiny hairy feathers which may be left after
the plucking.
2. Heat the oil in a heavy casserole. Put in the pigeons and turn them
in the hot oil. Add the onions and garlic cloves and fry them for a
moment. Pour in the sherry and tuck in the bay-leaves and juniper
berries. Season.
3. Bring to the boil, turn down the heat, lid tightly and leave to
simmer for 50–60 minutes, until the pigeons are quite tender.
4. Take off the lid towards the end, and bubble up
to evaporate the juices, leaving the pigeons bathed
in aromatic oil.
5. Serve one bird per person, making sure each
plate has its share of garlic cloves – creamy and
gentle-flavoured when slow-cooked like this.
It's lovely with a tomato salad and fat chips
salted first and deep-fried twice in olive oil.

struck me with blinding clarity. The following day, I put the feed-corn to soak in cooking brandy. Next morning, I delivered the children to school as usual – like all murderers, the last thing I needed was four witnesses to my crime. With trembling hands, I scattered abroad the avian equivalent of the poisoned chalice.

So far so good. The birds loved the stuff. Crops bulging with fermenting grain, they surged blearily back to their perches. Here they hung like so many ripe fruit, rocking morosely in the morning sun. I remained confident. It could only be a matter of time before the liquor produced the desired effect. I settled down to wait. Within the hour, the birds' mood of brooding resentfulness had changed to drunken optimism. There were birds swinging bat-fashion from branches, birds smacking into windows, birds lurching all over the roofs. By midday, I was already regretting my perfidy. Black coffee? Cold baths? Still they lurched on.

That afternoon, the school run returned the children to what looked like the aftermath of a monstrous pillow-fight.

'We're ashamed of you, mother,' said the tender-hearted daughters. 'Honestly, mother,' said Cas, sternly surveying the debris.

From that moment on I gave up the unequal struggle. None the worse for their hangovers, the birds bred merrily on – but this time they invited the local residents to join the party. A new strain of feral fantails still populate the valley, a living, breeding monument to Kentucky Norah's passion.

While poultry and barnyard beasts were considered women's work, fur and hoof were the responsibility of the men. In Andalusia the goat replaces the sheep as the meat animal – even after 400 years, lamb was still considered a little Moorish, one of those tastes which in the old days would have earned you a starring role in the Inquisition's *auto-da-fé*. Kid was the traditional meat for weddings and other such celebrations, and the goatherd took responsibility for his own slaughtering.

First-hand experience came early, at the roofing-out ceremony for the house. The foreman, a diminutive Tarifeño blessed with the libidinous name of Dionysius, took charge of the arrangements. The feast was to be spit-roasted kid – the whole beast slung over an open fire in the garden and basted from a bottle of salt and water as it turned. The kid arrived on the hoof. The slaughtering and skinning took place *in situ*. The roasting, too, was men's business, and the labourers downed tools for the day and gave the matter their full attention.

The celebration was held on a Saturday, so that all the community could attend. Rural Andalusia takes its pleasures when it can – any event is always an excuse for a party. Wives and children, grannies and grandads arrived as soon as the sun went down. By now the meat looked and smelt delicious – crisp-skinned and brown as a nut, and scented with the smoke from the juniper and thyme which provided the brushwood for the fire. There was dancing and singing afterwards – the formal patterns of the elegant *sevillana* traced out in the fallen leaves by jeans-clad girls and aproned matrons. We made the music ourselves, using the staccato handclapping which provides both rhythm for the dancers and accompaniment for the singers.

It was the children's baptism of fire, their first experience of the communal life of the people of the valley – the most exciting thing which had ever happened to any of us.

That we kept neither goats for milk nor chickens for eggs was considered a little eccentric. A pig was a different matter. Failure to keep a pig was in direct contravention of the unwritten laws of good husbandry. At that time in Andalusia, a pig was an essential member of every rural household, solving at a stroke the perennial problem of waste disposal and providing the yearly supplies of bacon and ham. The household pig – to distinguish him from the cash-crop pigs which foraged the woods for acorns – had a built-in sell-by date. He met his demise in the autumn, just in time to be salted down for the Christmas feast. Each spring a newly weaned piglet – bought from the pig-boy who herded the semi-wild flocks – was installed in his place.

It was Manolo the dustman who decreed that something had to be done about my shortcomings in the pig department. He broached the matter with Ana and José. The other two were in complete agreement. José was despatched to the end of the garden to rebuild the tumbledown piggery. Ana was delegated to tackle the mistress of the house.

'Señora, it is not well seen in the valley that you throw out so much food. You must have a pig. Manolo has a suitable animal.'

The following day, Manolo appeared with a small pink piglet. The pig settled down to the life of Riley in blissful ignorance of his future. He throve mightily on the debris from my kitchen, delivered daily in a blue bucket which he recognized as his own. He was soon big enough to bludgeon his way out of his muddy enclosure and come up to the kitchen door to fetch his supper for himself, rooting up the geraniums and helping himself in the vegetable patch on the way.

José inspected the damage with gloom characteristic of all gardeners everywhere: 'It is a simple matter of hormones, señora. This pig is no longer a piglet but a hog. We must send for the pig-castrator. You will not know this, señora, but certain precautions are necessary. The first is that the time of the moon must be right. The second is to ensure that the pig-castrator has not lain with a woman the night before he does his work. Should either of these rules not be obeyed, the pig will fall sick and die.'

We both considered the hog gloomily. José sighed. 'We have a problem, señora – not least because it is well-known in the valley that the pig-castrator has a woman in Tarifa.' He brightened. 'I have the solution. The pig-castrator shall spend the night with me. And in the morning I will deliver him untouched.'

The day was arranged, the celibacy of the pig-castrator assured. I have no doubt that the man was a master of his trade – what I did not expect was that he would do the deed with his teeth. Piggy had his revenge on me – his efforts to do his own foraging redoubled, and he would frequently appear at the door in the middle of the night, demanding his bucketful.

The slaughtering and butchering of each household's pig was a communal affair. My initial suggestion that I was a soft-hearted foreigner and the thing might be done in my absence was met with stern disapproval. She who had cared for the pig in life was not permitted to abandon it when it met its end.

The men arrived at dawn and immediately set to work to build a fire. I did not enquire as to the purpose too closely – I only knew that great cauldrons of water were put to simmer, planks were set in place, knives sharpened. Hurriedly, I whisked the junior division off to school before the slaughter began – rather hoping they might get on with the job without me.

I returned just in time to face the music – the moment of truth courteously delayed until my return. I did not care to admit it was

my first pig-killing. There's a time and place for girlish admissions –
and this was neither. The squeamish will be relieved to hear I shall
now draw a veil over the process by which Piggy was despatched.
Suffice to say that we all rolled up our sleeves and hung on – all
except me, who was delegated to hold the bowl for the wherewithal
to make the black puddings.

After this came the real work.

The carcass had to be scalded and scraped – the reason for all the
boiling water. The scrubbed body was then hung up on a tree to be
eviscerated. The intestines had to be washed in the stream, and the
tripes thoroughly scoured with salt. Everything was piled on the
kitchen table, and we were ready to begin. Maria, Ana's sister and
the valley's culinary expert, had already taken charge of the
preliminaries – chopping garlic, pounding oregano, crushing pepper and coriander seeds for the spicing. By midday there were half a
dozen of us in the kitchen – and plenty for all to do.

First the bacon flitches had to be packed away in salt in a wooden
drawer which was kept for the purpose. Then the lard and belly-
pork had to be melted down for paprika-spiced conserves for later
use in stews and soups. The hams were salted and put aside to be sent
up to a certain mountain village to be cured in the high cold air.
Fortunately, Maria's aunt had married a man from this village, which
was famed for the excellence of its hams.

The last job was the most important of all, the stuffing of the
intestines to make *chorizos* and black puddings. We scrubbed and
chopped, salted and minced our fingers raw. My job was to push the
mixture into the casings with the aid of a plastic funnel.

'Didn't your mother teach you anything?' asked Maria in exaspera-
tion as she untangled me from yet another cat's cradle of sausage.

The *chorizos*, like the hams, had to be sent to the mountains to be
cured and air-dried – but the black puddings, blood sausage *morcillas*
spiced with pepper and paprika, had to be cooked immediately. I was
delegated to take them out to the boiling cauldrons and watch to see
they did not burst. Maria decided that this at least was a task within my
grasp. But first, the warning: 'The water must tremble – no more. It
must certainly not be allowed to boil or the *morcillas* will all be spoilt.'

How would I know when they were done? 'They're ready when
they sing.' And sing indeed they did – a gentle little whistle which

escaped from the tiny holes in the casing as soon as the puddings had reached the right temperature.

My reward – even more valuable than the pile of beautifully cooked *morcilla* – was Maria's smile as she delivered her verdict on my work. '*Bien hecho, mujer. No 'sta mal – aunque sois extranjera.* Well done, woman. Not at all bad – for a foreigner.'

I laughed, and everyone with me. To be an *extranjero* – foreigner – was not a compliment in rural Andalusia – implying that you were someone with more money than sense.

The true rewards of that day came not so much in the achievement of a well-stocked winter store cupboard, but in the acknowledgement that I, as an *extranjera*, knew that the work was worth doing. None of the neighbours was in any doubt that as a family we could afford to buy that which had cost us so much effort to acquire for free. But everyone knew that what we had done was better by far than anything which could be acquired for money in the market-place.

Looking back on our years in the airy house among the cork oaks in the valley, I am confident that although the decision to move there was taken without much thought for the consequences, it was no mistake. Not only did it give four urban urchins a chance to grow up in a place where children are loved and valued, but we were constantly aware that we lived among people accustomed to give thanks for their daily bread; who respected each other's skills; who, at their best, treated the earth with courtesy but without sentimentality.

We found much to be admired in a way of life which is vanishing as fast as snow in summer; much for which to be grateful in the traditions of rural hospitality which allowed such easy acceptance of strangers; much to learn from those to whom birth and death – whether animal or human – is no more or less than part of the natural cycle of renewal.

CHAPTER FOURTEEN

Celebrating Christmas

'We still set our plum pudding and our mince pies on fire,
explaining the custom by considerations of easier digestion and
increased wholesomeness; but really we are, as it were, invoking
and placating a mysterious and dimly apprehended power, who
may thus be induced to wax brighter and warmer, to consume
the clouds and the darkness, and to shine beneficently upon us.'

Lady Jekyll★

OUR OWN FAMILY CHRISTMAS TRADITIONS WERE ESTABLISHED IN SPAIN.
Since then, perhaps because we instinctively felt it more appropriate, our Christmas celebrations have always been rural. And every

★In *Kitchen Essays*.

year, we always try to find at least one 'stranger' to share the festival –
motivated not only by altruism, but also because families, brought
together at such a time, are inclined to quarrel and the presence of an
outsider ensures this doesn't get entirely out of hand. We learnt on
our travels that we were in good company: primitive Christmas
customs stipulate the lighting of a candle in the window, the laying
of a place for the unexpected visitor at the feast.

Grafted onto more ancient celebrations, Christmas is the second
most important feast of the church – only Easter outranks the
festival. Before Christmas, there's all the fun of Advent. Until
recently, it was a time to observe the rules of a fast, just as Lent
is the run–up to Easter – a self–imposed slimming diet designed to get
everyone in the mood for the festivities.

We did not observe the fast deliberately, although necessity meant
that we ate very little meat and plenty of pulses and vegetables in
preparation for all the expense of Christmas itself. Anyone who'd
like to follow the rule strictly should start with the closest Sunday to
30 November. No sweet things and no liquor are the basic
requirements, and no meat, no fish, no cheese, or olive oil is the
rule among strictly orthodox Catholics. The rest of Christendom
traditionally abstains from those things it likes best.

When we moved to Andalusia, far from the temptations and
diversions of the city, we spent the four weeks of Advent preparing for
the festival, and we soon discovered that the midwinter celebrations
were quite different from our own. In many Mediterranean lands the
festival of Christmas takes the form of a fasting supper, followed by a
vigil in church on the Eve, and a feast at home on Christmas Day –
sometimes in the small hours of the morning immediately after
midnight mass. But the big day for children, the moment when
they receive their presents, is 6 January – commemorating the arrival
of the Three Kings with their precious gifts at the Bethlehem stable.

As for the culinary traditions, we needed little instruction in how
to adapt ourselves to the prevailing customs when the markets of
Algeciras and Tarifa themselves dictated the menu. As always in rural
communities, we had to work hard for our festive supplies.

In early November came the olive harvest – and we, following
our neighbours' example, bought them fresh and pickled our own.
The bitter little green fruits had to be cracked with a mallet – a merry

task for the children, and there was acid green juice sprayed all over the kitchen for days. The olives were then soaked in several changes of clean water for a week, and submerged in brine flavoured with garlic and fennel in deep earthenware jars topped with a wooden lid. By Christmas they were sweetly pickled, still firm-fleshed and delicately flavoured with their herbs, ready to be set on the festive table.

The Christmas meat in rural Andalusia is the best of the products of the autumn pig-killing saved up for the midwinter feast. The big treat is *jamón serrano*, the Christmas ham – salted and wind-dried, the meat lean and chewy, protected by a jacket of salty skin and rich yellow fat – and it's hung in a corner of the kitchen so that anyone who is hungry may carve off a sliver.

To bulk out these stores, under Maria's instruction, we put up another earthenware jar of preserved pork – chunks of lean meat simmered in its own lard, flavoured with oregano and paprika, a preparation not unlike a French *confit*. The meat was delicious as a quick meal – eaten either straight from the pot with a thick chunk of bread or slapped onto a hot griddle first. And the lard served as a superior dripping to spread on bread, or a spoonful went to enrich the bean stew, or to fry potatoes.

There were Christmas birds, naturally. At this time of year, the Algeciras market-place turned into a menagerie of clucking chickens and gobbling turkeys. The skinny, bronze-feathered New World birds were known locally as Jesuits for the Brotherhood which once held a monopoly on their breeding. Ana, never one to miss a dig at the church's least popular officers, maintained the birds were named for the resemblance their wattled faces bore to their sponsors.

We did not bargain for a market fowl. Ours was selected several months in advance from the flock at the Pelayo bakery – it was a matter of fattening up the bird on acorns and bread from the previous day's baking, so these things had to be planned well ahead. And, as usual, I was responsible for the slaughtering.

In the market, too, Christmas was the season of dried fruits – raisins still on their little stalks, wrinkled prunes all black and rich, sunny piles of dried apricots. Pyramids of oranges and leafy baskets of tangerines, heaps of lemons and downy quinces, the fruit of Venus which goes to make the plum-dark paste – *dulce de membrillo* – which is always served at weddings and church festivals in the

Mediterranean. Only at this time of year, the spice-lady had supplies of fresh chestnuts, moist-skinned walnuts. Most expensive of these luxuries were the almonds, still in their furry green jackets, cropped from trees first brought from the Jordan valley by the caliphs of Granada.

One corner of the market was turned over to the stalls which sold *belénes* – miniature figures to people the Christmas crib. The children of the Catholic Mediterranean set up a Bethlehem crib six days before Christmas, just in time to mark the arrival of the Holy Family at the inn. A small version of the grand display in the church, this is a three-dimensional Advent calendar starring little pottery models, not only of the Holy Family and the usual cast of Christmas characters, but also local tradesmen and workers. We added more to our collection every year. Nicholas, easily bitten by the collecting bug, became collector-in-chief, and we now have several hundred of these little models picked up in the course of our travels – the entire rural population of the Mediterranean littoral in miniature.

But most exciting of all for the children were tables piled with the vast range of almond-and-honey sweetmeats whose preparation was once a speciality of those same sybaritic Moors: *polverones* – 'dusties' – crumbly biscuits like soft shortbreads, shiny discs of baked marzipan centred with green pistachios. Nougat – ten different varieties at least; and almonds crusted with crystallized honey. There were sugared pine nuts and scraps of liquorice in snowy sugar coatings. Most addictive was *turrón* – the true halva – sandy-textured golden slabs of crushed toasted almonds and caramelized honey, made in the little mountain village of Jijona near Alicante.

The children's first Christmas task was to make the pudding (some habits are too nice to shake) in early November – and this had to be done from scratch. Suet was bought from the butcher, and the little pearls of fat separated from the caul with well-floured fingers – an activity which particularly appealed to Cas. Pops and Fran pipped and stalked the raisins and sultanas, while Honey's job was skinning the scalded almonds – popping the ivory kernels out of their furry brown jackets until the tips of her small fingers were as wrinkled as the nuts themselves.

We made our own Advent calendar each year – everyone supplying the artwork according to their skills. As soon as school broke up for the holiday, the making of presents took priority over all other activities. With six of us in the family, this was a serious undertaking. Our family cake always had to be cut too many ways to yield anything but small portions – enough for home-made artefacts, but never enough to pay for much in the way of manufactured goods. So the children hoarded their pocket money and bob-a-job payments through the autumn months, while Nicholas and I saved small change in a shoebox, to be shared out among us all.

Each evening we set ourselves up at the kitchen table for a working session. Some of us had more patience, some greater artistry, some manual dexterity – but everyone joined in. Francesca's speciality was trawling the Algeciras shops for scraps of cloth which might be sewn into pretty hankies or to make gypsy dresses for little wire-and-knitting-wool dolls. Cas hoarded wooden cigar boxes and made them into personalized treasure chests. Poppy, who now uses her talents backstage in film-making, made miniature market stalls loaded with tiny produce, manned by little stallholders: fishmonger, vegetable kiosk, grocery, fruiterer, butcher, spice merchant, *churro*-maker. The work took her weeks, but the results were exquisite – perfect small-scale models accurate in every detail. Honey – and anyone else stuck for ideas and strapped for cash – joined me at the stove and made chocolate truffles, macaroons, brandy-snaps, peppermint creams, coconut ice. These were carefully packed into jars and decorated with hand-painted labels, ribbons and evergreen twigs.

Those who found themselves particularly financially embarrassed made pictorial promissory notes for future services: an IOU which was redeemable, say, against one session of washing-up; or a machine-load of ironing; or even an hour or two of reading aloud. Cas's services in this last department were much prized by Honey, who loved stories but could only read in Spanish.

In the week before Christmas we set up the crib – the *Belén* or Bethlehem – which in Mediteranean households ranks as the most important ritual of the Christmas celebration. Cas built a little hill with shoeboxes; Fran gathered moss and leaves to cover the slope; Poppy made a stable from pieces of cork-oak bark. Finally, when all preparations were concluded and approved, it was Honey's task to set Mary and Joseph to shelter in the stable, and arrange the animals,

Chocolate Truffles

Rich and luxurious, these are easy to make and much more delicious than bought chocolates. This is a very simple recipe, and the raw materials dictate the excellence of the result, so choose the best chocolate you can afford. Look for a content of over 50 per cent cocoa solids – you can get it up to 80 per cent. If your basic chocolate is on the sweet side, a pinch of cinnamon or a teaspoon of coffee powder will set it right.

─────────── YIELDS ABOUT 1½ LB/750 G ───────────

1 lb/500 g plain chocolate   *4 oz/100 g cocoa powder*
½ pint/300 ml whipping cream

─────────────── OPTIONAL ───────────────

2 tablespoons rum, crème de menthe or whatever liquor you please

1. Break the chocolate into small pieces and place in a roomy bowl.

2. Bring the cream to the boil in a large saucepan. Remove the pan from the heat as soon as the cream begins to rise. Two things to watch: don't let the cream boil over – it can erupt like Vesuvius over Pompeii. Second, if the cream is too hot when you pour it over the chocolate, the mixture can separate and you will find yourself with a film of oil on the surface.

3. Let the cream subside and cool for a moment, then pour it into the chocolate, along with the (optional) liquor. Chocolate liquefies at blood temperature, so it will melt easily into the hot cream.

4. Beat the cream and the chocolate together thoroughly with a wooden spoon.

5. Leave to cool at room temperature for 3 hours. Then whisk with an electric beater until the mixture is smooth, creamy and full of air.

6. Sieve the cocoa powder into a bowl. Drop teaspoons of the mixture into the powder. Roll them into little balls.

7. Box them up beautifully. They must be eaten fresh, but will keep for a couple of weeks in the fridge.

Almond Macaroons

These crisp little biscuits are a traditional Christmas treat – delicious with hot chocolate, or for grown-ups to dip into a glass of spiced wine.

MAKES ABOUT 24 MACAROONS

8 oz/250 g caster sugar
4 oz/125 g ground almonds
2 drops almond essence

2 egg whites (medium eggs)
2–4 sheets rice-paper
Flaked almonds

1. Mix the sugar, ground almonds and essence, and egg whites – there's no need to beat the whites first.
2. Oil and line 2 baking sheets with rice-paper.
3. Heat the oven to 350°F/180°C/mark 4.
4. Using a teaspoon and a wet finger, form small balls with ½ teaspoon of the mixture. Space the balls out on the rice-paper.
5. Top each ball with a flaked almond.
6. Bake the macaroons for 10–15 minutes, until lightly browned.
7. Remove and cool on a wire rack.
8. Tear off excess rice-paper and bag up in little sandwich bags. Decorate with ribbon and holly.

Brandy-Snaps

The warm biscuits have to be curled round a wooden-spoon handle before they cool and become brittle. With practice, it's the perfect task for small fingers.

──────────MAKES ABOUT 3 DOZEN BISCUITS──────────

8 oz/250 g plain flour
8 oz/250 g butter
8 oz/250 g demerara sugar

8 oz/250 g golden syrup
1 heaped teaspoon powdered ginger

1. Sieve the flour.
2. Butter a couple of large baking sheets.
3. Put the butter, sugar and syrup into a small pan and melt the mixture over a gentle heat.
4. When everything has dissolved, take it off the heat and leave for a moment to cool.
4. Beat in the flour.
5. Preheat the oven to 375°F/190°C/mark 5.
6. Drop teaspoons of the mixture onto the buttered baking sheet – leave them plenty of room to spread. Bake for 10 minutes, when they will be bubbly and golden but still soft.
7. Now comes the fun. Butter the handle of a wooden spoon and wrap each biscuit round the handle to give the characteristic tube shape. Leave it for a minute or two to set brittle. Slip it off and continue until all the biscuits are curled. If they cool and harden – warm them up again and they will soon soften.
8. Pack into pretty jars, decorate and label.

P.S. For a Christmas treat, stuff the snaps with whipped cream flavoured with cinnamon and a little chopped crystalized ginger.

shepherds and village people all around. As the youngest, it was her responsiblity to remember to pop the Baby in his manger after midnight mass on Christmas Eve. Afterwards, through the twelve days of Christmas, the Three Kings were daily moved nearer to the stable, until they joined the Holy Family after sundown on 5 January – the last day before Twelfth Night, when everything was packed away for next year. This final post-Christmas chore was never popular.

The nativity play was the high spot of our pre-Christmas festivities. The first year, we had five young cousins and their attendant adults staying in the house to swell our numbers. The next year, we had to recruit elsewhere. Among the available neighbours, a wild diversity of ages and mother tongues meant that a formal theatrical presentation was never possible. Instead we held a kind of themed Christmas bun fight. Because our neighbours were Roman Catholic to a man, they were initially suspicious that our non-conformist version of the Bethlehem story might contain undesirable additions or omissions. Worries were set to rest when we stuck to the gospel accounts: powerful stuff, it needs but little attention from the rewrite merchant.

From first rehearsal to public performance, it was a one-day wonder. The young performers were delivered by their parents at midday, and by the evening we had to be ready to perform. The cast list grew organically out of the dressing-up trunk – a motley collection of hand-me-downs and Sixties' flowerchild debris with full access permitted to my fake-jewellery box. We had to be flexible – cowboys and Indians, soldiers and ballet-dancers would arrive in full regalia, and lines had to be included to accommodate their preferences. One recruit who insisted on full military camouflage was given the role of Herod's chief child-murderer – and he had to be kept under close surveillance whenever we had a real newborn baby for the crib.

Nicholas, as producer and director, had the last word on casting – although in reality the allocation of roles was a raggedly anarchic process of self-selection. As you might expect, there was heavy competition for the villainous characters. The selection of the Innkeeper, a bibulous character given to swaggering around with a wine bottle, was once settled by a bare-knuckle fight, and it was not unknown for rival King Herods to come to blows. There was little competition to play the goodies – even poor old St Joseph was only considered interesting when he was locked in a battle of wills with the Innkeeper.

The in-house four formed their own cabal. Francesca drifted naturally into the role of the Virgin Mary – not because of any inherent saintliness (far from it) but because the other siblings considered babies her department. Poppy, far from angelic but capable of a convincing stage presence, met the job description of the Angel Gabriel, being both blue-eyed and blonde. Honey ran wildly excited interference round the edges, popping up now as a shepherd, now as a page, now as the innkeeper's assistant – holding up the action by delivering her lines with a gloriously uninhibited stutter. Cas, our star reader, held the whole thing together as narrator – a position of considerable responsibility since the troupe had a short attention span and had regularly to be called to order.

Once the cast list was agreed, it was time for lunch. The food was of the simplest – home-made chips, crisp and hot with tomato sauce for dipping, and hamburgers for those who wanted something a little more sustaining.

With a meal behind us, the first rehearsal allowed everyone to get to grips with their roles. All were encouraged to deliver their lines in their native tongue. Those who could not remember their words were perfectly at liberty to read them. The first and only rehearsal was followed by sustaining cake and ice-cream – the commercial sort, naturally (home-made was not a treat).

At five o'clock make-up and beginners were called. The audience arrived at six. The performance was delivered, willy-nilly and de'il take the hindmost, with much recourse to the prompt. As assistant stage-manager, I was in charge of rounding-up the multi-lingual stragglers – nothing mattered except that every toddler should have its way. On such a day, with excitement running at fever pitch and every parent rooting for its home team, there was no room for anything but a roaring rumbustious, not-a-dry-eye-in-the-house success.

After that the festival swung into the home straight. Decorating the tree was the final task, reserved for Christmas Eve. We had a tree in the garden which we left in its pot, and dug up again every year and set up by the big log fire which was all the heating we had. All artistic decisions were taken by those most passionately involved, with Nicholas in charge of wiring up the lights. Then the presents were tucked underneath, the labels read and speculation on the contents encouraged. As Father Christmas's *alter ego* I was excused tree-duty, and spent Christmas Eve wrapping up small parcels for the stockings – in strictly enforced secrecy. No prizes for guessing why somehow I could never manage to get this organized ahead of time – none but I knew the bliss of those tranquil moments alone.

The stocking-presents had to include something to wear, something to eat, something to use and something for pleasure. Something for pleasure was a new book. Useful things were soap, shampoo, pencils, rubbers, notepads, home-made lavender bags, cotton-wool balls and paper tissues. The something to wear always included a new party garment, stitched up by me in secrecy and to be worn for the first time that evening at Christmas dinner.

The girls judged that the best ever, made one year when the purse-strings were more than usually overstretched, were full skirts made of brightly coloured lining-silk, each with a bold appliqué of a green Christmas tree decorated with real tinsel and little silver baubles, with T-shirts to match – red for Fran, yellow for Poppy and turquoise-blue for Honey.

Some years the family income dictated the wrapping paper was newspaper fastened with glitter-tape. In better years it would be coloured tissue-paper – each child allotted a colour to avoid mistakes. Santa Claus is apt to get among the champagne of a Christmas Eve, and a few goodies inevitably landed up in the wrong stocking. There was never a Christmas when there didn't have to be a trade-off in the morning. Cas would get a pair of frilly knickers and a copy of *The Yellow Fairy Book*, while Honey would get a Swiss army penknife and a pair of thick football socks at least four sizes too big.

After the delivery of the stockings by the last adult to bed, it was all over until the morning. I didn't go looking for trouble, whatever the din. Inevitably Honey or Fran would wake up at four a.m. and start investigating the edibles. Either was sure to be sick after consuming an entire packet of *turrón* or imported chocolate. Cas watched the whole thing with detached amusement, and Poppy slept through everything, including thunderstorms. This was none of my business – what the eye doesn't see, the heart doesn't grieve over. On Christmas Eve, as long as my beauty sleep was not disturbed, who was I to question scufflings in the dark?

No earlier than eight o'clock on Christmas morning, the stockings were brought into our bedroom and everyone climbed on the bed to share the excitement. There was high drama as the contents were unpacked, admired and discussed. Part of the pleasure was that parents had to guess what the parcels might contain and express creative astonishment: 'Good heavens, what on earth can this be? A wooden leg? A baby camel?'

Long after they were grown up, everyone optimistically hung up their stockings on Christmas Eve – although nowadays small presents go round the tree, still in their own distinctive wrapping. Years ago, I attempted to discontinue the stockings when Father Christmas's cover was blown one windy Christmas Eve, and Nicholas, as Santa's self-appointed representative, had, if I remember rightly, been out for a late wassail and tripped over a chair when negotiating darkened bedrooms. He was caught red-faced and red-handed, and that, I thought rather regretfully, would be that. Not a bit of it. The children protested that it was not whether *they* believed in Father Christmas – it was whether Father Christmas believed in *them*. And there the matter has rested ever since.

The ritual of the day itself evolved gradually over the years, stretching to accommodate new family members as they were born, and by the time we settled down in Spain it had acquired its own shape.

The morning was mostly taken up with preparations for the festive meal. Nicholas's family always had Christmas lunch, but as chief turkey-stuffer, my vote was decisive, and it went unequivocally to my own family's tradition of a meal in the evening. I love candlelight. Anyway, if you dine at nine there's all the time in the world to enjoy the preliminaries. I have never been one to peel the tatties and top-and-tail the sprouts until absolutely necessary, so everyone was welcome in the kitchen to lend a hand with the stuffing-making and vegetable-scraping.

The bread sauce was Cas's speciality, Poppy liked beating up the brandy butter, and Fran – always the style-queen – was in charge of cleaning the silver and scraping out the candlesticks. Honey added the spice of anarchy, surreptitiously squeezing presents, peering hopefully down the tiny hole in the crackers to see if she could identify the contents, dictating where the silver charms went in the Christmas pudding.

Lunch was always light. A tortilla and a salad perhaps, or maybe a handful of our home-made olives and a slice off the *jamón serrano* sandwiched between dense textured slabs of Pelayo bread, with big juicy oranges to finish. Everything stopped at two o'clock for the Queen's speech, relayed via Gibraltar radio. Listening to the Christmas message was our major concession to expatriate priorities: the familiar 'My husband and I — ' rippled across the air waves, a bizarre reminder, in our echoing mansion in the cork-oak forest, of that orderly world of Commonwealth and corgis we had left behind.

The conclusion of the speech was the signal for present-opening. Nicholas, never a man for kitchen duty, saw his role as organizational: the distribution of the parcels from under the tree, the note-taking on which aunt or uncle or set of grandparents had sent what to whom, the clearing away of the debris. This ritual occupied most of the afternoon, with occasional forays into the kitchen to baste the turkey, until it was time to bathe and dress for the evening festivities and set the table for the feast.

At Christmas the dining table became a *mesa camella*. Topped with a heavy brown underblanket and a white tablecloth, underneath were slipped the two metal dishes full of glowing coals so that the diners could warm their feet with the blanket tucked round them. Candles blazed all round the room, and all surfaces were heaped with tinsel and ivy and oranges and nuts and as many crackers as my budget would allow – and that was always far more than might be considered proper. Whatever else was in short supply, there's no such thing as too many crackers.

We were never less than a dozen at table for the Christmas meal and often twice as many. There were always childless neighbours or in-house visitors to swell our numbers. Cas, who was the best at spelling, was in charge of the seating arrangements – place names had to be handwritten for everyone, family and guests alike. Nicholas's responsibilities stopped at the wine – copious rather than elegant, and the girls and I were back on kitchen duty.

Imagine, if you will, the glory of that meal – the heavenly scent of the roasting bird, the delicate perfume of the herbs in the stuffing, the butteriness of the vegetables, the creaminess of the bread sauce, the richness of the gravy, the crispness of the roast potatoes. The pleasure of plates piled high, white napkins and shining silver and gleaming glasses, the glitter of candlelight, the glimmer of the tree and the warmth of the coals on the toes.

Imagine all of this in the silence and sweet tranquillity of our house in the cork forest – with all the wild around us and the lights of Africa's ports across the Straits. And afterwards, in the glow of the embers, the reading of a bedtime story to sleepy children, pink-cheeked and replete, with the debris of the festivity left until morning.

CHAPTER FIFTEEN

Home remedies

'He who does not mind his belly, will hardly mind anything else.'

Dr Samuel Johnson (1709–1784)*

THERE WAS NO SUCH THING AS THE NATIONAL HEALTH SERVICE IN our cork-oak forest, let alone St George's Hospital's Casualty Department just down the road. This risky state of affairs would serve to concentrate any mother's mind on what to do in an emergency.

I made my enquiries when we first set up house. In our valley, I was told, the nearest thing to a family doctor was Cura, the white witch who lived in a lean-to on the far side of the ravine. Cura, although her reputation as a healer was considerable, was an uncertain quantity, a witch being a witch for all that.

*From Boswell's Life of Johnson.

Should I choose not to put my trust in Cura, we might try our luck in the hospital of the Sisters of Charity – the only medical provision in Algeciras at the time. This, Ana warned me, was a little on the primitive side. The nuns, she explained, put more faith in the intercession of the Virgin Mary than the limited resources of the local medico.

I discovered the truth of this caveat during the first winter we spent in Spain. As the forest was everybody's playground, it was inevitable that someone should break a limb by falling out of a tree. It was a little unfortunate that the day Cas inadvertently selected to deliver this disaster was 6 January. As the most important of the Christmas feast-days, it's a national holiday, when every working person is at home with the family having a jolly time and plenty of wine.

We arrived – all of us – at the hospital on this inconvenient day with the broken arm cradled in a blown-up plastic bag to stop it bumping around. Had Cas not been extraordinarily brave, we might have been in more of a panic. The nuns, summoned by a large brass bell, shrugged and smiled. There was no-one but the Lord at home – and He was still only a baby. The surgeon, a grandee of the town, was celebrating the feast with his brother-in-law the mayor.

With some hesitation since the nuns were unwilling to disturb the great and the good, they produced the mayor's address. The promise of ready money prized the grandee loose from the family bosom, but the ordeal was not yet over. The chemist – the only stockist of the necessary drugs – also had to be dug out of the family bosom. Ready money once more ensured the necessary. So far, so good. We had the surgeon, we had the drugs, we had the patient. We arrived back among the nuns. We were ushered into the operating theatre. The cavernous room had a large kitchen table, a lamp with a naked bulb, a long strip of fly-paper and a cupboard with a red cross roughly painted on it in nail varnish.

Then I started to panic – but the rapidly swelling arm confirmed there was no choice. We all rolled up our sleeves. The painkillers were administered by the senior nun. Cas faded into fuzzy semi-consciousness. The nuns and I yanked, the surgeon pulled. Cas woke up, gritting his teeth. He hung onto the table with his good arm and yanked right back. It clearly hurt like hell. We all pulled together. Miraculously the bones clicked into place.

Flushed with success, the surgeon vanished. The nuns took over, wrapping the arm into its plaster with surprising expertise. This task completed, they showed us to the door, and then hesitated. Would we like to stay in the hospital overnight? It was cheap, and they had heard that foreigners liked to do this. There was no nursing available, of course, so I would have to remain overnight with the patient. As far as the townspeople were concerned, it was thought that post-operative children were much better off at home. But there was a small chance the surgeon, hangover permitting, might look in in the morning. And then there were the antibiotic injections to be administered – although no doubt I could do this myself, as was normal in Andalusia.

Cas took his own decision at the mention of his mother's capacity to administer injections. He had had enough of the hospital, and more than enough of injections, whoever was responsible for them. We went home – and quite right too. You catch things in hospitals. The following day, Ana's sister Maria was called in to adminster the jabs. As a mother herself, she clearly thought me a little delinquent in my duty since I had not learnt the skill. From then on, we were on our own with the aspirin bottle and camomile tea.

In due course – some three months – the plaster came off, to reveal a perfect mend. Nevertheless, I had learnt my lesson. Florence Nightingale herself would have been proud of me. I took a first-aid course and laid in enough plaster and splints to patch up an entire regiment of walking wounded, enough wide-spectrum antibiotics and hypodermics to repel an outbreak of the Great Plague.

Well equipped as we now were, we did not often have recourse to the medical pharmacopoeia. We *did* have one case of snake-bite (Nicholas), an injury he put down to an argument with a thorn-bush, until a coin-sized bit of his calf-muscle dropped out. We escaped the attentions of the lice, scorpions and fleas which were a normal hazard of those parts.

Our Belgian neighbours up the way, wealthy owners of the paper-mill in Algeciras, who had their own swimming-pool and tennis court and absolutely no need to bother with donkey-transport, were not so lucky. Their three offspring – contempor-aries of my own four – suffered a terrible infestation of warts, and *they* attended a very expensive private school indeed, where warts were a terrible disgrace. The medical profession failed to solve the infestation. We, keeping less exalted company, were untouched. In consultation with her best friend Emma, who lived close by and as an only child was an honorary member of our household, Poppy decided to approach Cura on our neighbours' behalf. This had to be done in secrecy, as everyone knew that the afflicted ones' strait-laced parents would run a mile at the thought of a witch's remedy.

Lacking children of her own, Cura acted as surrogate mother to Emma, and Poppy was always welcome in the witch's hospitable lair. For all her reputation, Cura's bark was a great deal worse than her bite. Her hospitality included acorn coffee with condensed milk, thick and sugary, lavishly laced with anis brandy. After a visit to Cura's shack, the two little girls would reel home with spinning eyeballs.

Cura gave the problem her full professional attention. She advised rubbing the warts with snail goo, shutting the snails up in a matchbox, and then burying the box. When the snails passed to the great snail-trail in the sky, so would the warts. In strict confidence, the proposal was put to the Belgian children. The warty ones concurred. The snails were caught, the protuberances rubbed, the boxes buried. The warts vanished within a week. No doubt the Belgian parents thought it was the doctor's costly unguents. Poppy and Emma knew better.

Cura's remedies often included snails – both as a cure-all and as a pick-me-up for invalids. Her treatment for summer colds was snail broth – much more delicious than it sounds. Snails are a popular rural treat, much appreciated in the *tapas* bars of the little villages. Cura herself showed me how to prepare the molluscs, and I would often make a potful when we had been wild-gathering of a Sunday.

Cura the white witch was not all spells and snails. She had a wealth of modern advice for dealing with the minor ailments to which children are prone. It was she who passed on the tip that boiled Coca-Cola was good for tummy upsets. A dab of household bleach, she advised, was an alternative to the hydrogen peroxide used in Mediterranean countries as a wound-healer and first aid for burns. Failing this, a strong solution of salt and boiled water is a first-ditch disinfectant – in fact, the salt jar, she concluded, is the most readily available panacea for many evils.

I added a few panaceas of my own, discovered through trial and error. An application of cold tea on a flannel takes the heat out of sunburn. And although we never had to follow it, I had our London dentist's advice on losing a tooth in a football match: if someone knocks a tooth out, make every effort to find it as quickly as possible, rinse it and shove it back in. If you're lucky it'll re-root itself. It sounds obvious – but you might not think of it.

We did a lot of walking on our Sunday outings, which made sturdy shoes a vital item of equipment. Although most clothing was passed down or acquired second-hand, shoes were always your own and no-one else's. We were adventurous walkers, and the ravines of the little river which ran past our house and down the two kilometres to the sea made a fine training ground for climbers. We lived in a designated military zone, so there were no maps, and Cas and I often found ourselves in charge of a little squad of assorted children, making our way slowly and dangerously across some precipice which had caught us unawares. One fine summer's evening, just as the sun was setting, we almost came to grief by following a goat-track which ran across a sheer cliff face which plunged fifty feet into the oleanders.

We had reached the halfway point before we realized that the way back was as hazardous as the way ahead. Not quite the Himalayas, but we had to jettison all unnecessary loads in the way of picnic materials, and six small children had to be roped together with an assortment of belt buckles and knotted hankies before we could continue. Then, with Cas as the leader and me bringing up the rear, we inched our way to safety. The small ones never knew the danger we were in, but the moon was already high in the sky by the time we finally made it home. Afterwards, I added a rope and a torch to the picnic equipment, just in case.

Our Sunday outings into the countryside to cook a paella had their natural hazards. The cooking of food attracted the attentions of Andalusia's considerable and varied insect population. Nature, red in tooth and claw is capable of turning a rural idyll into a nightmare, and never more so than on a hot day in the breeding season.

On one such day in May, with a little bird-watching in mind, we were making our way through a clump of olive trees towards a sandstone ridge where a colony of jewel-feathered bee-eaters – cliff-nesters – had taken up residence. Where there are bee-eaters, naturally enough, you might expect to find bees. We had not noticed until we were right in the middle of the olive grove that a migratory swarm of the busy little insects were cropping the nectar-laden blossom on the olive trees, or that the birds were taking full advantage of this manna from heaven to feed their hungry fledglings. Unfortunately the confused insects mistook us for the source of their troubles. Pursued by an angry black-and-yellow cloud hell-bent on revenge, we dropped our baskets and ran for cover. The bees, fortunately for us all, had a short attention span, and soon lost interest. But by then we had all been severely stung and the antihistamine had been abandoned along with the lunch.

Reading up on the bee-eaters before the outing, I had learnt that bee-eaters protect themselves from the acid in insect stings by producing ammonia. The remedy was obvious to any cook whose budget would only run to the cheaper cuts of meat – kidneys must be soaked in vinegar or lemon juice to get rid of the ammoniacal taste. Logically, the chemistry must work in reverse: if an insect sting is acid, fresh urine is almost neat ammonia. I delivered my suggestion – normally my solutions are greeted with howls of disbelief, but this was an emergency. After a brief intersibling conference, Cas was selected by the sisters as the easiest source. He obliged with the necessary – and boy, were we grateful. The panacea proved its worth – the stings subsided, and the rest of the family voted Cas a medal for courage and creativity above and beyond the call of duty.

It was mostly in Andalusia that the usual ailments of childhood came our way. Mumps and measles and chickenpox followed in quick succession. If one child caught something, everyone else went down in sequence, like dominoes. This arrangement had its compensations: nursing a sick child is a full-time business, so it's perfectly convenient if everyone is sick together.

Ana's remedy for all ills was a raw egg beaten up with olive oil and good Scotch whisky – a liquor which she pronounced far more efficacious than Spanish brandy. The children preferred Cura's ministrations – they might not taste any nicer, but they came in a wider variety. The witch was a mine of information on the use of the herbs which could be wild-gathered in the scrub-thickets round about: sage for soothing a fever, fennel for the digestion, rosemary and thyme for skin troubles, lavender for wounds, water-mint for the throat, lemon-verbena as an insect repellent. All this notwithstanding, the most active ingredient in her brews was either the imported whisky or, failing that, the local fire-water – a distillation of grape liquor flavoured with aniseed.

I was more inclined to put my trust in good strong chicken broth and a hearty rub with eucalyptus oil, with maybe an infusion of camomile or lime-blossom administered to the feverish last thing at night. For a cold, I would make gallons of lemon-water: the fresh fruit chopped up whole, with a few sprigs of Cura's water-mint to disinfect the throat and honey to sweeten the mix, all infused in boiling water and allowed to cool.

As for the invalid's diet, all three of us – Ana, Cura and I – were in agreement that the old wives' advice to starve a fever and feed a cold is worth taking. No-one has much of an appetite with a raging fever, but a cold needs plenty of nourishment. The invalid had the last word on the matter – children have strong notions of what's good for them when they're ill. Bovril with toast-soldiers was the favourite meal. But if the bedridden one longed for ice-cream and chocolate – ice-cream and chocolate is what it got.

I have great sympathy for any small person confined to bed. Bedrest is boring, and even more irritating for an invalid who is convalescent but still covered in a thick scarlet rash. After the first flush of temperature when no-one can do anything but sleep, invalids need entertaining. With six of us in the family, a partner could usually be found to play board-games or racing demon or battleships-and-cruisers. And there was always a pack of cards for a game of patience.

But the best idea of all was the graffiti wall, introduced during a measles epidemic. There was no doubt that a sloping eave painted a tempting white cried out for creative attention, and before it was declared a free-trade zone, someone was always sneaking in a little drawing or two. But when you were ill, you were allowed free-range, although the invalid's pyjamas were protected by an old piece of sheet with a hole cut out for the head, poncho-style. The result was a do-it-yourself Bayeux tapestry done in felt-tip pens: Noah's ark and all the animals, every face in the school crocodile, medieval armies, everything and everyone who had been part of the invalid's experience meandered up and down its snowy heights – with a corner for noughts and crosses down by the floor.

The graffiti were always pictorial – I don't remember any writing on that wall. One year, when we had been on the gypsy pilgrimage to the sanctuary of the Virgin of the Rocio, the wall was covered with an intricate snake-procession of wagons and horsemen. When there was no more space, out came the pot of white emulsion, everything was painted over, and the artist could start all over again.

In spite of the first-aid course, I remained an instinctive rather than a practical nurse, believing that caring for the sick is all about confidence. If a child knows that a kiss makes a bruise or a scrape feel better – better is what it is. Throughout the childhood years, I didn't even own a thermometer. It seemed to me that there was no point in taking temperatures. Any child of mine could run a fever up or down at will. Fran was the supreme exponent of this magic trick: she once managed to push her temperature up to 104°F, registered on a borrowed thermometer, in anticipation of a birthday visit to a performance of *Toad of Toad Hall*. Even more astonishingly, she managed to sink it to normal as soon as the visit was cancelled.

After that I took temperatures by putting my own forehead against the invalid's, and judging which was the hotter. It's a bit rough-and-ready, but at least neither of us was unduly scared by fluctuations.

Not all emergencies could be faced with such tranquillity. We all have our Achilles' heel. Mine was Honey. At birth her prematurity had manifested itself in a severe case of jaundice. On the day of her birth by emergency Caesarean section, Nicholas – told that she was unlikely to make it through the night – had had her baptized. As a last throw of the dice, he gave her Stonewall for a middle name – summoning to her aid the spirit of that granite-hewn survivor of the battle of the Alamo, General Stonewall Jackson. She won through – but for the first few weeks while her blood was being changed, she was the colour of mustard. One rainy September evening in the cork-oak forest, she turned bright yellow all over again. By morning, she had gone all floppy.

At this, I panicked. A house conference was called. Cura prescribed sage tea and bedrest. Ana made her usual brew – yellow as the invalid. I refused all advice. For one desperate day, I trailed round Algeciras's small posse of medics, the ochre-tinged child asleep on my shoulder. We had aspirin and sympathy from one doctor; shrugs and delayed hospital appointments from the next. No further risks could be taken. I knew I had to get her back to medical civilization as soon as possible – for preference, Great Ormond Street Hospital.

Honey was no stranger to London's most famous children's hospital – they had all her records as she had already had three operations to correct the muscles of eyes which, from birth, resolutely refused to pull together. She was three when she had the second operation. To distract both of us after she came round from the anaesthetic, I carried her down the corridor to admire the lines of infants in their glasshouses. The last isolation ward contained a single tiny infant. 'Two babies,' said Honey enthusiastically. We stared at each other – I in horrified surprise that the operation had had this ungovernable effect; she in obvious delight that two babies could possibly look so alike.

It took several months before she could make both eyes work in tandem. Mysteriously, her elder siblings were by no means convinced that the adjustment could be counted an improvement. Pressed for an explanation, they revealed that there was money in boss-eyes. They had learnt this the previous summer in London, from an oil sheik whose morning constitutional coincided with their daily outings in Hyde Park. The sheik had been in the habit of slipping a tenner into Honey's infant fist – it was to bring him luck, he said. In Saudi, he explained, cross-eyes were a sign of great beauty and good fortune – a little of which might rub off. Honey's newly acquired ocular co-ordination threatened a modest but dependable source of income. Tough, I explained. One person's cloud is another's silver lining.

Faced with what I saw as a new threat to my most hard-won infant's survival, I tucked up the other three children with Ana, and booked immediate passage for us both on the first available tourist run from Malaga. Great Ormond Street's admissions took one look and diagnosed not a recurrence of the jaundice, but infectious hepatitis. We were packed away to an isolation ward for the hospital equivalent of bedrest and sage tea. Cura had been right after all.

Honey and I were away for a fortnight while she turned gradually back to the colour of pale tea. On our return, a little late for the evening meal, Ana greeted our arrival with relief and headed back for her home. Honey was tucked up to continue the bedrest, and it was business as usual.

'What's for supper, Ma?'

Tortilla Española

This is a potato omelette, a thick, juicy egg-cake. Whatever culinary skills she may otherwise lack, every Spanish country girl whips up a beautiful tortilla, and serves it straight from the pan, or just warm (the best temperature for it), at any meal.

SERVES 4–6

6 medium-sized potatoes	*Olive oil*
½ large Spanish onion	*6 eggs*
(or 1 ordinary one)	*Salt*

1. Peel and dice the potatoes: there are also those who favour slices and those who prefer chips. Skin and chop the onion finely: some housewives leave out the onion, some add a little chopped parsley.
2. Put the oil to heat in the pan. Fry the potatoes and the onion gently in the oil. The vegetables should soften and cook through, but not take colour. Transfer the potatoes and onion to a sieve over a bowl to drain and cool.
3. Beat the eggs lightly with a little salt and add them to the cooled potato mixture. Pour most of the oil out of the pan, leaving only a tablespoon or two, heat it again and tip in the egg mixture. Fry gently, lifting to let the raw egg run underneath, until it begins to look set. The heat should be low or the base will burn before the eggs are ready. As it cooks, neaten the sides with a metal spatula to build up a deep straight edge to the tortilla. When it looks firm, slide it out onto a plate, then invert it back into the pan – a little more oil may be necessary to cook the other side. Remove to a plate. Pat with kitchen paper to remove excess oil.

Accompany the tortilla with the classic Spanish salad of chopped cos lettuce, chunks of tomato and cucumber, rings of mild purple Spanish onion and perhaps a few olives, dressed with olive oil, wine vinegar and salt.

Starvation-Diet: Rice-Bowl

The standard rice-to-water proportion is 5:8, a little more rice than is required for the classic risotto proportions of 1 cup of rice to 2 cups liquid. Japanese rice, *kome*, is round-grain, but not as sticky as 'pudding' rice. Chinese and Indian rice is long-grain.

———————————— SERVES 2 ————————————

5 oz/130 g rice   *8 fl oz/250 ml cold water*

1. Rinse the rice thoroughly in a sieve under the tap until the water runs clear. Measure the water into the pan, tip in the rice, and leave it to soak for half an hour.

2. Bring the panful rapidly to the boil, turn down the heat a little, lid and boil for 5 minutes, until all the water has been absorbed.

3. Turn the heat right down, and let it dry out, still covered, for 15 minutes more.

4. Turn the heat off and leave it for another 10 minutes before serving. Bowls and chopsticks are essential for this. Hunger is better satisfied when each grain is savoured. Ask any Chinaman.

P.S. Side dishes of pickled vegetables, radishes and grated carrot improve the shining hour.

I was well aware that in the kitchen Ana was something of a blunt instrument. As a scrubber of faces and floors she had no peer. As a teller of spooky tales of the wolf-man in the woods, she was unrivalled. But when it came to cooking, her repertoire was strictly limited. Bread-porridge – gazpacho – was the standard midday meal in her own house, and this the children absolutely refused to eat. Otherwise, she could cook only two dishes. Both involved eggs. One was a Spanish tortilla, the second hard-boiled eggs with bread, pure and unadorned.

I made a brief tour of the store cupboard.

'How about delicious boiled eggs with toast soldiers?' I enquired cheerfully.

'Oh no. Not eggs again,' was the unanimous chorus.

At that moment, perhaps from relief at Honey's rapid recovery and a desire to mark the occasion with a little sackcloth and ashes for the rest of us, I saw red. Most of the world was on a starvation diet, I declared. We, too, would take an educational gastronomic tour of the Third World.

Packed lunch for school was downgraded to bread rubbed with garlic and oil. In my defence I can only say that it was really *good* bread, and plenty of it: proper wood-oven bread, with a dense creamy crumb, a crisp mahogany crust and everything left in, including a pinch of lime for the teeth. I *did* tuck a carrot, an orange or an apple in the lunch basket, because I am, of course, a responsible mother. Supper was more varied, but remained an unadorned diet of the world's staples, dished up according to ethnic habit.

On Monday we ate Spanish lentils with garlic. On Tuesday we ate plain-boiled Chinese rice with salt-pickled vegetables. On Wednesday we ate Moroccan broad bean purée with a dressing of oil. On Thursday we ate Italian corn-porridge with cheese. On Friday we had Scottish barley broth with greens. On Saturday we ate jacket-boiled tatties with buttermilk, Irish style. On Sunday – well, I'm sure you catch the general drift.

My nerve held for a month. Cura and Ana did not approve at all. The episode entered family mythology.

CHAPTER SIXTEEN

Birthdays and other celebrations

'Dining partners, regardless of gender, social standing, or the years they've lived, should be chosen for their ability to eat – and drink! – with the right mixture of abandon and restraint. They should enjoy food, and look on its preparation and its degustation as one of the human arts.'

M.F.K. Fisher*

NATURALLY ENOUGH IN A HOUSEHOLD SUCH AS OURS, FAMILY celebrations centred around a meal.

With six birthdays a year, we had plenty of practice in marking rites of passage. In addition to the chance of a feast, it was all good theatre – an opportunity to hone performance skills. Sure enough, as

*In *The Art of Eating*.

the children grew older, their parties evolved through a one-act toddler's tea party to a full theatrical performance with the presentation of gifts as the overture, followed by a three-course feast, and a curtain call supplied by post-prandial games.

Birthdays are one of the few chances for a child to acquire a little capital – however temporarily. The most difficult thing for any small person to get their hands on is ready money. Still more so if you're one of four siblings in foreign parts and therefore lack the casual hand-outs which might come your way from a generous uncle or doting godmother. This made birthdays doubly important in the early years. On someone's birthday, there was always the chance that something wonderful might arrive in the post. This optimism was sometimes ill-founded – maybe all relations were absent-minded or temporarily financially embarrassed.

After one particularly impecunious year, I took to intercepting the birthday mail so that the shortcomings, say, of a grandmother who sent a birthday card without a fiver inside, could be tactfully rectified. Many was the enthusiastic thank-you note written to bewildered relations who had failed to come up with the necessary.

And then again, I was perfectly capable of insisting that all of one year's donations should be shipped off to those more needy than us. One year, I remember, Cas was obliged by his intemperate egalitarian mother to hand over a huge sum, a birthday present from a godfather, to some charity or other whose purpose now escapes me. I tell myself such experiences account for his financial skills in adult life – but I think he might not agree.

The birthday rituals took account of season and geography and the problems of reconciling a busy household with the need to mark the day as special. In other words, a birthday must have a focus, a moment when the star has the full attention of the whole group. Even when everyone was still at home, this could not be fixed at a particular hour, since all six of us had to coincide.

The solution, as so many things, was locational. All in-house gifts, outside contributions and cards were piled into a basket which could not be touched until the party was about to begin. This arrangement had the advantage, too, that it was not so obvious if someone had forgotten the event, and I squirrelled away a small stock of emergency gifts to make up the shortfall. Presents did not have to be expensive as long as they were prettily wrapped (Poppy was the best wrapper, although Nicholas could turn in a mean parcel), but it was *quantity* which was important. Quantity denotes a large audience, making the star-for-a-day feel properly celebrated.

The piled-up basket was then hidden in a secret place, and someone would be elected to make up a treasure hunt. Scraps of paper with clues, each one leading to the next, were tucked around the house. The clues were expected to be in rhyming couplets – demanding a fair degree of creative skill. Cas was the star of this literary firmament, and his clues were always accorded the supreme compliment of being pasted into the birthday person's commonplace-book. Each child had one of these scrapbooks – big enough to take pressed flowers, poems, cuttings from magazines, photographs, autographs, anything which deserved preserving for posterity.

When the moment for the treasure hunt arrived – consensus dictated the timing, although the hunt always preceded the birthday meal – the birthday person hurtled around the house from clue to clue, trailing the rest of the group behind. This was more of a stampede than a procession – it was a very noisy business, generating its own excitement. All clues were read out at full volume, dissected and finally solved.

When the treasure was discovered at last, it would be taken back to the kitchen table finally to be publicly unwrapped and visibly appreciated. Audience participation is of the essence. This ritual applied to adults and children alike in the early years, but the basket and simultaneous unwrapping remains the centre of birthday celebrations now we are all adults. Crackers and party poppers remain obligatory, and a birthday is no birthday at all without a cake – decorated with one candle for each year and one for luck, so that you can be sure you'll reach the next birthday safely.

The point about cake is the glamour and the candles. The basic sponge can be carved up and decorated – a house, a train, a teddy bear, in short, anything which might be of interest to the recipient. Children will eat the icing and leave the cake – so the decorating is all that matters.

Cas and Honey both celebrate their birthdays in October. When we lived in Spain, these birthdays were marked by fire-festivals which could take place out of doors since the weather usually held until the New Year. The first guests to arrive assembled a ring of stones and enough brushwood to make a cooking fire. When the flames had burnt down to embers, we set the racks from the oven across the stones to make a rough barbecue. Chicken was the festive meat of choice. Baked potatoes finished in the embers of the bonfire took the edge off hunger while people were waiting for the chicken to be ready. To refresh the perspiring cooks, there were big slabs of water melon – really messy stuff. For the triumphant conclusion, Cas always had a chocolate cake, and Honey's was a buttery madeira topped with lemon icing.

Fran's birthday is in January – the rainiest and coldest month of all, even in Spain. Hers was an indoor party with indoor games – 'Sardines', 'Musical Bumps', 'Statues' and the like. Her cake was made with ground almonds – in plentiful supply post-Christmas – iced and flavoured with the bitter oranges which arrived in the market in January. Poppy, as an April baby, was born with the lambs and blessed with the new fruit of spring, flowers in full bloom and the weather just warm enough for games in the garden. Her cake was a cream-stuffed sponge topped with the first strawberries.

It was not until we settled in Andalusia that we had a chance to enjoy the pleasures of the Spanish *feria*. These municipal celebrations – unlike the pre-Lent festivals of Mardi Gras – are held at any time from Easter through to Michaelmas. Sometimes coinciding with the day of the patron saint or local Virgin (some Virgins are more equal than others), sometimes declared by the city fathers with an eye to increasing trade, sometimes timed to accommodate the travelling circuses and sideshows which move from one village to another. Each community has its turn at the swings and roundabouts – queuing up to peer at the fat lady and the mermaid in her tank.

From our valley, we had access to two *ferias*, just as we had access to two market-places. The first of the year was in Algeciras at the end of June. Her *feria* – as befitted the prosperous port from which the old dictator Franco set his course for the counter-revolution – was the longest, richest and smartest in the province. It ran for a full fortnight – the length and breadth of the burghers' purses. With four children along for the ride, *feria* was an expensive affair for us. As soon as Christmas was over, once again we set out the communal collecting box for the hoarding of small change.

Lemon Birthday Cake

This is the classic French *quatre-quarts* – four-quarter cake. named for the equal quantities of everything. It's quick, easy – and the sharp lemony icing contrasts beautifully with the opulent buttery cake crumb.

SERVES 8
---

4 eggs
Same weight of butter (1 large egg weighs about 2 oz/50 g)
Same weight of castor sugar
Same weight of self-raising flour (it works with plain flour, too)

A little milk
1 lemon, grated zest and juice

ICING
---

8 oz/250 g icing sugar, sieved   lemon juice and water

1. Weigh the eggs and then weigh out the butter, sugar and flour to match.
2. Soften the butter in a warm bowl, and beat in the sugar with a wooden spoon. Beat the mixture until it is pure white and fluffy – a

mixer will do the job for you in no time. Beat it some more. Then beat in the eggs whole, one at a time. After you have incorporated three of the eggs, the mixture may look a little grainy and you will need to stir in a spoonful of flour (sprinkle it in through a sieve) to soak up the extra moisture. When all the eggs are beaten in, sieve in the flour, a spoonful at a time, and fold it in with a metal spoon. Add enough milk to give you a soft smooth mix which drops easily from the spoon. Stir in half the grated lemon rind.

3. Preheat the oven to 350°F/180°C/mark 4.

4. Butter a small roasting tin and line the base with greaseproof paper cut to size. Drop in the cake mixture and push it well into the corners. Smooth down the top.

5. Bake the cake in the middle of the oven for 45–50 minutes. By this time it should have shrunk from the sides and be well-risen and golden brown – if it feels soft to your finger and is still hissing, put it back in for another 5–10 minutes. Leave the cake to settle in the tin for a few minutes, and then tip it out onto a rack to cool. Peel off the paper.

6. Mix the icing sugar with enough lemon juice (you may need a little water) to give you quite a runny icing. Stir in the remaining zest and spread the icing over the top and sides of the cooled cake. Decorate as pleases you, and finish with candles.

Chocolate Birthday Cake

This is the best cake for cold-month birthdays. Rich and delicious and very chocolatey – you only need a small piece.

8 eggs
8 oz/250 g castor sugar
8 oz/250 g bitter black
chocolate

4 oz/125 g butter
8 oz/250 g ground almonds

ICING

6 oz/175 g bitter black chocolate
1 oz/25 g unsalted butter

4 tablespoons water
4 oz/100 g sieved icing
sugar

1. Whisk the whole eggs with the caster sugar until thick and white (this takes twice as long as you think).
2. Melt the chocolate and butter, let it cool, then fold it, alternating with the almonds, into the beaten egg and sugar.
3. Pour the mixture into a large cake tin lined with greaseproof paper. Bake for 25 mins at 400°F/200°C/mark 6. This is a cake which should be undercooked: let it shrink before you turn it out.
4. When absolutely cold make the icing. Melt the chocolate, butter and water together gently. Allow to cool.
5. Beat the mixture into the icing sugar, and ice the cake with a knife dipped into boiling water. Finish with candles – one for each year, and one for luck. Make a wish when you cut the cake.

Honey, as the youngest, always screamed when the cake was cut – to let the devil out.

Orange and Almond Birthday Cake

Bitter marmalade oranges are nicest, although you can make it with ordinary oranges.

──────────────── SERVES 6 ────────────────

4 eggs
6 oz/175 g castor sugar
8 oz/250 g ground almonds

2 tablespoons honey
2 Seville oranges, grated zest

──────────────── ICING ────────────────

2 oz/50 g butter
6 oz/150 g icing sugar

2 Seville oranges, juice

1. Line a cake tin, 6–7 in/15–17 cm in diameter, with a circle of paper. Butter the tin and the paper thoroughly and sprinkle with a little sugar.

2. Heat the oven to 375°F/190°C/mark 5.

3. Whisk the whole eggs together until frothy. Sprinkle in the sugar and beat the mixture until it is white and stiff enough for the whisk to leave a trail. This is easiest done with an electric beater – it takes twice as long as you expect.

4. Fold in the ground almonds, honey and the orange zest gently but firmly. This is called 'tiring' the mixture. Tip it into the buttered cake tin lined with buttered paper.

5. Bake for 45–50 minutes, until the cake is well browned and firm to the finger. Leave it to settle for 5 minutes and then transfer it to a plate.

6. When the cake is cool, make the icing. Beat the butter with half the icing sugar until white and fluffy. Beat in the orange juice – depending on how much juice the orange produces, you will need extra water or extra icing sugar to make a spreading consistency. Ice the cake with a flourish, and decorate with candles.

Strawberry Birthday Cake

This is a classic fatless sponge – the richness comes from the cream filling. Any other soft fruit can replace the strawberries – choose whatever is in season.

SERVES 12

8 eggs
1 lb/500 g caster sugar
1 lb/500 g flour, sieved

A little vanilla essence (or bury a pod in the sugar for a week or two)

FILLING

2 lb/1 kg strawberries, wiped and hulled

1 pint/600 ml double cream, whipped and slightly sweetened

ICING

8 oz/250 g icing sugar

Water

1. Whisk the eggs until frothy. Whisk in the sugar gradually. Continue to whisk until the mixture is absolutely white and keeps its shape, like soft meringue.

2. Fold in the flour. Don't be afraid to turn the mixture well over to 'tire' it. Add the vanilla essence, if using.

4. Preheat the oven to 375°F/190°C/mark 5.

5. Divide the mixture between 2 large sandwich-cake tins lined with buttered paper. Don't worry if it comes right up the sides – the mixture won't rise much more. The cooking process sets everything – it's already quite puffed up.

6. Bake for 25–30 minutes, until firm to the finger and shrunk from the sides.

7. Let the cakes cool for a moment, then tip out onto a cake rack and peel off the buttered paper.

8. When the cakes are quite cool, assemble with the filling. Slice and fold all but a few of the best strawberries into the cream. Use this to sandwich the cakes together.

9. Mix the icing sugar with enough water to give a runny cream. Ice the top of the cake, letting the icing trickle down the sides, so that everyone can appreciate the beautiful strawberry cream in the middle. Decorate with cake candles shoved into the remaining strawberries.

Ana took charge of the accumulation of finery essential for the proper presentation of the girls. I had been busy with my needle in previous years, stitching up skirts in polka-dot patterns and splashing out on new tops and matching rope-soled sandals. But now we were honorary Andalusians, Ana considered my provision woefully inadequate. Off-the-peg flounces, she explained sternly, would do nothing for our reputation. We came to a deal, Ana and I. Each daughter was to be equipped in turn – but only one a year. The dresses would be made by Juana, José the gardener's wife, a graceful Andaluz beauty famed far beyond the valley for her skill with the needle. *Feria* frocks were her speciality – run up in the traditional pattern on the treadle sewing-machine which was a family heirloom.

Meanwhile, Fran had earned herself a place in the Los Pinos troupe of dancers, and a proper frock was not only advisable, but vital. Two expeditions were mounted: the first down the valley to Juana's little *cortijo* so that measurements might be taken; the second to Algeciras so that Fran herself might choose her fabric. It could not be any old fabric – there are rules which govern what is or isn't suitable for a *feria* frock. Although the classic material is a plain polka dot, the ladies of Algeciras changed their fashions yearly – and there were a thousand permutations to be explored. The haberdasher stocked an entire room with *feria*-dress materials of every hue and pattern. The one Fran chose was scarlet cotton sprigged with tiny blue flowers. It was agreed by everyone in the shop that it looked wonderful with her *andaluz* colouring – deep brown hair, dark eyes and sun-browned skin.

The next decision was quantity required – depending on how many layers of frills, whether the sleeves and the hem be long or short. Yards and yards of scarlet cotton were measured out from the bolt – more than enough, it seemed to me, to set up a full-grown Cinderella for the ball. It would be economical in the end, Ana assured me, as Juana would be able to allow plenty of turnings for growth. Next came a bolt of crisp blue nylon to stiffen the flounces, and curtain wire and white broderie anglaise to finish the edges. And all of this before we had even started on the accessories – fringed shawls, matching hair combs and silk-petalled flowers, plastic gypsy-ear-rings and bangles, and (most essential of all) real proper high-heeled shoes. I had always dug my toes in at the high-heeled shoes –

but this time, with a practical purpose in view, I had to concede defeat. Fran had her high-heeled dancing pumps, with little straps across the insteps, in blazing fire-engine-red leather.

In addition to this costly trousseau, as much money as possible was necessary for all the fun of the fair, both active and edible. The former featured everything you might expect from a fairground – shooting-galleries, diving ducks, big dippers, dodgems. As for the latter – there was candyfloss, sugared almonds, nougat and crystal-lized fruits, nuts, salt-crusted sunflower seeds, *kikos* – roasted corn kernels (my favourite), potato crisps and dough fritters straight from the frying vat, soaked yellow beans to nibble, tiny kebabs on steel knitting-needles, toffee-apples, tiger-nut milk, vanilla-scented hot chocolate.

The municipality took its *feria* seriously and personally – not so much as free entertainment for the citizenry, but as a chance to display that the town had made a success of itself. The festivities began with a mile-long procession of floats – every respectable enterprise in the town was expected to sponsor one and all vied with each other to produce the most lavish display. The young of the town jockeyed for a place on the floats – a vantage point from which friends in the crowd might be pelted with sweets. There was fierce competition for the tinsel crown of the carnival queen – but no-one was particularly surprised when every year the prize was claimed by one of the town councillors' unmarried daughters.

White-frocked and tinsel tiara'd among her attendant princesses, the carnival queen presided over flamenco and *sevillana* dancing which the well-drilled local schoolgirls – including Fran and Poppy – performed on an open-air stage specially erected in the small central park. Proud parents bulked the audience. There was, too, a firework display concluding with the obligatory blazing set piece celebrating some official event – one year the message was 'Thirty years of peace'; another, it was to mark the announcement that the heir to the old Generalissimo was the old Pretender's son, still another to welcome the building of a new oil terminal in the bay.

Some years after our arrival, the fairground had been moved to the outskirts of the town – a reflection of Algeciras's increased prosperity since the amusements could no longer be contained in the central square and park. In the bullring four full-scale bullfights

starred the legendary old toreros: the gentlemanly Antonio Bien-
venida and the great Litri; the manic gypsy Curro Romero – poised
to run for the train if he didn't like the look in a bull's eye; our friend
Miguelin, the local hero; a brace of Domecqs, the cream of Jerez,
offered the horse-borne version of Spain's national sport.

For comic relief, the Fireman Torero appeared with his Dwarfs, a
knock-about special for children – the fighting bulls and dwarfs were
real enough, as was the skill of the fire-engine-driving clown-
bullfighter who could have given many a serious torero a lesson.
By this time the children were well used to grown-up bullfights.

As if this was not enough, there was also a circus. The inhabitants
were left in no doubt as to who had hit town, as the clowns
themselves waylaid the children as they came out of school. You
could smell the greasepaint and the elephant dung all the way round
the harbour – shading delicately into the ripe fumes billowing out of
the sardine-canning factory.

We all loved the circus. It was a proper old-fashioned affair, with two
elderly African elephants; a moth-eaten pride of lions with their loin-
clothed trainer; a family of knot-muscled Russian high-wire artistes;
tumblers and the full brigade of clowns; a pair of camels which, the
publicity avowed, had starred in the film of *Lawrence of Arabia*; and a
flounce-frocked lady with a troupe of performing poodles.

For those who enjoyed a little more adult entertainment, there
was the Teatro Chino, a travelling music-hall featuring a magician, a
stand-up comic, and a troupe of chorus girls. The daughters loved
the Teatro Chino – every small girl is a music-hall star at heart. The
artistes were either on their way up – young, green and keen to
move on; or on their way down – guitarists who had spent too much
time on the fire-water and dancers who could no longer draw an
audience in the nightclubs of the cities.

The gypsies came into their own in the days of *feria* – doing a busy
trade reading fortunes and putting on professional cabarets in the
casetas – private pavilions financed by those who had provided the
floats. Even Puri, our gypsy-minder in the market, was far too busy
on *feria* days to look after us. The pickings were richer among the
tourists.

As the *feria* swung into its stride – all the schools were closed for
the duration – we made our way down to the town each evening.

The children came and went with their schoolfriends, while I took up semi-permanent residence in one of the *casetas* where the best dancing was to be seen. I particularly loved the flamenco singers.

In those days, Algeciras was a busy seaport, and as such, permitted and licensed a handful of brothels, some rougher than others. These, I learnt, were where the best flamenco was to be found. Of these, the *Pasaje andaluz* was famous for its *guitarista*. A perfectly respectable bar adjoined the working girls' business quarters. It was here that the world and his wife and children congregated in the small hours, just in case Dona Manuela might feel inspired.

No-one knew how old Dona Manuela was, except that she was very old indeed. It was rumoured that, as the madame of the brothel, she knew more about the town's dignitaries than anyone had a right to know. Her profile was pure Edith Sitwell; her grey hair cropped short as a boy's. Most incongruous of all, even in the heat of summer, she always wore a man's suit of English tweed, the outfit neatly completed with a white shirt and dark tie.

Dona Manuela would sometimes come and sit with me, the odd woman out, an *extranjera* with my sleepy children on the bench beside me. She was the daughter of a gypsy herself, and amused to find an *extranjera* with a passion – an *afición* – for the dances of Andalusia. No-one danced when she played. Manuela's guitar needed no embellishment. But when she had finished, some of the young women would take the floor under her instruction, and she would favour me with a running commentary on their skills.

'See that? The truth of the flamenco is not in the correctness of the movements, although the discipline must be obeyed – it is in the heart. All the excitement, the passion, lies *beneath* the surface – a promise just about to be kept. A good dancer or singer is like an explosion which has not yet happened. All the energy is rammed down. You know it's there, you feel the heat in the snap of a finger, the lift of an eyebrow, the curl of a lip. Beauty and fear – it's exactly like bullfighting. The patterns of the dance mirror the bullfighter and his bull – the *criatura* he must bend to his will. *Duende* is what has to be shown: on the man's side, his complete domination; on the woman's side, the worthiness to be dominated. When you have the two together, you have art. You'll find it in places like mine, where I make sure all the girls have a good streak of gypsy-blood.'

And then again, later. 'Flamenco is a gift which cannot be bought. Passion is not for sale: I'm a professional and I know. It's the life-blood that you hear in the guitar and the snap of the palms, the *toca* – it's the noise your babies heard in the womb. In the grace of a dancer's arm you may see the curve of your mother's breast as she suckled you. You must listen not with your mind but with your heart.'

Now *there's* a lesson for a wise child. You don't get that kind of information in sex-education classes.

The Tarifa *feria* in September was a different kettle of fish altogether.

The ancient fortress-port, guardian of the Pillars of Hercules since Phoenician times, could only manage to sponsor a three-day event accommodated on the palm-fringed esplanade which led to the walled-off naval harbour. The main attraction was a little ghost train which rattled round a small circle, ducking in and out of a darkened tent draped with rope cobwebs and luminous painted skeletons. Two young men dressed as a broom-sticked witch and a skull-and-crossboned pirate beat up the passengers when they emerged from darkness.

The municipality could only afford to stage one bullfight. However, the little harbour town had its own secret ingredient – the patronage of Don Antonio Ordoñez, often described as the greatest bullfighter of all time, the legendary torero whose exploits brought Ernest Hemingway back to Spain to chronicle his rivalry with his brother-in-law Luis Miguel Dominguin, another giant of the corrida, in his book *The Dangerous Summer*.

That particular summer was long gone by the time we came to live in Andalusia, but sometime during it Don Antonio had conceived an affection for Tarifa's little sunken bullring, which nestled deep into the sandy cliff to protect it from the wind. Tarifa is famous for its raging sea breeze – a trick of geography which has recently brought the town prosperity as a windsurfer's mecca. Whatever its friends, the wind is the matador's mortal enemy – wrapping the heavy scarlet cape against his body so that he becomes an easy target for the bull's horns.

Although in the twilight of his career, Don Antonio was still running the bulls, and each year he would sweep into town with his *cuadrilla* of picadors and *banderilleros*, accompanied by his two beautiful daughters and his bullfighter son-in-law. The local bull-ranchers were honoured to send the finest of their bulls for the legend to confront, and each year the citizens of Tarifa would be treated to the best bullfight anyone could hope to see.

The bullfighting tradition in Spain is rooted in rural life – reaching back to the days when people brought the steers to market for sale at the end of summer. The beasts were brought in from their pastures and run through the streets of their market town, to be corralled in the central square. The stampeding bulls would chase unwary loiterers, catching stragglers on sharp horns, affording robust entertainment for the spectators and an opportunity for the young bloods to show their mettle. This tradition of bull-running still survives in a few small villages – with the annual festival of Pamplona the most visible urban survival. In those days the chase was all that mattered – it was not until the formalization of the modern bullfight that the killing itself was considered of any theatrical importance.

In Tarifa, although a good kill was appreciated, the old tradition still held and the fight was not always to the death. Instead, the bravest bulls were sometimes permitted to return to their pastures as breeding stock. Breeding for the ring remains an important source of income for the cattle ranchers of Andalusia, and we could admire the *toros bravos* from a respectful distance as they cropped the broad flower-carpeted pastures by the shore when we were on our way for a beach paella at the *chozo* which produced Jane the rickety cat.

The country people of Andalusia, smallholders and subsistence farmers, lived with and husbanded their animals, knew each one by name, and took responsibility for their lives, and the fights were intimately linked to the agricultural cycle. Each September, shortly before the *feria*, Cas joined the other boys of the neighbourhood in the little ring which served the valley's community – the bulls were only first-year calves, but they could send a sturdy twelve-year-old like Cas flying across the sand.

Bullfighting became part of our lives. We all went to the Tarifa bullfight, queueing for the best tickets weeks in advance. Even Poppy, who would always turn off the bullfights her father wanted to watch on television (never the best place to see a bullfight) knew that this one was special. Whatever you may think of the bullfight, its principle function is to concentrate the mind on mortality.

The costumes worn were not the suits of lights – the flashy sequined *traje de luz* worn in the big rings – but the elegant sombre grey uniform of the *andaluz* cowboy, short-jacketed, leather-chapped and booted against the mountain thorns. Tarifa, too, was notorious for its leniency towards the *spontaneo* – the would-be bullfighter who leaps the wooden barrier to grab the cape and make a few passes in the hope of catching the eye of a professional. There was never a *feria* without a *spontaneo*.

Everyone, young and old, rich and poor, lived for that annual carnival. When the bullfighters are the finest, the bulls are the bravest, the mantilla'd señoritas the most beautiful, there is no more thrilling spectacle than the corrida. Afterwards, the poor of the town enjoyed the only meat they tasted all year – sold cheap as *carne de lidia* in the market. We lined up with the rest for our ration of fillet, or tripe, or shin – it was first come first served, and everything cost the same.

The opening of Tarifa's fiesta was marked by the rural equivalent of Algeciras's floats – a *romería*, an all-day pilgrimage on foot and on horseback into the hills behind the town.

The official purpose of the outing was to fetch Tarifa's miracle-performing Virgin, Our Lady of the Light, back to the town to join the party. The Mediterranean has many such Holy Ladies, guardians of the well-springs once patronized by the mother-virgin-goddesses of pagan times. Dressed in her finery, embroidered and flowered, the Mother of God was brought back on the shoulders of her devotees to take up temporary residence in the cathedral church in the town whose well-spring she guarded. Although the pilgrimage had a more ancient purpose – licensing the town's young people to escape the vigilance of their elders for a little flirtation – all were welcome on the road.

There was much deliberation in the household, that first year, over whether or not Bernardo the donkey was a proper form of transport for a *romería*. José and Manolo, Tarifa countrymen both, were in no doubt of his suitability. But Ana, as a sophisticated Algeciras townie, shook her head firmly. Donkeys were all very well on a business trip, but a *romería* is a social occasion, worthy of the finer things of life.

Cas came up with the answer. He negotiated with a neighbouring landowner the loan of Furia, a handsome young stallion with a flowing black mane, on which he was learning to ride. This arrangement suited both of them, since Cas gave the young animal a thorough daily workout in return for his riding lessons. The *romería*, Cas proposed, would be a fine opportunity to test his somewhat ungovernable mount's roadworthiness.

Everyone agreed we were a fine little group when we took to the trail – what with Fran in the new *feria* frock and our booted and hatted horseman for an escort. There was no doubt that a well-mounted cavalier gave us the all-important *categoria*, even if we did have to dodge the prancing hooves.

Man cannot live by bread alone: there must be music and dance. The procession would stop every few hundred yards for a little traditional refreshment – the pale dry wine of Chiclana. When throats were well-wetted the dance would begin. A rural *sevillana* needs no formal accompaniment but the singing of the participants and the briskly expert handclaps of the spectators.

The most important of Andalusia's pilgrimages is the Whitsun *romería* which crosses the marshes and dunes of the great estuary of the Guadalquivir to pay homage at the shrine of the Virgin of the Dew – the *Virgen del Rocio*. Our first excursion as pilgrims to the shrine took place when we were invited to join the Hermandad de Sanlucar, a brotherhood from the little port from which Columbus took sail, for the week-long journey.

Each of the brotherhoods came from one of the towns which surrounded the marshes, or from Seville itself, Spain's most important southern city and once the capital of the New World.

The Virgin's legend is a romantic tale of love lost and found. In the early thirteenth century, a hunter from the little village of Almonte on the edge of the Guadalquivir delta, some three days' foot-journey in the marshes south of Seville, was out with his dog, scouring for nesting birds in the spiny cistus scrub. The dog insisted on guarding a particular thicket. There his master found to his surprise not a brooding water bird, but a carved wooden statue of the Virgin. He pulled the statue free, shouldered it and set out for home.

Very soon, exhausted by the increasingly heavy burden and the midday heat, he lay down and fell asleep. When he woke, the Virgin had vanished. Retracing his steps the hunter was amazed to find the Virgin reinstalled in her hiding-place. The next day, the bewildered man returned with companions from his village. They pulled her out again. Then they, too, fell asleep, once again waking to find the Virgin back in her thicket.

The village priest took the matter up through the church's hierarchy to the Bishop of Seville, who eventually decided that the Virgin had selected her own home, and there it was that she should have her shrine.

The Virgin of the Dew, and the Whitsun pilgrimage which the villagers of Almonte made to her, grew in reputation over the centuries. The little pueblo of Rocio, its sandy streets lined with hitching posts for the horses, was only occupied for the week of Whitsun. The rest of the year it lay dormant, inhabited only by the cloud of white doves who quickly colonized the chapel's bell tower and have given the Virgin her pet name, *la Blanca Paloma*.

Gradually the White Dove was acknowledged as the purest of all Virgins (with the tacit consent of the Church), and the neighbouring villages and towns, and even Mother Seville herself, joined the pilgrimage to her shrine, carrying with them their own statues of the Virgin to receive her blessing.

The pilgrims, faced with the usual dangers that awaited travellers in medieval times, compounded by an inhospitable landscape, joined together for safety. Some had to cross as many as seven rivers and make a journey of many days. The groups soon formed themselves into brotherhoods, each of whom built a chapter house and shrine to shelter their own visiting Virgin in the village of Rocio.

In those days the journey was only possible on foot or horseback. More recently tractors and Land Rovers have been pressed into service as means of transport – although even they can get bogged down in the dunes. Knowing this, we hired a mule and cart from a gypsy in Sanlucar – the rent inflated in case the capital foundered by the wayside – and joined our hosts at the edge of the river for the ferry which took horses and carts across into the pine forests which were once the hunting grounds of the kings of Spain. The little cart lurched and thumped as we crossed the wide mouth of the estuary on the flat-bottomed boat, and the children scampered from side to side to avoid the nervous horses and rocking wheels.

On the other side stretched the great empty marshes, dunes held together with scattered groves of pine trees, interspersed with clumps of reeds and linked by great swathes of thorny scrub. For three days and nights we journeyed with the brotherhood, taking turns at the head of the recalcitrant mule, carrying all our stores inside the cart. If the sand was heavy, the carriage wheels buried themselves deep, the mule came to a halt, and everyone had climb out and join him on the shafts. Once or twice we had to be pulled out of a particularly deep dune by a cheerful scarlet-faced farmer who was making the trip with his wife and family on a huge mechanical harvester.

Every few hours the carts had a chance to catch up with the horsemen when they stopped to sing and dance. Unlike the elegant ladies of the cities, the women of Sanlucar did not care to ride side-saddle behind their men, preferring to ride astride their own mounts. Gypsy-flounced but sturdily booted, they descended from their mounts to trace on the beaten earth the formal patterns of the *sevillana*. Their music was the click of castanets, the snapping of fingers, the quick drumbeat of the handclapped *toca* and the accompaniment of voices raised in the newest ballad, especially composed for that year's pilgrimage. But the main purpose of the halt was to slake the thirst with as much of the straw-pale wine of Sanlucar as throats and bellies could accommodate.

The Sanlucar wine is manzanilla, dry and salty and heady – as highly prized as the wines of Jerez. Water was carried in leather bottles, too – in Andalusia only drunkards take wine without water. But even so, there is an obligation on the pilgrim to drink the fruit of the grape to the glory of the Virgin.

The first two nights we slept by the embers of the camp-fire among our companions of the brotherhood, huddled together under a canopy of summer stars. The wilderness was as busy by night as by day. Nightjars whirred in the underbrush, and owls hunted low over the cistus scrub. A gang of little tuft-eared lynxes paid us nightly visits – we found their tracks around the camp-fire each morning.

By day, broad-winged eagles kept us company from the skies. Flocks of rosy flamingoes stalked the shallows by the ocean, and the sand of the shore bore the tracks of *jabalí* – wild boar – which would always set a party of horsemen scampering in pursuit. Hoofed creatures of every kind came down to the edge of the water each evening to drink from the sweet waters which flowed into the sea. Storks and spoonbills, community-builders, kept an eye on our passage from their stacked tenement nests in the few trees which had managed to endure the winter storms from the Atlantic.

Soon after dawn on the third day, we rode out of the wilderness and into the maelstrom which was Rocio. The sandy streets of the tiny village were crammed to overflowing with a milling mass of pilgrims like ourselves. Even then, long before any road to the shrine was built, there must have been 10,000 of us, at least. In the wide streets with their wooden-verandah'd brotherhood houses was an endless passing and repassing of riders and foot-travellers, a rattling of carts and a trundling of wagons.

In the dusty square which surrounded the sanctuary was what might well have been a medieval market-place, so constant was the business of greeting and leavetaking; so many long-lost cousins to be acknowledged, so many old friends to be greeted among the throng of hawkers and drunks, lovers and rivals, dancers and singers, poets and storytellers, old and young, rich and poor – and all bound together by the unwritten rule of that holy pilgrimage: no quarrel might be continued once the name of the patron Lady had been invoked. Just as well, since many a child was born nine months after the pilgrimage and blessed with the name – and protection – of the Virgin of the Dew.

The wine flowed freely – but what would you expect in Andalusia? Even the children – our own among them – quenched their thirst with fizzy lemonade sharpened with a splash of new wine. Among the sherry-brotherhoods it was obligatory to offer each visitor a *copita* of your own making, with a handful of olives or salted almonds, a sliver of *jamón serrano*, a chunk of bread. Generosity indeed, when nothing could be bought in the village, and all supplies had to be brought on the carts or in the saddle-bags of the pilgrims.

Each of the brotherhoods followed a different route across the estuary, the way dictated by the starting point – the Rocio ballads celebrate the comparative hazards of those who must cross river and forest, marsh and dune. Each brotherhood, too, had its own special identity – the different colours of the favours worn by each troupe scarcely necessary to distinguish one from another. The weatherbeaten farmers of the little whitewashed fortress-pueblos of the hills – Arcos, Vejer, Medina Sidonia – crossed the eastern marshes on their sturdy working nags. We, the vintners of Sanlucar, crossed the river at its widest point, and rolled our barrel-laden carts along the southern strand.

The aristocratic horsemen of Jerez, severely tailored in the dark *traje corto*, mole-grey sombreros tilted over fine-boned faces, picked their way through the dry scrub of the king's hunting grounds on pure-bred Arab stallions. The grandees of Seville, their patrician ladies riding side-saddle behind, pranced through the northern pine groves. Behind them followed their servants in huge ox-drawn covered wagons, the interiors brilliant with a palace wardrobe of shimmering silk shawls and richly flounced skirts – even on pilgrimage the fashionable ladies of Seville changed their outfits twice a day.

In spite of all this splendour, the most favoured by the Virgin – those who were permitted to carry her silver-encrusted litter when the time came on the last day for her to give her blessing to the throng – were the foot-soldiers of Almonte.

After mass on Whit Sunday, the descendants of Cortes's conquistadores fought each other for the privilege of hefting the wooden platform on which the doll-faced Lady bounced and swayed. Oh, the beauty of her, sighed the crowd – the perfection of her flowers, the glory of her crown, the sweetness of her smile, the tenderness with which she cradled her infant in her arms. And oh, the holiness of the blessing she alone could give. A man could commit a thousand sins and save his soul, so long as he had the benediction of the Sinless One, the White Dove, the Virgin of Rocio.

The return journey had a different quality – a tiredness, a sense of triumph, a mission completed. We rode and slept and rode again, the mule ambling gently along in the shafts. The brotherhood trudged homewards, stopping as before for a draught of wine, a dance, a song – but now the singing and dancing was subdued, gentle – as if we were only reminding ourselves of past glories. The cart rattled through the same dunes, following more easily down the wide track of the outward journey.

Today, the brotherhoods have swollen into an almost unmanageable throng, and a road fit for tourist buses now joins Rocio to

Seville. There are day-outings for those who wish to visit the shrine. No doubt the Lady knows her own – only a foolish foreigner would think her blessing could be so easily earned. And yet and yet – the pilgrim's way gets into the blood. There are still many who – in penitence for sins, or recognition of mortality, or for the joy of human companionship – take the old way through the marshes and across the dunes and over the rivers to reach the sanctuary.

That last night we slept again under the stars – this time on the beach, waiting for the flat-bottomed ferries to come over to collect us in the morning. Wearily we pushed the wagon aboard, too tired to take leave of our companions or they to acknowledge our departure. The next year, and the next, we resolved we would return.

And we did – until circumstances dictated we must leave our house in the cork-oak forest, our pavilion pitched on the slopes of paradise, and the way through the marshes was no longer ours to take.

CHAPTER SEVENTEEN

France: Pastures new

'Don't underestimate yourself.'

*Reverend Sydney Smith**

IT WAS 1978 AND TIME TAKE STOCK – NOT LEAST BECAUSE OUR years of going native in southern Spain had turned the four children into *andaluzes*.

'Speak English!' I would yell at the chattering mob.

They paid absolutely no attention. All social communication was in the thick patois of the region. The four tried to reassure me they could also do 'madrileño' – the Spanish equivalent of the standard BBC vocabulary and accent. I wasn't convinced.

*Advice to a young lady in low spirits (*c.* 1830).

In the end it was Cas who decided that something had to be done. At thirteen and the spokesperson for the junior division, he carried considerable weight in the household.

'You'll have to face it, Mother,' he explained patiently, rather as one addressing a retarded child, 'you have only yourself to blame. Either we're going to be Spanish – and that means eventually we'll be off to universities or whatever in Seville or Madrid. Or we'll have to go back to English schools. So make up your mind.'

Of course, he was perfectly right. I considered the options. From my own experience, I knew that bilingual Spanish could be counted as an eccentricity. But if one's trilingual, if you can speak also French as both Nicholas and I did, it's not only an asset but a qualification. I made up my mind.

Within the family I had always been responsible for deciding the minor issues, the button-sewing, one might call it: disposition of income, choice of education, where we lived and what we ate. Nicholas occupied himself with the major problems of existence, the dragons: whether to bomb Colonel Gaddafi, the selection of England's test team, the consequences of chopping down the rain forests – and earning our living (the sound of a tapping typewriter is music to my ears).

I proposed we return to Britain but spend a year in France on the way.

Lessons in French began immediately round the kitchen table. As a little taster of future pleasures, I began by running through my repertoire of French dishes. *Hachis Parmentier* replaced the beans-and-bones dishes of Andalusia. *Tarte au citron* became the Sunday treat. We read Saint-Exupéry's *Le Petit Prince* each evening and borrowed a batch of Asterix books from the Belgian neighbours.

We were off on another adventure, a French sabbatical. We arranged to borrow a little stone-built farmhouse belonging to Auberon and Theresa Waugh, who used it as a summer home. The house was high on the windy plateau of the Languedoc, and we had no idea what we were in for before we arrived.

Telephone calls established that the nearest CES school at the nearby town of Castelnaudary would be happy to welcome us. The French authorities appeared to consider our application entirely

Hachis Parmentier

There's no-one like a French housewife for careful management of the family budget, and this is no more than the cottage pie 'à la française'. It was the great Monsieur Parmentier, eighteenth-century chemist and politician, who persuaded the Gauls that the potato was fit for human consumption. His reward was culinary immortality – a repertoire of potato dishes which bear his name.

--------------------------------- SERVES 4 ---------------------------------

1 lb/500 g cooked meat	2 tablespoons plain flour
2 oz/50 g butter or dripping	1 tablespoon chopped parsley
1 large onion, skinned and	½ teaspoon thyme
finely chopped	½ pint/300 ml stock
1 garlic clove, skinned and	(or white wine and water)
chopped	Salt and pepper

--------------------------------- TO FINISH: ---------------------------------

2 lb/1 kg potatoes, boiled and	1 egg yolk
mashed with salt, pepper, butter,	Large nugget of butter
hot milk and a little nutmeg	1 tablespoon grated cheese

1. Chop the meat finely, discarding any gristle.

2. Melt the butter or dripping in a saucepan and fry the onion and garlic very gently until they soften and take a little colour. Stir in the flour and fry for a moment. Sprinkle in the parsley and thyme. Add the stock and let all bubble up. Let the sauce reduce for a few minutes, then stir in the chopped meat. Bring back to the boil, then turn down the heat and leave it to simmer for 15–20 minutes. Taste and correct the seasoning.

3. Butter a gratin dish and spread a layer of mashed potato in the base. Cover with the meat in sauce, then with another layer of potato. Repeat until all is used up, finishing with a layer of potato. Fork up the potato, gild with egg yolk and dot with butter. Sprinkle with grated cheese.

4. Finish in a hot oven for 20–30 minutes to reheat the layers and brown and crisp the top.

Tarte au Citron

These beautiful sharp-flavoured lemon tarts were sold in our local patisserie in Castelnaudary.

─────────────── SERVES 8–10 ───────────────

─────────────── FOR THE PASTRY ───────────────

6 oz/175 g flour   6 oz/175 g cold butter
1 teaspoon salt   2 egg yolks
1 oz/25 g sugar   3 tablespoons water

─────────────── FOR THE FILLING ───────────────

4 lemons   5 eggs
4 oz/100 g unsalted butter 5 oz/125 g caster sugar

1. Make the pastry first. Sift the flour into a bowl with the salt and sugar. Make a well in the middle and grate in the cold butter. Mix it in lightly. Fork the egg yolks with the water. Work them into the flour and butter until they form a ball. Knead lightly for a short time.

2. Roll out the pastry, then lay in a tart tin, easing it into the corners. Cover and put aside to rest in a cool place.

3. Preheat the oven to 350°F/180°C/mark 4.

4. Make the filling. Grate the rind of one of the lemons and squeeze the juice from all of them. Melt the butter. Beat the eggs and the sugar together until they are light, white and fluffy. Fold in the lemon juice and the butter.

5. Pour the filling into the tart case and bake for 40–50 minutes until set.

normal and understandable. They felt that anyone who *didn't* want to be educated in France was making a terrible mistake.

The only condition was that our new home had an inside toilet. The French equivalent of Family Welfare enquired solicitously if we had one – because if not, there were grants, you understand. On learning that Maison Wog, as Waugh is pronounced in France, was indeed equipped with the necessary, we were assured we were officially inscribed on the school roll. No further formalities were required.

We arrived at our quarters early one cold September morning, after a chilly night on the road spent under canvas with my sister Marianne, the favourite aunt (who later provided that essential safe haven for family runaways in the teenage years). We had struck camp and travelled on as dawn broke, too chilled to the marrow for sleep. It was not an auspicious beginning – and we envied Nicholas, kept behind by work in the comfort of London.

Our hearts dipped even further as we bumped up the track that led to lonely Maison Wog. We already knew that the farmhouse, aproned with wheatfields and sheep pasture, had never been intended for winter occupation. What we did not yet know was that the windy plateau was the region's watershed, hurling the deluging rain and icy snow either towards the Atlantic or the Mediterranean. Or that in winter, the winds would roar across Europe from Siberia, howling down the plain until they curved upwards over our roof and blew the owls from their perch in the eaves, the mice from their nests in the rafters.

The next morning, the first of the educational year, we made our way to the town. There was no difficulty in locating the school. It seemed as if everyone in Castelnaudary – man, woman and child – was heading towards a large grey stone building on the hill. We joined the throng. To me, accustomed to English officialdom universally suspicious of motives and provenance, the school's decision to accept us without question seemed almost too good to be true. I was more than a little nervous as we followed the stragglers through the warren of old streets until we reached a wide flight of steps which led up to the school door.

A bell clanged. Everyone vanished. We were left gazing round, uncertain how or where to begin.

'*C'est n'est pas par hasard la famille Luard?*'

We turned to confront a red-faced gentleman in a tweed suit with a watch-chain across his waistcoat. It could only be the headmaster. I breathed a sigh of relief.

'*Suivez-moi.*'

We followed him into his office. He considered us thoughtfully – clearly we were as dubious a bunch of foreigners as any schoolmaster has ever been expected to take under his wing.

'How good is the little ones' French?'

'*Comme-ci, comme-ça.*'

We spread our hands and shrugged in what we hoped was a suitably Gallic manner. We had, after all, put in a little ground work on the idiom – enough to be able to count, decipher the days of the week and answer simple questions about age and name. Apart from that, I hoped for the best, crossed my fingers and trusted that knowledge of one Latin language would lead to an early grasp of another.

'No matter,' said the headmaster. 'We have Algerians, we have Catalonians, we have Vietnamese – and now we have *les Anglais*. You will soon find yourselves at home.'

The three eldest, the headmaster explained, were scheduled to start in the lowest form – the right age group for Poppy, youngest of the three – and her brother and sister would move up to the appropriate level as soon as their command of the language was adequate. The three were to catch the daily school bus at six-thirty a.m. prompt at the crossroads a mile below our house. The cost of transport, declared the headmaster with a shrewd glance at our elderly camper-van, would be paid in advance. School books were the responsibility of the parents – and there was a second-hand exchange which kept the cost to the minimum. No uniform was necessary.

Cas, Fran and Poppy vanished into a classroom – three small figures among many, while the headmaster turned his attention to Honey. At seven years old and not yet a candidate for the big school, he had arranged that she should attend the École Maternelle in Montmaure, the infant school in the village nearest our address. There was no hurry, he explained, as *les petits* weren't due to start for a week.

Honey and I returned to the farmhouse.

As the wind howled through unmortared stones, I was beginning to think the whole thing was a terrible mistake. If we were not to be defeated before we had even begun, something had to be done about the cold – and done immediately. We stuffed the holes in the walls with newspaper, hung blankets over the doorways, and laid in supplies of wood for the fire.

In spite of these precautions, I knew we would need exercise to keep warm – and this would have to be taken indoors. The house was divided in two by an open arch where farm machinery could be brought under cover. It was large enough to take a table-tennis table. We consulted Madame Guillermat, our nearest neighbour and keeper of the house's keys. She told us there was a do-it-yourself section in the *hypermarché*, and her son, a mechanic in the town, would be happy to bring anything we wanted back on his lorry.

Honey and I needed no further prompting. We bought trestles, a huge sheet of hardboard, a pot of green paint, a net, four bats and a supply of balls, and we were in business. That evening, we had a fine table – a little rickety, to be sure, but it would serve its purpose.

Then there was the matter of hot baths – without which in the bleak midwinter I cannot do. The problem was not the heating of the water, but its disposal. A large notice in the bathroom stated the cesspit was prone to the vapours and could not cope with more than two baths a week. A similar problem had occasionally struck in our house in Spain, and I had a fair idea of what to do. Investigations revealed an industrial length of hose in an outhouse.

I jammed one end of the hose in through the bathroom window and shoved the other end out into the sorghum field which sloped conveniently away from our little plateau. We had a gravity hose – even if, every time, it was somewhat inconvenient scampering down the hill in the cold and damp dressed in little more than a towel, in order to establish the proper suction. Later, in the spring, Monsieur Escrieux, the owner of the sorghum, was mystified by the sudden fertility of a small patch of his crop.

The next essential was the rental of a television – not so much for entertainment, but because it is the quickest and most accessible way to learn a new language. A shop in Castelnaudary was happy to oblige, and the owner came out to install it immediately, trailing a spider's web of wires across the roof.

Our preparations took all day. With supper simmering on the stove, Honey and I drove down the hill to collect the others. I questioned the people anxiously. How had it gone? They looked at me speculatively.

'What's for dinner, Ma?' was their long-familiar noncommittal reply.

As with their first day at the school in Pelayo, my three wise monkeys would not be drawn. We ate our supper and I asked no further questions. I knew the scrubbed boards which served as the kitchen table must become an undemanding raft of safety in an uncharted sea.

The daily timetable was set by the school run. I rose at five, lit a fire in the kitchen, set the milk to heat for café au lait, heated the oven to warm the croissants fetched by Cas each evening on the house's little motor cycle from the delivery point on Madame Guillermat's porch, and breakfast was ready. By six o'clock the three eldest had to be dressed, fed and ready for the bumpy drive down the cart-track to meet the school bus.

Winter came early that year in the Languedoc. We had scarcely established our bridgehead when the first snow fell and our mud track vanished under a thick white blanket. Icicles rimmed the eaves. Each morning the van's doors froze unless I remembered to drive its front part under the archway the night before. On the second day of snow, following my own tracks back, I skidded into the ditch and had to be winched out by Monsieur Escrieux's tractor.

Such a display of vulnerability endeared us to the two families who farmed the fields which surrounded our house. Madame Escrieux and Madame Guillermat conferred. It was clear that, with a young family, I needed all the help I could get – particularly since, so far, there was no husband in evidence. They decided to take us in hand. We needed access to proper food for the children – not the rubbish you bought in the *hypermarché*, but reliable food whose provenance could be guaranteed.

Lacking the necessary smallholding, it was certain I would not be able to achieve much on my own. No matter. Both ladies kept a barnyard and well-stocked *jardin potager* – and we were welcome to the surplus at a lower price than we would have to pay in the market. These transactions all had their logical length – they could not be hurried, and had to include time for a gossip. As foreigners, we were a source of endless amusement. The free entertainment we provided was willingly paid for in kind when we had to be rescued from yet more disasters of our own making – overloaded electrical circuits, no gas for the cooker, running out of firewood.

There was a geographical limit to how foreign anyone could be. Those who came from beyond a thirty-kilometre radius were simply *les gens de Paris* – 'people from Paris' – and we were no more or less foreign than they. As foreigners, we were plied with culinary advice. Passionate public discussion of the raw materials is an essential part of any provisioning in France. The selection and preparation of the daily dinner, once the entire preoccupation of the human race, remains a subject of universal interest in the Languedoc – a matter for the heart, with silence descending only when the business of eating takes precedence.

As with all self-sufficient households, our neighbours never let anything go to waste. Lacking domestic creatures of our own, we nonetheless kept a bucket to be filled with scrapings and peelings for the benefit of our neighbours' animals. Our leavings, being considered rich pickings, went to the geese. The Languedoc is the heartland of the goose, and Madame Escrieux's Christmas corner-of-the-apron money came from selling the birds she kept for *confit* and foie gras – stocking her own larder first.

The goose, explained Madame Escrieux, is a generous bird – and not just for its meat and delectable liver, although that was trouble enough by the time you had finished fattening the birds up on the walnuts from the tree in the yard. The eggs made a fine omelette and the feathers and down went to stuff mattresses and quilts and provide warm winter waistcoats for the field-workers and huntsmen. The traditional Sunday dinner in the two households was the stupendous cassoulet, a mighty layering of conserved goose and haricot beans.

Honey was delivered to her École Maternelle the following week.

I wrapped her up warm and sent her down to the end of the track to meet the school round. Tucked into her satchel alongside her new pencil-case was her favourite lunch: egg-and-butter sandwiches, an apple, a slice of cake and three squares of chocolate, neatly packed into a plastic lidded box.

I worried all day. Madame Escrieux, from whose farm-gate the school round collected her, assured me that all would be well. She had even prepared a little edible surprise for *la petite* – just to set her on her way.

As the sun set over the humpback hills I watched for her return. She came trundling up the track with Madame Escrieux's warm *pain au chocolat* in one sticky fist and a face as pinched as a sour plum. I ran to meet her, my worries confirmed. Obviously the other children had bullied her and the teacher had been mean.

She gazed at me gloomily. None of those things. Everything was fine – everything except the packed lunch. And that wouldn't do – it wouldn't do at all. What she needed was what everyone else had – a hot lunch, brought to school in a canteen. She had borrowed her new best friend's just to show me what she meant. A canteen, it appeared, was a little metal bucket, square-edged and rubber-sealed like a kilner jar. Inside, it had a small removable metal tray for the hors-d'œuvre, with space for a helping of savoury stew underneath. The dinner lady, explained the daughter patiently, collected the canteens from all the children when they arrived. At lunch-time, having first removed the cold hors-d'œuvre, she set the canteens to heat in a vat of boiling water. Everyone compared each other's ladleful of daube or cassoulet. Sandwiches just weren't up to it.

Another area of discord surfaced at bath-time. Honey's clothes weren't up to it either. They must be covered with a *tablier* – a front-and-back pinafore. Everyone else had a *tablier*. In fact, she couldn't go to school at all unless she had a *tablier* – or she would stick out like a sore thumb. That evening I cut down a Laura Ashley smock for her pinny. The following day I bought a canteen. Honey professed herself content. She might not have the language, but she had the street credibility.

Each day the older children cautiously delivered snippets of information on the big school. All were agreed it was different. For a start, they vouchsafed, the school work was far harder than it had been in Spain. Much was asked of them in the way of literature and philosophy – not subjects that had been bandied about in Los Pinos, where modernity ruled and science was all. The school playground was a battlefield – and you had to be tough to survive it. The main problem was the Algerian orphans. Lacking material goods, the young *pieds-noirs* practised a junior form of extortion, lying in wait for unwary greenhorns foolish enough to take

Boeuf en Daube

This is the Languedoc's favourite midday meal. The better the wine the better the dish – within reason. The beef should be mature and well-hung. Put the meat in the marinade overnight.

―――― SERVES 4–6 – APPETITE AND CLIMATE DICTATES ――――

―――――――――――― FIRST STEP ――――――――――――

2 lb/1 kg beef (top rump or
any piece of lean stewing beef)
Sprig of thyme,

2 bay-leaves,
½ teaspoon juniper berries
1 bottle strong red wine

―――――――――――― SECOND STEP ――――――――――――

3 garlic cloves
2 oz/50 g lard
2 onions
3 large carrots
3 large tomatoes
1 medium-sized potato
2 oz/50 g bacon, cubed small
3 tablespoons oil

1 sprig thyme
1 sprig summer savory
2 bay-leaves
6 juniper berries
2–3 cloves and a curl of
orange peel (dried is best)
½ bottle red wine
Salt and freshly ground
pepper

1. Cube the meat and put it into a bowl with the herbs and red wine, cover and leave all in a cool place overnight. Turn it in the marinade a few times.

2. When you're ready to cook, take the meat out of the marinade and pat it dry (save the wine marinade). Rub a casserole with a cut clove of garlic, transfer it to a gentle heat and melt the lard. When it is hot, put in the pieces of meat. Leave the meat to brown gently while you prepare the rest of the ingredients.

3. Peel and chop the onions and garlic. Scrape and slice the carrots finely. Scald the tomatoes to loosen the skins, and then peel and chop them. Peel and cube the potato.

4. Put the bacon to melt in the oil in a frying pan over a low heat. When the fat is running, add the chopped onions and crushed garlic. Cook them gently until they soften and gild. Add the carrots and fry them until they soften. Put in the chopped tomato, cubed potato and add the wine marinade. Bubble it up fiercely for 5–10 minutes until it is reduced to a thick sauce. Add the sauce to the meat in the casserole with the herbs and spices. Pour in the second bottle of wine and lid tightly.

5. Put the daube to cook slowly in a low oven, 300°F/150°C/mark 1–2 for 4 hours at least. The meat will then be so soft you can eat it with a spoon, which is as it should be, and the sauce rich and thick. Taste and adjust the seasoning, and mash the sauce a little before you serve it. A green salad is the best accompaniment.

barterable goods to school. The children's schoolmates warned that Cas's treasured Swiss army penknife and the girls' Snoopy pencil-boxes were temptations best left at home.

What about their social lives, I enquired apprehensively. The sisters' faces became thoughtful. In their polite middle-class school in Spain, social intercourse had been conducted within strict parameters. Not so the French. The French, not to put too fine a point on it, were sex-mad.

This preoccupation, however, could sometimes be turned to their advantage. The sisters established a profitable little trade in bubble gum by flogging the seat next to their brother on the bus. Unfortunately the boys pinched the girls' bottoms – a painful liberty which would have been considered quite out of order in Spain. The main danger zone for these unwelcome attentions was the lunch-time queue. At the mention of lunch, everyone cheered up.

Lunch was terrific – a three-course, sit-down, knife-and-fork affair. It might start with a *rémoulade* of celeriac, a slice of salami and a little tomato salad, and progress through a rich meat casserole cooked with wine, via a green salad with goat's cheese, to a dessert which was certain to be something delicious – maybe a *petit-suisse* with fresh grapes, or an orange with a *crème caramel*.

As their confidence increased, the children chose companions among their new schoolmates. Soon they were invited to stay in neighbouring farmhouses at weekends – and our social life was up and running. Poppy found a friend whose parents, Swiss by birth, kept goats – a fine flock of pedigree beasts whose cheese was much esteemed in the neighbourhood. Fran's best friend was the dark-eyed daughter of immigrant Spaniards who ran the town's super-market. And Cas's chosen companion went by the unlikely name of Anthony Llewellyn – French to the core, his blood line traced straight back to the rugby-playing Welsh valleys.

Honey spread her net wider: celebrating her autumn birthday, she invited the entire École Maternelle home for games and birthday tea. To my surprise, a group of what looked to me like well-grown young men appeared on bikes and hoovered up the inappropriately smartie-encrusted birthday cake. Even more surprising, Honey demonstrated an energetic grasp of the finer points of the attacking game during the football match that followed in the muddy field behind the house. Quite the little tearaway was her well-earned reputation, and it came as something of a shock. I had always thought she looked so adorable with her flower-fairy face, studious little specs and that delicious floral pinny.

The École Maternelle – an unlikely forum for political manoeuvrings – provided us with our first direct experience of French politics. As the Revolution bore witness, there is no animal more political than the peasantry of France. Far from being something remote which concerns only *les gens de Paris*, politics are woven into the very fabric of rural daily life. From the allocation of the trading space in the market-place to the choice of society in the café, everything has a political dimension. Everyone knows this particular trader is the right-wing candidate in next month's muncipal elections, that particular bar is where the communists take their morning pastis.

Madame Lelong, the lady responsible for the school run – an official position carrying some small remuneration and much responsibility in the way of vehicle safety and insurance – called a meeting of all those who used the *transport scolaire*. The subject to be discussed was the selection and insurance of a new vehicle. As parents, we were bidden to attend along with the half-dozen other parents similarly involved. The meeting was at six-thirty in the evening. We thought, Nicholas and I, in our foreign innocence, that the discussion could not possibly last longer than half an hour. We went to it supperless, imagining we would be home in two shakes of a goat's tail.

Not a bit of it. The meeting was attended, not only by those who had recourse to the school run, but also by an equal number of parents who, living in the village, had no need of the *transport scolaire*.

'We shall be here until midnight, *ma pauvre amie*,' whispered Madame Lelong as we took our places beside her. 'I hope you have had your supper.'

I sought enlightenment. '*La politique*,' said my neighbour rolling her eyes towards the assembly.

'Politics? Over the school run?'

'*Mais oui*.'

The political dimension was plain, she explained gloomily. The rural dwellers who used the service were independent farmers, smallholding employers of seasonal labour – as such they held conservative principles. The village dwellers, the mayor included, were landless workers, dependent on the farmers for seasonal labourings – and as such might be expected to vote for the socialists, or worse.

Madame Lelong's fears were confirmed as soon as the meeting was declared open. Battle was enjoined immediately. The socialists declared it was a matter of conscience: the meeting was élitist, a denial of the right to equal representation. Three hours later, the flames of political passion still raged.

'Soyons raisonnables, messieurs,' shouted the protagonists on either side, knowing full well that reasonableness has never been the stuff of politics. Right and left were still slugging it out at midnight when we finally plucked up courage to abandon our political responsibilities and crawl starving home to bed.

I never did discover who won the battle of the school run. But by the end of the evening we had learnt an important lesson: never attend a school run meeting in rural France on an empty stomach.

CHAPTER EIGHTEEN

France: Round the kitchen table

*'Two things are essential in life: to give good dinners and keep
on fair terms with women.'*

Charles Maurice de Talleyrand*

WINTER CLOSED IN ON THE MAISON WOG.

Lacking a telephone, we had to write letters. Lacking central
heating, we kept good blazing fires. Lacking old friends, we were
obliged to make new ones. Lacking easy entertainment, we had to
rely on our own.

As with any geographical displacement, we had to learn not only a
new language, but find a new balance for our daily lives. Because the
house was small – far smaller than our home in Spain – and the

*Attributed.

207

weather harsh enough to discourage any thoughts of escape into the great outdoors, it was as well that we had plenty to occupy us.

At first, as in uncharted seas, we took compass readings and watched out for wandering albatrosses. For the first weeks, we stayed close to home – getting the measure of the neighbourhood, finding our way round the network of narrow unsignposted lanes, checking out the little villages for useful shops and welcoming cafés.

At weekends we took trips into the mountains, tracing the ravines of the beautiful Gorges du Tarne where ravens nest among the crags and all the early vegetables are grown for the Paris market. We visited the limestone caves at Roquefort and returned home in triumph with a whole cheese, blue-veined and chalky, bought from the master-cheesemaker himself. We climbed the tall brick tower of the thirteenth-century cathedral at Albi for the view of the vineyards and streams which water the plains of Cahors. Below in the nave, we shuddered at *The Last Judgement* painted to warn the citizenry of the terrible consequences of disobeying the church. Across the square, the little Musée Toulouse-Lautrec housed the painter's own collection of his work, and a brief sweep round the rooms could be concluded with a *chocolat chaud* and a *tête-de-nègre* in the best *chocolatier* in the Languedoc.

On weekdays, with the children away all day at school, Nicholas and I established our work spaces. In the annexe on the far side of what had now become the ping-pong room, warmed by a rattling gas stove, Nicholas's new novel, *The Orion Line*, began to take shape – a spare, bleak thriller to match his surroundings.

Choosing the only other warm room in the house, I set up my painting board at one end of the kitchen table and began work on my first London exhibition, scheduled for the following summer at the Tryon Gallery. For the first time since family life began, I felt there was a real possibility of a career when my children no longer needed a full-time mother.

As a water-colourist – botanical and natural history – I have always needed to paint from life. The Tryon believed birds were the saleable items. But a *peintre animalier* – as I overheard Madame Guillermat describe me – does not have an easy time of it in midwinter. For models, I had to be content with the resident pair of tawny owls who hunted our eaves for mice, a few solitary gulls and the occasional fall of fieldfares stripping the last of the autumn's berries. I bundled myself up for sketching forays – the quickly completed water-colours supplying a record, not only of images half-glimpsed, but a visual diary, a record of our daily lives.

In the evenings, pushing the remains of supper aside, the children would join me at the kitchen table with their homework, while I painted details for my pictures. In return for help with their school work, a laborious undertaking involving much recourse to verb tables and dictionaries, the children collected furred and feathered wayside casualties, stacking small corpses in the ice compartment of the fridge until I was ready to tackle them. The health and safety police of today's EC would have had a fit had they opened our cold store.

In spite of the *nature morte* which threatened to crowd us out of the kitchen, we ate wonderfully well. The Saturday market in Revel, a bustling little town with a market square ringed by medieval arches, became the high spot of our week. Here was all the plenty of the Languedoc in winter. Bundles of white-stemmed chard and woolly-stalked cardoons, heaps of Jerusalem artichokes, all knobbly and brown. Bouquets of baby turnips and hanks of black-skinned salsify; clumps of bitter-leaved dandelions. Most luxurious were the wild-gathered fungi proudly displayed on bleached white napery – apricot-fleshed *girolles* and spike-toed *pieds-de-mouton*, fat round *bolets* and delicate *grisettes*. Later, the seller confided with pride, there would be truffles.

Even the fruits were unfamiliar, their labelling a lesson in geography: one little village was known for its sunny yellow *reinette* apples; another was famous for its freckled William pears – their stalks dipped in scarlet wax to seal in the sap; from another still came winter melons with sweet golden flesh.

If there's anything a French housewife knows how to do it's how to shop. Ask anyone with a well-loaded basket and you will be told which baker makes the best cakes and tarts – great cartwheels of sugar-crisp pastry filled with egg-custard cushioning black damsons, golden plums, sugar-blistered apples, or – most deliciously wintry of all – crackle-glazed caramel stuck with nuts and raisins. Or which particular butcher knows how to trim a bit of shin and tie up a perfect *plat de côtes* – lean rib of beef – for Saturday's boiled beef and vegetables. They know too that you must buy your free-range chicken – its scrubbed grey legs and pliant beak proclaiming its race and tenderness – only from the stall of this particular farm-wife, who can be relied upon to have fed her barnyard fowl on the most delicate and purest of diets.

We took advice from those waiting to be served on the proper cuts for the stews and soups which were the everyday staples of a Languedoc winter. There seemed to be no set recipes – all was open to discussion: the amount of garlic proper to a *pistache d'agneau*, the correct spicing for a *blanquette de veau*, the best wine to moisten a daube. The *traiteur*, the man who provides the housewife with her fast food cooked to his own family recipes, would have: white *boudin*, made with veal and cream and spiced with nutmeg; his own pâté – rough-chopped, lard-rich, pistachio'd, peppery. The *char-cuterie* displayed a dozen varieties of wind-dried, pepper-spiced sausages and home-cured hams – the cold breezes from the mountainous Causses, the '*vent de l'altar*' as the patois had it, ensuring the perfect conditions for conserving such delicacies.

'*Régalez-vous, mesdames, messieurs!*' cried the stallholders, 'Spoil yourselves, ladies and gentlemen!'

We needed no such prompting to fill our baskets. Weekday menus were dictated by what the season delivered and the purse might stretch to – but Saturday's meals were special.

On our return from the market the painting board was pushed aside and the baskets tipped out onto the table so the week's meals might be planned. Saturday lunch was easily come by – French housewives have little need to cook on market day. We had fresh bread, hot from the baker: crunchy *ficelles* and crusty baguettes, or maybe a *fougasse aux gratons*, a flat slashed bread enriched with little scraps of pork crackling.

There was a dish of salads to be assembled at will: dark-leaved winter spinach, bitter little dandelion rosettes, a handful of tender corn salad; roasted beetroot, wrinkled and treacle-sweet; pickled vegetables and salty olives; a posy of radishes, round and scarlet as berries, to be eaten with rough salt and sweet butter sliced by the cheese-man off a creamy pyramid. Our greatest extravagance was cheese, irresistible in its perfection: a creamy slice of Bleu de Causses, a thick slab of firm-bodied cantal, a broad wedge of slippery Brie.

Saturday dinner was always *pot-au-feu* – the peasant dish which is neither soup nor stew but both in one, with the meat slow-simmered till it's soft enough to eat with a spoon. The rich broth is ladled out first, to be sopped up with bread rubbed with garlic, and the meat and vegetables come afterwards, served with sharp little pickled cherries and capers and maybe a thick yellow *aioli*. We made our *pot-au-feu* to the butcher's instruction – rib for flavour, shin for body, and a sawn-off bone for the richness of the marrow. For the children to drink, there were beautiful jewel-clear syrups, fragrant as the fruit itself, ice-cool with water from the spring.

Sunday lunch began with a treat from the *traiteur* – artichokes, sliced and dressed with oil and lemon, potatoes with mustard and onion and dill, a smoky scoop of aubergine purée. Then came roasted guinea-fowl – supplied to order by Madame Guillermat. Her flock of grey-laced, blue-wattled, half-wild birds pecked around in the yard by day, and roosted high in the rafters of her kitchen at night. She called them her *poules de luxe*, flighty and wilful as a king's mistress, and sold them to us neatly prepared for the oven.

At the end of the autumn term, we packed ourselves into the camper-van for the journey south to celebrate Christmas in Andalusia.

As we passed the farmhouse at the end of the drive, Madame Escrieux, convinced we were heading into a gastronomic desert, pressed emergency supplies into our hands: her own foie gras in a glass pot, a big jar of pickled wild plums, thick slices of salty pink ham from her own pig, a large basket of winter salad leaves; and, most welcome of all to the adults, a bottle of walnut brandy, dark and strong, and distilled by Monsieur Escrieux himself to an old family recipe. In France, the right to distil remains in the family as long as the ancestral acres remain in the family's hands – and Monsieur Escrieux's hands were as ancestral as they come.

On our return, having celebrated Christmas with the proper ceremony in our own familiar surroundings of the cork-oaks, we were back on parade in Castelnaudary for the first day of the spring term. Good news greeted us. The school was well-satisfied with the progress of *la famille* Luard. Cas was to be promoted to the form above, and the girls had done all that was expected of them and more.

Later that first day, Honey and I called in at the farmhouse to deliver the almond nougats and orange brandy we had brought from Spain to repay our neighbour's generosity. Southern sunshine had reminded us of spring, we said gazing hopefully at Monsieur

Pot-au-Feu

This is our winter favourite in the Languedoc. The classic French cuts of beef used are *plats de cotes* (breast-meat on the bone) and shin – the first for flavour, the second for strength.

─────────── SERVES 6 ───────────

*2 lb/1 kg bone-in beef,
flat rib or flank
2 lb/1 kg boned-out
beef shin (tied)
(optional) 2–3 short
lengths marrowbone
6 pints/3.5 l water
2 onions, unpeeled and halved*

*1–2 large carrots,
scrubbed and chunked
2–3 celery stalks (or the
green from a whole head)
Bay-leaf, sprig of thyme,
a few parsley stalks
½ teaspoon peppercorns
Salt*

─────────── TO FINISH ───────────

*2–3 carrots, scraped and chunked
2–3 potatoes, peeled and
chunked*

*2–3 leeks, washed and chunked
½ cabbage, cut into thick
wedges*

1. Put the meat and bones into a large pot with the water. Bring to the boil, skim off the grey foam which rises. Add the rest of the ingredients, bring back to the boil. Turn the heat right down, cover loosely and leave to simmer quietly for 3–4 hours, until the meats are tender.

2. Remove the meats and marrowbone (if used) and reserve. Discard the soggy vegetables – they've given all they can to the broth.

3. Bring the broth back to the boil and add the carrots and then the potatoes. Reboil, turn down to simmer. After 10 minutes, add the leeks and lay the sliced cabbage on top. Lid loosely and simmer for another 10 minutes, until the vegetables are tender.

4. Slice the meats and reheat in a little of the broth. If there's any marrow in the bone, spread it on a bit of toast and serve as a tiny hors-d'œuvre.

Dish up the vegetables and meat in hot deep plates, well-sauced with broth. Accompany with a garlicky mayonnaise, radishes, gherkins and capers – with bread to mop up the juices, naturally.

Escrieux's freshly turned plough. Madame Escrieux shook her head gloomily. She could assure us spring would be in no hurry to return this year. You could tell, she explained, by the depths to which the snails had dug themselves in. When a hibernating snail thinks it necessary to bury itself six feet under, it will be May before the frost is gone.

We returned to our quarters, chopped down the icicles, restocked the store cupboard, and resolved to make the best of what winter could throw at us.

January brought cause to be grateful for the snow which still lay thick on the ground. Each year, the school took advantage of Castelnaudary's proximity to the Pyrénées – visible from our own eyrie on a clear day – to offer its pupils a subsidized sojourn on the ski slopes used to train the army.

The French take a national pride in their prowess on the ski slopes, and the exercise was as much as anything to allow the authorities to identify future Olympic champions. The accommodation in the military barracks would be a bit rough and ready, we were told, but equipment could be cheaply hired and the tuition was free. The opportunity was too good to miss – and Honey, the headmaster confirmed, would be welcome to join her siblings on the trip.

The family budget would just about stretch to the basic costs. For the rest, we searched the market for fieldworkers' waterproofs, padded jackets, thick socks for fingers and feet – whatever might be adapted for the needs of the skiers. I delivered everyone to the bus, and they vanished for a full ten days.

On their return from the mountains, brown-faced and sparkling-eyed, the four reported proudly that this had been no recreational skiing holiday, but a serious training exercise. An official extension of the school's usual working timetable, the army instructors saw to it that their pupils were up at dawn and worked the slopes till dusk. At the end of the training, every child was required to show he or she could climb up a hill on skis without the help of a ski-lift, and slide down it again without a single tumble. Much pleasure was taken in outwitting the instructors – one of the girls had indeed toppled into a snowdrift, but happily out of the examiner's line of vision.

What's more, they boasted joyfully, they had official certificates – stamped, signed and properly witnessed – to prove it.

The first sign that spring was on its way was neither the emergence from hibernation of the snails, nor the appearance of the first buds on the blackthorn. The first sign of spring was the arrival of the French Foreign Legion.

It was Nicholas who first realized we had nightly company on our bleak wintry upland, and his discovery added a new dimension to our lives. When it seemed as if the words would never flow and even the black wine of Cahors failed to inspire, he was accustomed to wander around the fields at night with a torch, looking for company.

'Badgers and things,' he said vaguely.

There was far more than badgers in our icy moonlit pastures. The bushes were full of shadowy camouflaged figures. Nicholas, who had worked with legionnaires behind enemy lines in the Hungarian uprising of 1956, was enchanted to find out that the Legion had claimed the use of this least hospitable of landscapes as a training area for their élite recruits.

Drilled behind the high walls of their Castelnaudary base by day, the Legionnaires were unleashed on our blasted heath by night to practise winter survival techniques. A group of young captains were in charge of this chilly ordeal, and as soon as Nicholas came across them on one of his forays, they recognized him as a man they could talk to – indeed, one who was willing to provide safe haven in a storm.

Soon the exercises were re-routed to include a key checkpoint at Maison Wog, and the bone-chilled officers would come in to join Nicholas round the kitchen table for a cup of coffee while the rest of us were tucked up safely in our beds. We turned over and snuggled beneath our blankets as the murmur of military talk drifted up between the floorboards.

In return they would invite him back for dinner at their mess in the barracks. One Saturday evening, taking the two eldest children on a shopping trip in Castelnaudary, he stopped by the mess for a quick drink, parking the car outside, its British number-plates fully in evidence.

While their parent was inside taking refreshment, the children returned to the car. A formidable mustachioed figure marched up and tapped on the window.

' "Please, sir, can I have some more?" *Oliver Twist*, no?' He roared with laughter. It turned out later that these were the only words in English he knew.

Sergeant-Major Bradjic was a legendary figure among his fellows – a recently retired veteran of many of the Legion's campaigns, the Czech-born Bradjic had stayed on with France's mercenary force to run, among other things, its chess club. Many Legionnaires come from eastern Europe where chess is a national passion. Inevitably, chess has become the Legion's game.

'You have a grand master in your country, I'm told,' said the Legionnaire. Could the two of them, he enquired, play chess?

As the answer was in the affirmative, he proposed that Cas and Fran – both already competent chess players – join the Legionnaires' Saturday games of chess, since their father was already an honorary member of the mess. After a month proving their worth, the two were invited to play for the Legion's team.

Monsieur Bradjic managed to convince the headmaster of the CES that a few weekend absences (Saturday morning was a school day) were in the best interests of improving international relations. Also, he pointed out, chess had long been a required subject on the school curriculum in Russia.

With the headmaster in agreement, who were the parents to object? From then on, like footballers bought and sold to the highest bidder, the two children would set off regularly at the weekends with the burly Legionnaires to play competitive chess all around the Languedoc. To my feminist amusement, they reported it was Madame Bradjic, the sergeant-major's even more formidable wife, who was the real team manager, ruling her flock and her husband equally with a rod of iron.

Free tournament lunches provided by various grateful munici-palities were the reward for their travels, providing me – albeit second-hand – with a gastronomic map of the region's specialities. In the mountain village of Rodez they ate *aligot* – a rib-sticking, garlic-scented fondue of cream and potatoes and cheese. In the shepherd's stronghold of the Cévennes, they had their first taste of *cabbasols*, a scented daube made with lamb's tripe flavoured with mountain herbs. They came to grief only once – over a purée of stockfish, a pungent Norwegian-imported delicacy which they reported had the texture of mashed sock and smelt like very old sneakers.

The high spot of the Castelnaudary's chess year was the town's all-comers tournament – a municipal event hosted by the town fathers and held in the town hall in mid-February. The defending team consisted of the town's best players. The competitors flocked in from all over the Languedoc. Toulouse radio station installed itself in a mobile studio to report the action. Inside the hall, double lines of trestle-tables were laid out with boards and time clocks. At the appointed hour the protagonists lined up on either side like tug-of-war teams. The townspeople bundled up against the weather and turned out in force to cheer on their favourites – and by now the two young foreigners were famous enough to command considerable personal support.

Team chess, unlike the solitary sparring matches when the Goliaths of the game do battle, is a social occasion. The spectators wander round the tables, discussing the merits of each position, while the players hunch over their pieces. Cas's style was the more physically aggressive of our two players – the completion of each move punctuated by a triumphant thump of the time clock. In competitive chess, the end of each game was always marked by the boys with a session of speed-chess, a flurry of machine-gun clock-punching with each player completing his game within sixty seconds. But Fran, one of no more than a handful of girls who played against the men on equal terms, would sit in her pool of perfect tranquillity, oblivious to all around her, motionless until the game was over. Between contests, she would simply sit in her place and dream.

To a French municipality, a festival without a feast is no festival at all. The players in Castelnaudary were fortified during their endeavours with slabs cut from a vast chocolate cake. The mayor announced with pride that this munificence, chequer-iced and topped with six-inch high marzipan chess pieces, was donated by the patisseries of the town.

Both our team-players won their games – but what would you expect, with the Legionnaires as trainers and chocolate cake under their belts? Sergeant-Major Bradjic basked in reflected glory, explaining to anyone who would listen that – as an old ally of the English against the imperialist adventurings of France – he had felt it his duty to equip *les jeunes Anglais* for the battleground of life. The game was, the *Français* might like to note, the great Napoleon's favourite pastime on the long haul to Moscow. '*Souvenez-vous de Waterloo*,' said Nicholas, swiftly effecting a strategic withdrawal before the gallant soldier could mount a counter-attack.

At home, in our snowy citadel on the windy plateau, we all played chess of an evening round the kitchen table – even me, normally excused games duty on the grounds that I had to do the cooking or the ironing. There's something about chess which appeals to me. It's a game in which instinct counts as highly as intelligence, temperament as much as skill, in which weakness can be as useful as strength. The real challenge lies in judging how everyone's peculiarities might be turned to advantage.

Nicholas enjoyed the military precision of the opening, when all the pieces must be moved into their attacking positions, but I loved the romance of the end game – when the queens and castles have all been sacrificed and the game turns on a single pawn. Poppy, although the very soul of patience when making her tiny models or sewing a garment, had no time for the subtleties; she played the attacking game, her pieces reeling round the board like drunken sailors, sometimes scoring a knockout, but more often coming to grief.

Honey, constantly on the lookout for something at which she might beat her siblings, could throw in a mean defence – reeling back a bit if she lost a major piece, but capable of staging remarkable feats of recovery. But none of us was ever a match for Cas, whose steady nerves and analytical mind defeated us all. The only one who could occasionally beat him was Francesca – who, in her teenage years, was to play internationally for England.

It has its social dimension, the great game. A universal language, it cuts across social barriers, age differences and national boundaries. In Spain, Cas's first chess partner was a Swedish count well into his eighties; Fran's favourite opponent was a much-trophied bullfighter who found the game improved his concentration in the ring.

Set up a chessboard in any corner of the world and you'll not be alone for long. Some time later, Cas did exactly that when, backpacking round Australia in his year between school and university, he needed to waylay a few dollars to pay for room and board. He established a bridgehead in a local café, set up his chessboard and offered to take on all comers against a stake of $5.

As he explained crisply at the time, it sure beat slaughtering sheep in the abattoir, the only alternative employment available to a Pom in Alice Springs.

CHAPTER NINETEEN

French sunshine

'The difference between landscape and landscape is very small,
but there is a great difference between the beholders.'

Ralph Waldo Emerson*

IT WAS MID-MARCH BEFORE THE CLOUDS BEGAN TO LIFT – AND OUR
spirits with them.

The days were lengthening: dawn was already breaking by the time
we left the farmhouse each morning, and when we returned in the
evening, the honey-coloured stone was bathed in long rays of pale
golden twilight. Our muddy track turned into an avenue of almond
blossom. Our neighbours emerged from hibernation – through the
depths of winter their doors and windows had been shuttered and

*In *Essays*.

barred when we drove past on the early school run. But now the two ladies threw their shutters wide, hung feather-beds and blankets to air in the morning sunshine, and celebrated with bright flowered pinnies.

Tight-curled rosettes of green on the limestone plateau promised a profusion of orchids – not the showy air-rooted blooms of tropical forests, but ground orchids, most curious and beautiful of Europe's native flora. Each unfurled its single stalk of blossom as the spring drew on: first the freckled early marsh, the roots of which were once used to make strengthening drink for invalids; next the fat purple cones of the lady, dense-packed flower-heads with a faint perfume of vanilla; then the rank-scented monkey orchid, tall as a toddler; rare soldier-orchids with little green helmets; butterfly-orchids, creamy-bloomed and fragrant. I gathered each in turn – only one from each clump – before the sheep could graze them, and brought them back to the kitchen to paint.

The first appearance in the market of spring vegetables – *primeurs* from the sheltered valleys of the Gorges du Tarn – was echoed in the wild. On my winter rambles in search of subjects to paint, I had found the asparagus thickets familiar from Spain – even though in winter only the prickly skeletons were to be seen. Now, in the spring, Madame Guillermat confirmed my suspicions.

'Indeed they are *les asperges*. The place is famous for them. There'll be a wonderful crop in a week or two. We like to eat them in omelettes, chopped up like little peas – *tian d'asperges*. When my children were small, they used to crawl underneath and fetch out big bunches. Now my sons crawl under cars instead of asparagus bushes, so *vos petits* are welcome to pick all they please.'

My *petits* did not need telling twice, and we feasted all through April on the tender green shoots. Better still, tucked away in a corner of a dry chalky pasture, we found our first wild fungi, the honeycomb-patterned morels, which are, after the black truffle, the most prized of all wild crops.

One morning in early April, Madame Escrieux called us into her kitchen. On the table was a bucket piled high with snails.

'You see this?' she held up one of the creatures, its pinhead eyes vanishing into the speckled shell. 'This is the next crop for *les petits*. As I told you they would, the snails have emerged at last. My husband collects them when he sees them, and puts them on his

Tian d'Asperges

Choose a shallow earthenware dish (the eponymous *tian*) for Madame Guillermat's way with wild asparagus.

———————————— SERVES 4 ————————————

1 lb/500 g thin asparagus
(sprue)
4 eggs
½ pint/300 ml milk
½ pint/300 ml cream

½ teaspoon salt
Freshly ground white pepper
2 oz/50 g Cheddar or Gruyère
cheese, diced small
Butter for greasing

1. Trim off the woody ends of the asparagus and chop into very short lengths, like peas.

2. Beat the eggs with the milk, cream and seasonings. Stir the cheese and the chopped asparagus into the egg mixture. Pour into a well-buttered shallow earthenware casserole.

3. Bake the *tian* at 350°F/180°C/mark 4 for 35–40 minutes until just set – still a little trembly in the middle. Serve warm with a cold glass of the pink wine from the sands of the Camargue – *vin gris*.

vines to fatten. Then he can be sure of a good flavour, and no *mauvaises herbes*, so they will not need to be starved. There is plenty for all round here. You will find them particularly in the clump of broom by the chalk-pit, where I have seen you, *Madame Elisabeth*, at your painting.'

She smiled at my expression of disbelief.

'It's not surprising you overlooked them. The snail is as cunning as any other wild creature. Unless you spend all your days in the fields, as my husband does, you will only find the creatures just before dawn, when they climb to the top of the broom-twigs. You have to be ready at exactly the right moment, they are only there for those few minutes just before sunrise. As soon as the sun lifts over the horizon, they vanish into the grass.'

The task of snail-gathering in the dawn-lit bushes fell to Honey and me. After the others had been delivered to their bus, we had an hour to do as we pleased. As Madame Escrieux had instructed us, we waited until the sun was rising and plucked the fat molluscs like little apples from the branches. From experience in Andalusia, we knew they would need two weeks until they had digested everything for which we could not vouch. Mindful that it might be stretching hospitality a little if we popped them onto Monsieur Escrieux's vines, we stored our snails in a bucket in one corner of the kitchen, feeding them with sprigs of thyme and rosemary and the trimmings from the salad.

You had to be careful to keep the lid well-weighted. A troupe of snails can heave up a carelessly closed bucket lid in a trice. 'Snail breakout!' was the signal for everyone to drop whatever they were doing and retrieve the peripatetic uniped Schwarzeneggers from their hiding-places under the table, beneath the sink, on the ceiling, clamped to the television aerial, inside gumboots, beneath chair seats.

The snails trailed a substance which could slice through vegetable matter like a wire through cheese. In fact, in the twinkle of a pinhead eye, they could decimate our stores. I came down to the kitchen one morning to find that the small raiders had managed to clip the corner right off Volume I, A-to-Markworthy, of the *Shorter Oxford Dictionary*. It was a perpetual battleground. After their adventuring, the snails had to be starved all over again in case they had ingested lead paint along with the literature.

Working all day while the children were at school, I was beginning to accumulate enough bird paintings for the scheduled summer show – including a pair of hoopoes just arrived from Africa who, dainty in russet frills, patrolled the bomb crater which served as a rubbish dump. Even so, I still needed a few really dramatic subjects such as those I had sketched in the Doñana – more raptors and the larger birds like herons, storks and spoonbills. I selected Easter as a convenient moment to move everyone to the Camargue for a spot of bird-watching. We arranged professional company for our expedition – Michael Taylor, secretary of the BTO, a skilled ornithologist and an old friend from our days on the avian flight path in Andalusia.

Spring comes earlier to Provence than it does in the Languedoc, and I had high hopes of what we might find. On the first day of the Easter holiday, we packed our camper-van, collected Michael from the airport at Montpelier and made our way across the marshland of the Camargue. On Michael's recommendation, our headquarters were on the Crau, the stony plateau which borders the great bird sanctuary in the marshlands, where we had booked a pair of caravans – one for the senior and one for the junior division. Michael had done his homework: his maps were marked and the local ornithological bigwigs had been alerted to our arrival.

Mike was not one to see a holiday as a chance for a slouch. Cas, our star birdsong identifier, was declared chief spotter. Stragglers excepted, we rose each dawn to catch the early bird, worming. Midday found us skirting the Marseilles rubbish dump, where, as our nostrils filled with the thick vulture smell of rotting debris, our guide introduced us to Europe's largest population of red kites, magnificent in their red-gold plumage among the flapping plastic.

In the afternoons we searched out the birders' birds (LLBs, which stands for little brown bastards) which only the true expert can love. Of such was a flock of small waders scavenging among the pebbles down by the shore. Lacking our mentor that day – he had been taken off by the French ornithologists in search of nesting flamingoes – we puzzled over them for hours. They had markings like miniature hen pheasants, all scalloped edges and freckled backs, and they ran straight-legged down the sand like chickens. A flock of reeves, Mike explained delightedly when we described them on our return – and surely an all-girl outing, on their way back from Africa. We went looking for and found the lek, the fighting arena – a beaten earth circle, like a miniature bullring – over which the ruffs, magnificent in their feather collars, battled like miniature fighting cocks.

After the first week of peripatetic sketching, I needed to settle down to detailed work. Artistically speaking, a bird in the hand is worth fifty in the bush. Ask any bird painter. The great John James Audubon shot 'em and strung them up on wires. We were made of more delicate stuff. We found a zoo.

Honey and I kept company together, and while everyone else tramped around among the free-range raptors on the marsh, we repaired to the calm of the enclosures. Here were all the denizens of the wild going about their spring affairs within inches of our noses. In netted areas of reed and tamarisk were speckled bitterns, egrets with ochre-tipped plumes, mop-topped squacco herons and bright-eyed spoonbills. A clump of willow sheltered a colony of rare night-herons – creamy breasted, their sleek backs the colour of wet slate.

We had eagles, we had hawks, we had falcons, we had harriers – for me, at least, we had paradise. Honey dabbled gently along in my wake – until, being of an age when all a person wants to be is a horse, she discovered a herd of white Camargue ponies coralled alongside the zoo. From that moment on, I scarcely saw hide nor hair of her. The next day, as it was Easter Saturday, there was an all-day outing on the marsh, and she managed to talk herself into joining the group.

The following day, with Honey safely occupied until sundown, I settled down for a peaceful day at my work. I had a stork in mind as a sitter – a solitary bird whom I had watched building an untidy nest on the roof of the zoo's little entrance pavilion. The keeper – by now the zoo's employees were quite accustomed to me – had already told me the stork's history. He was a young bird who had been orphaned in the egg and brought up in an incubator. Hand-reared, he was not pinioned and always returned each year at breeding time.

I began to paint his portrait – only to find my intentions open to serious misunderstanding. Unfortunately my subject had fallen to the wrong conclusions about the species on whom he should be lavishing his attentions.

Encouraged by my interest, the stork began his mating display. The courting stork does not hide his light under a bushel. Quite the reverse. He treats the object of his affections to the full unequivocal display: such a raising of crests, a tossing of heads, a clattering of beaks, a throbbing of wattles, a flashing of scarlet protuberances of every imaginable kind as might be guaranteed to draw an audience from miles around.

The stork, as everyone knows, is the bird of good fortune, the avian messenger who brings the baby. And babies was certainly what my feathered suitor had in mind. Being the first day of the Easter weekend, the zoo was unusually crowded. In fact, the entire junior population of southern France seemed to have crammed themselves into the limited space between the marshy cages and the visitors' track.

The schoolchildren were in no doubt about the direction in which events were unfolding. Few have smuttier minds than French schoolchildren. Few birds could be better equipped to stimulate them. Absently-mindedly I sketched on. The stork redoubled his efforts. Such wooing deserved some response, and I was clearly woefully inadequate for his purposes. No Leda I – I knew my limitations. I threw in the metaphorical towel, packed up my sketch-book and fled.

Meanwhile, Nicholas had led the rest of the gang off for a day patrolling the perimeters of the Marseilles rubbish dump, where the greatest concentration of red kites in Europe scavenge happily among the steaming heaps, their red-gold plumage all the more brilliant against a background of flapping black plastic. This unsavoury scrap heap, they reported, also supports a breeding colony of rare night-herons – elegant in clerical grey with ruby eyes.

Each day's bird-watching was balanced by another spent exploring the pleasures of Provence – both cultural and gastronomic. The markets of Provence are a cornucopia at any time of year, but especially at Eastertime, when the scent of spring flowers fills the air, and the stalls are piled with new-cropped honey and the first berries of summer.

The beauty of Provence appeals to all the senses. It has something to do with the landscape – with hill-slopes ridged with lavender; red-earthed groves of olive trees with rope-twisted trunks and silvery leaves; sloping fields of poppies; sunflowers turning their bright faces to a heat-hazed sun. Something to do with jasmine hedges and wisteria starred with swallowtail butterflies, with little white-walled villages cascading down hillsides carpeted with juniper and thyme.

It has, too, something to do with the history of the people which can be read in the landscape. Here are olives trees whose root stock goes back to the Greeks. The wines of the Rhône have been famous since Roman times. In Chateauneuf-du-Pape, among the vines which grow miraculously in fields of polished pebbles, the captive Popes of Avignon once spent their gilded summers. The Moors reached the fortifications of the Rhône, their passing marked by the almond sweets and honey-preserved fruits you find in every corner *confiserie*.

It has something more to do with the people themselves, with wherever a cluster of Provençal matrons are gathered together explaining to each other exactly what they mean to do with whatever vegetable or fruit or wild-gathered fungi has reached its prime in that particular week. The inhabitants of Provence – like those of Andalusia – live most of their lives outdoors. The day is one long street theatre, what with the morning visit to the bakery or meeting a friend at the pavement café under the plane tree for a *café crème* or a pastis. There is time to spend on the important things of life – the pleasures of the table. And whenever possible that table is laid under the grape arbour; or in the courtyard under the shade of the mulberry tree, relic of the silk-worm industry; or in the dappled sunshine of the terrace.

Except, that is, when the mistral howls down from the mountains, driving the hardiest inhabitant behind the safety of sturdy wooden shutters. It's as much in the mind as the body, the mistral – the snake in Paradise. The wind spreads mayhem right down to the old men playing *boules* in the village square – causing rifts between lovers, *monsieur le maire* to pick a fight with *monsieur le curé*, quarrels between devoted wives and husbands, the most saintly of children to throw tantrums.

The mistral struck on the last day of our holiday in Provence sweeping across the Crau and rattling our temporary shelter like a terrier shaking a rat. Eardrums ringing, we retreated back to our

Cèpes with Potatoes

The peculiar gluey texture of the *boletus* family of mushrooms is delicious with potatoes – look for a floury variety which bakes well.

──────────── SERVES 4 ────────────

1 lb/500 g *cèpes*
4 oz/100 g butter
3 lb/1.5 kg potatoes
1 garlic clove

Salt and pepper
Approx. 1 pint/600 ml hot
home-made chicken stock or
boiling water and white wine

1. Pick over, trim, wipe and slice the *cèpes*. Don't, as some manuals instruct, strip off the spongy underparts – they make just as good eating as the caps.

2. Fry the sliced *cèpes* gently in half the butter for a few moments – longer if they were picked on a wet day and need to be dried out.

3. Peel the potatoes and slice finely. Rub a gratin dish round with a cut clove of garlic, and butter the dish. Lay alternate layers of sliced potato and *cèpes* in the dish, seasoning with salt and pepper as you go. Start and finish with potato. Pour in the hot stock or water and wine. Dot the surface with the rest of the butter. Cover.

4. Bake in a bread-baking oven – 350°F/ 180°C/mark 4 (uncovered after the first 40 minutes), for about an hour, until the potatoes are tender and the top is crusty and brown. If the dish is deep, the potatoes will take longer to cook.

upland pastures – now no longer snow-blanketed but starred with spring flowers – for the final term of our French sabbatical. On the first day of school, we learnt that Cas and Fran were both, as promised, to be moved to the form appropriate for their years. With Poppy already in the class of her own age group and Honey making good progress in her École Maternelle, honour was well satisfied.

It was time to look ahead a little to anticipate our return to English education after our expatriate years. It seemed that Cas was likely to be the most vulnerable to the system – re-entering it in the first year of O levels, we feared he might lose an all-important year if he didn't have something tangible to prove his competence. In order to circumvent the danger, every Wednesday and Saturday throughout the year, I had collected him from the CES at lunch-time, and we spent the afternoon bringing his maths up to O level standard. Although maths was my favourite subject at school, I was never more than one lesson ahead of him.

In May, Cas and I paid a flying visit to London to allow him to sit three extramural O levels – Spanish, French and Maths. The languages were the obvious choice, the mathematics less so, but it was a risk we had to take, even though we had nothing but previous papers against which to measure his capabilities. 'I think, Ma,' he said quite casually as he came out of the examination room, 'I may have forgotten the value of "pi".' I gazed at him in horror – it seemed to me that all our work had been in vain. I need not have worried. When the results came through, he had scored straight 'A's in all three subjects.

On the last day of school, we threw a party for the children's schoolmates to mark the end of our French sabbatical. It was an emotional parting which took place in the little stone house on the windy plateau. The neighbours emptied their store cupboards for us.

Madame Guillermat sent a pair of her famous *saussison à l'ail* and a huge tray of buttery cake with lemon icing. Madame Escrieux supplied a basket of fresh eggs for an omelette, and three bottles of home-made mulberry *sirop*.

Poppy's best friend Pascale arrived already in tears, with a parting present of white kid skin she had salted and tanned herself. Honey's squad of muscular admirers from the École Maternelle presented her with an autographed football. Cas's soul mate Tony Llewellyn, whose ambitions lay in the building trade, pledged himself to find and restore for us a Languedoc house of our own – a promise I fully intend to take him up on some day. Fran's best friend Spanish Maria appeared with a huge pan of paella her mother had made.

We feasted together and swore undying friendship until the sun had set over the sorghum fields. We sat round the kitchen table long after our guests had gone, chewing over the events of that year, tumbling into our rickety beds at last by the light of the moon – serenaded for the last time by the hooting of the owls and the night wind in the rafters.

The next day we packed up our belongings in the camper-van. It had been tough, an adventure certainly – and we had found much to enjoy and even more to learn. As we bumped back down the stony track to bid a final farewell to our neighbours, it was with a feeling of triumph, of a task completed against all the odds.

Poppy – always the one to put her finger on the nub of things – summed up what we all felt. 'We did it, Ma – and I'm glad we did. Nothing else will ever be as tough again.'

Later, as our lives changed as all lives must, when fate brought us sorrow as well as joy, we were to remember that year and be glad that we could draw strength from experience shared, comfort from challenge confronted, pride in pleasures not granted but earned.

CHAPTER TWENTY

Home again

*'See as much as you can of those people that respect and like
you. And of those acquaintances who amuse you.'*

The Reverend Sydney Smith*

WE SPENT A FINAL SUMMER IN SPAIN AFTER OUR FRENCH SABBATICAL.
Then it was time to return to our life in London. We had all agreed
that was what we would do, and that was what must be done.

My exhibition at the gallery in London took place in June.
During the month it was on, all the paintings found themselves
homes – owls and flamingoes, spoonbills and storks (my suitor
immortalized), hawks and vultures. I like vultures best of all. I've
always felt in sympathy with nature's dustmen – there's something

*Advice to a young lady in low spirits (*c.* 1830).

which appeals to me about their necessary function, the good housewifeliness of it all. I realize that not everyone feels the same: I'm afraid at least one eager purchaser who fell in love with what he thought was an eagle went home with a scavenger to hang on his walls.

While I was in the city for the show, I made preliminary enquiries of the London Education Authority as to how best we might rejoin the educational stream. The Authority expressed its surprise. My stories of schooling in Spain and an *année scolaire* in France were treated with circumspect disbelief and considerable disapproval – clearly I was trying to post a bunch of educational liabilities into the system.

I racked my brains for an alternative. Maybe we might try the Lycée, a just-affordable democratic halfway house between private and state school? On my return to Spain with the news of the possibilities the children turned the offer down flat. Everyone had had enough of what they considered to be hard slog and no games. Not even the thought of French school dinners drew them.

We tackled the Authority again on our return to London. The start of the new school year was nearly upon us, and it seemed someone must be persuaded we were not illegal immigrants. The credibility gap yawned wide. No-one had ever gone to foreign schools from *choice*.

Questions were asked, framed in the most egalitarian of language. Forms had to be filled in: 'We just like to take note of ethnic origin – purely so that we may recognize special needs,' explained the Authority tactfully, examining our foreign-sounding name with knitted brow. 'We have nothing against foreigners.'

The Authority conceded defeat. Eccentric as we might be, we were clearly entitled to schooling. Catchment areas limited our choice. For the two elder girls this was between Holland Park Comprehensive, fashionable among those who could afford private schools but believed in state education, and Pimlico, 2,000 strong, and at the time making headlines over sawn-off shotguns in the playground. The girls inspected the alternatives. Fresh from the rough-and-tumble of Castelnaudary, they did not hesitate. Pimlico had it, by half a league.

Honey was booked into St Peter's Primary for the last year before she was due to go to a secondary school, so she was well cared for.

Cas signed up with Westminster City, a boys-only grammar school just turned comprehensive, but which had retained a reputation for scholarliness – and a decent chess team. Apart from the absence of girls, an arrangement he had never come across before and found rather peculiar, it seemed to offer what he needed.

The elder two daughters, with more time to make up educational leeway, vanished into the glass and concrete of Pimlico. Here, they discovered new priorities. The passion for sex and food which had preoccupied the schoolchildren of France took second place to the British passion for appearance.

Although uniforms were not worn, the various groups invented their own to underline philosophical divisions. A capacity to fit into the chosen group depended on the purchase of the right bomber jacket, the correct brand of baseball boots, the right kind of jeans. In the jungle which was the playground, new associations had to be formed, new allegiances forged. For that first year at least, we were grateful that everyone could come home each evening – and life round the kitchen table provided a sense of continuity and community.

I, too, had new problems to confront, not least the realization that the battle for equality between the sexes which had so preoccupied me when I was first married had not yet been won. Both in the Languedoc and in Spain, my authority over the household had never been in question. Nicholas continued to ponder about the problems of the rain forest and the selection of the test team, and was happy for me to deal with the rest.

In other words. I was mistress of my own realm. In my native land, the state thought otherwise. One morning soon after our return, the state census-taker rang my doorbell.

'Mrs Luard?' She handed me a form. 'Can you get your husband to fill this in?'

I glanced down. 'It says here it can be filled in by the head of the household. Come in – I'll do it right away. It'll save you another journey.'

'Very thoughtful of you, Mrs Luard,' she shook her head politely. 'But it has to be your husband.'

'I'm afraid,' I replied, 'that who is the head of the household is a matter for my husband and myself.'

As one might expect, bureaucracy and I failed to reach agreement.

'I'll come back this evening when your husband returns,' said the state, banging the door as she retreated.

Nicholas, delighted by the chance to unbalance the state's books, declared his support for my position and refused to fill in the form. In due course he was summoned to court – failure to complete the census form properly is a criminal offence. He conducted his own spirited defence, was congratulated by the judge on his eloquence and moral correctness, but duly convicted as the statute required – and fined the statutory fifty pounds.

He smiled, paid and took his leave.

Nevertheless, someone out there had learnt a lesson. Next time the census came round, the form had no such stipulation. I like to imagine the nation's stoops stiff with irritated housewives claiming their headship of a million households.

Meanwhile, the London flat hadn't changed. It was still too small, and none of us had shrunk to fit. In fact, some of us were considerably larger and in even more need of our own space. We cast around for somewhere which we might beg or borrow at the weekends and for holidays, when the pressure was most keenly felt. We found a landowning friend, a peer, who farmed his own great acres and had taken various previously tenanted farms in hand. He had spare housing capacity – a Victorian farmhouse, capacious but unmodernized, whose barns were still needed for the lambing season.

At first it was a bolt-hole – so that I, at least, could escape from the city at weekends and holidays, dragging the offspring in my wake. They, naturally enough, were vociferously reluctant to leave the King's Road and their newly acquired street cred. The house was stone-built (with mortar, unlike our house in the Languedoc), and set like an elderly and not-too-watertight gumboot in a frosty pocket of Northamptonshire mud.

I investigated the provisioning. The Co-op was no substitute for Revel market – but there was an apple orchard and a rhubarb clump alongside the house, pick-your-own down the road with strawberries and sweetcorn in season, a local farmer's wife willing to supply us with eggs, and we had access to game from the estate.

The first spring, Honey and I – the wild-gatherers of the family – searched out everything which might be edible in the woods and

Northamptonshire Mud Pie

This is Poppy's recipe. It's quite scrumptious, a chocolate pastry base filled with a rich dark cream.

SERVES 6–8

SPECIAL CHOCOLATE PASTRY

6 oz/150 g flour
1 oz/25 g icing sugar
1 tablespoon cocoa powder

4 oz/100 g cold butter
2 egg yolks

RICH CHOCOLATE FILLING

12 oz/300 g chocolate
4 oz/100 g butter
4 oz/100 g cream

4 eggs and 1 yolk
4 oz/100 g caster sugar

1. Make the pastry first. Sieve the flour with the icing sugar and the cocoa powder. Chop in the butter until the mixture looks like fine breadcrumbs. Work in the egg yolks (you only need one in a hot country because the butter melts). You can do this in a blender. If the pastry's too short to roll, press it into the tart tin.

2. Bake the base blind (line with foil and weight with a few haricot beans) until the pastry has gone paler in colour – this is what happens to a chocolate pastry. Give it about 15 minutes in a coolish oven (325°F/170°C/mark 3) first, and then turn up the oven to crisp the pastry (you can do this in the reverse order). Remove the foil and beans and let it cool a little.

3. Meanwhile, make the filling. Melt the chocolate, butter and cream in a bowl over simmering water (a bain-marie). Put the bowl aside.

4. Now make a saboyan: whisk the eggs and the extra yolk with the sugar in a bowl until fluffy, and set the bowl over the

bain-marie. Whisk over the hot water until the texture firms a little. This will take about 10 minutes – take care not to scramble it. Take it off the heat. Fold in the melted chocolate mixture.

5. Pour the mixture into the tart case. Put the tart in a moderate oven – 350°F/180°C/mark 4 to set for 10 minutes – until the filling won't ripple if you push it.

6. Take it out. Let it cool. Serve with runny cream. Irresistible.

Pick-Your-Own Fruit Soup

This is an unusual northern recipe – delicious for a summer dessert or as the first course of supper.

———————— MAKES 2 PINTS/1.25 L ————————

2 lb/1 kg strawberries,   *1 pint/600 ml water*
blackcurrants, raspberries   *1 tablespoon sugar*
(whatever)   *1 heaped tablespoon cornflour*

1. Put the fruit, water and sugar into a saucepan. Bring to the boil. Lid and cook gently until the fruit collapses into a purée.

2. Sieve, return to the pan and stir in the cornflour, previously blended with a little water. Cook as briefly as it takes the soup to thicken slightly.

3. Babies like this warm. For the grown-ups, serve it hot with biscuits, or well-chilled with soured cream.

hedgerows. Honey imported two new friends from the city, and I provided the three of them with poster-sized paper and paints for recording their finds. Before being cooked, each plant had to be correctly identified (vernacular and Latin), and its portrait painted. Everyone had to work fast before the raw materials wilted and became inedible. Tasting notes were then incorporated in the poster. At the end of the holiday, each person had a beautiful poster and raging indigestion.

For the first time in my life, I felt I might make use of a freezer. Since we were miles from any shops, I told myself it would be wonderfully convenient. The freezer was a huge ex-Walls ice-cream store chest. To this day I can't think what possessed me. Conditions were Arctic anyway. We filled it with sliced white bread, strawberries from the pick-your-own and home-made ice-cream. We packed out the corners with a year's supply of Anchor butter which Honey won in a painting competition. Neither sliced bread nor frozen strawberries fitted the household's culinary habit, so I can only imagine we suffered a moment of collective madness. Happily, one balmy week when we were away, the power failed and we came back to find the freezer overflowing with a huge fluffy green-tinged summer pudding. The freezer was sluiced out with bleach, and never turned on again.

After three years of intermittent commuting and quarrelling over who was allowed to stay in London in the school breaks, I took a unilateral decision, and we settled down in Northamptonshire for another sabbatical with the three daughters – Cas by now had completed his secondary education and had headed off to backpack round Australia during his year between school and university.

The girls were absolutely furious. I was unrepentant. We needed, I felt, a year away from the smokestacks so that Poppy – threatened with remedial everything at Pimlico – might pass her O levels at Northampton Girls' School; and Honey might acquire a firmer grasp of the basics than an inner city school, gripped by the fever of educational innovation, seemed capable of imparting. Fran had already acquired a full hand of O levels and earned herself two A level years at Westminster School – and it was just possible for her to commute from Milton Keynes.

Creature comforts in Northampton were hard won: the house had not been modernized since the Second World War. An elderly Rayburn did the best it could with the cooking and the hot water.

Barley Risotto with Wild Greens and Peas

Barley takes about twice as long as rice to cook. It's the perfect vehicle for wild-gathered greens: nettle tops (top 4 leaves only), sorrel, chickweed, Good King Henry, young dandelion. Cultivated greens can substitute: spinach plus parsley, watercress and outside leaves of lettuce, and spring onions and greens.

SERVES 3–4

---

2 tablespoons olive oil
1 medium onion, skinned and finely chopped
1 green pepper, de-seeded and chopped small
8 oz/250 g barley

1½ pints/1 l stock
– or half water, half white wine
4 oz/100 g shelled peas
Salt and pepper
4 oz/100 g greens (wild or cultivated) well-washed and shredded

---

TO ACCOMPANY

Grated cheese (Parmesan, or any mature hard cheese)

1. Warm the oil in a wide frying pan. Fry the onion gently in the oil for a few minutes, and then stir in the chopped peppers. Let them soften a little.

2. Stir in the barley, moving it about until all the grains are coated.

3. Add the stock or water and wine, and let it all bubble up. Season.

4. Either turn down the heat, lid loosely and simmer for about 45 minutes, adding more boiling water as necessary. Or tip everything into an ovenproof dish and lid it, or cover with foil and bake at 375°F/190°C/mark 5 for an hour, until the barley is tender and the liquid all absorbed.

Just before the end of cooking, stir in the wild greens and peas. Fluff it up with a fork – a little butter makes it even more delicious.

It will keep quite happily in a warm oven until you are ready to serve. Hand grated cheese round separately.

Honey Ice-Cream

Use the basic recipe as a vehicle for different flavours – real
vanilla, chocolate, coffee, fruit purées – rhubarb is delicious.

─────── MAKES ABOUT 1 PINT/600 ML ───────

½ pint/300 ml full-cream milk   4 tablespoons honey
2 egg yolks   1 teaspoon cinnamon

1. Whisk the milk, egg yolks, honey and cinnamon in a bowl over a
saucepan of simmering water, till the custard thickens velvety
smooth and coats the back of the spoon.
2. Let the mixture cool.
3. Freeze it hard.
4. Take it out of the freezer and beat it: the volume
will double (here lies the commercial profit). Freeze
again until you are ready to use it.

There was no question of central heating, but a big open fire in the drawing-room gave everyone a chance to dry off.

That year ran a close second to the Languedoc's snowy excesses – all winter long we fought a holding battle against the icy drifts. One week we were evacuated in our entirety to the Big House itself. At other times, hot-water bottles and porridge were the order of the day – and once again Fran and I had to leave the house at dawn.

The two younger daughters had an extra hour – but even so, the going was tough. One morning Honey appeared at breakfast in the kitchen carrying the goldfish bowl she kept in her bedroom.

'Look Ma,' she said. 'It's not moving!'

I looked. The fish was indeed suspended immobile in the bowl – except that it wasn't water, but solid ice. We set the fish to thaw on the Rayburn while I did the school run. On my return, I'm ashamed to admit the goldfish was well and truly poached.

The advent of the lambing season took Honey's mind off the fishy tragedy. She joined the shepherds in the lambing shed each evening on her return from school, and soon they were fetching her in the middle of the night for midwife duty. With her small strong hands, she could reach right up the birth channel and turn a lamb trapped the wrong way round in the uterus. She volunteered as a foster-mother, and soon a succession of little orphan lambs were clicking on dainty hooves round our kitchen in search of their evening bottle.

It was Poppy, plucked from London in the middle of her O level final year, who took the move hardest. She had been awarded a coveted place in Northampton Girls' School, an old grammar school which had chosen to go private rather than comprehensive. The school upheld the old-fashioned virtues of duty and discipline. Poppy demonstrated her disapproval in subtle and not-so-subtle nonconformism.

She particularly hated the uniform – a royal-blue herring-bone A-line skirt with acrylic V-neck jersey to match. A skilled needle-woman since her early years, she simply took a pair of scissors to the pullover and turned it into a sleeveless vest, shortened and straightened the skirt, and wore it with St Trinian's tights with holes in them. As a dyed-in-the-wool sartorial nonconformist I could not but applaud her ingenuity. Her contemporaries were enviously awe-struck, the headmistress outraged.

'Mrs Luard – I don't think Poppy's uniform is at all correct.'

I pleaded ignorance and poverty in equal measure.

The headmistress was unconvinced. She was even less convinced as the first term wore on. We began to receive regular phone calls complaining of subversive London ways. Nicholas – ever on the lookout for something to take his mind off the hard business of writing – always took the calls.

'I'll have a word with my daughter, Headmistress,' said Nicholas helpfully.

Poppy, who had long nurtured a reputation for telling the truth, denied everything. Nicholas, a sucker for a pair of honest blue eyes, was entirely convinced of the injustice of the accusation and fought her corner tooth and nail.

'Your daughter, Mr Luard, has been seen hanging around on street corners in the mid-morning break. In *uniform*. Talking to unemployed youths,' added the headmistress.

Never one to pour oil on troubled waters without tossing in a match, Nicholas suggested that a lack of uniform and an employed youth would scarcely have been an improvement on the arrangement.

Honey fared rather better in Towcester. She learnt to read and write in her native tongue, rather than the English-for-foreigners which was all that had been required of her at Pimlico. With Honey, it was never an it's-or-its problem or the i-before-e syndrome. She did the job properly, tackling the unfamiliar right behind the knees and bringing it down phonetically several miles the other side of the touch-line: 'cort' for caught, 'shepad' for shepherd, 'kigin' for kitchen.

That year in Northampton marked the real end of the childhood years – and all four children began to organize their lives independently of each other.

My own work had by now evolved to include food journalism – a passion which had developed over our years on the road – and my skills as a painter were used as an illustrator. In the summer of 1983, Dr Miriam Rothschild, a neighbour in Northamptonshire and at that time embarking on her campaign to save our wild-flower meadows, and I, together produced *The Butterfly Gardener*. She supplied the text and oversaw my work, correcting the position of an insect or the set of a petal.

'Oh Elisabeth, you made that up,' she would say as she leant over my shoulder while I worked from nature in the tangle of her own wild-flower meadows at Ashton Wold.

The days in her sunny meadows, and the work itself, provided me with an escape from domestic responsibilities, a new certainty that there might indeed be life after children.

Nevertheless, in spite of these flurries of independence, once a mother, always a mother. I have never wanted to be a friend to my children – they are more than capable of choosing their own. Even so, there is a time when the ties must be loosened, the better to take the strain of independence – for parents no less than children.

The exam-taking years were the years of battle. As in wartime, you get used to it. Ducking the bombs became second nature. Exams come at quite the wrong time in a person's development. No-one can possibly put up their best performance with their hormones in an uproar – puberty, first love, first heartbreak. I imagine hormones also account for the prodigious amount of time young adults spend asleep. They may be horizontal, but they're busy as birds and bees – and very little of what's going on has anything to do with the intellect.

With the youngest on O levels while the eldest approached finals at Cambridge, there were seven years when one at least, and probably two or three, was on red alert and claiming priority treatment. This welter of warring interests dictated, among other things, that the household's culinary timetable had to evolve.

I cooked once a day, in time (more or less) for eight o'clock dinner. And that, in a nutshell, was that. Anyone who didn't arrive on time was given free range among the leftovers – and might rely on my advice, even if not on my participation. Leftovers remain the culinary exercise in which I can truly claim professional expertise. To this day I can do things with the contents of a fridge – *any* fridge, even one containing two rollmop herrings and a bag of elderly potatoes – which the common-or-garden chef would consign to the bin.

No-one can live on the intellect alone. There are certain domestic skills without which a person – male or female – cannot do. It's a matter of taking control of your environment. Everything becomes a threat if you can't fix it. Practically speaking, I admit I'm no handyman. I will never win the fairground competition to drive a nail in straight. Nature made me a jerry-builder, perfectly content to convert the potting shed into a cosy office by separating myself off from the pots with a line of recycled doors, insulating with old newspaper, waterproofing the floor with roofing felt, and lining the roof with cotton ticking to keep the computer dry when the corrugated iron lets in the rain. I think it comes from my South American childhood, when most people whose company I valued – the cook, the maids and the gardener – lived in newspaper and string hovels and threw up new cubicles overnight.

Nicholas, my resident handyman, has never been a natural house-husband. By inclination an out-of-doors man, confronted by indoor problems he goes for a saunter round the wildwood. He can only be galavanized into action when I've already jerry-built what he has been promising to do for months, weeks, years. So elementary electrical skills such as wiring plugs and changing a fuse were passed on round the kitchen table on a rainy day. Everyone had to know how to change a tap washer and unblock a sink.

Certain tasks can be shared – all the children were put in charge of redecorating their own rooms as soon as they could load a paint roller. Family washing was the exception – it can only be done *en masse*. Individual washes are not cost-effective – whether you do the laundry in the launderette or at home. As mine was the hand that flicked the switch, it was always I who shrunk the woollies, and turned all the underwear a murky violet. Nobody's perfect. And as soon as the children became teenagers, they were promoted to responsibility for their own ironing, which was separated out into named baskets and left on the stairs to be collected. Whether the clothes were ironed or not was up to each individual. Sheets, pillowcases and towels were and are my area of responsibility – and I admit to folding up the sheets and only ironing the top layer. I never found a way to deal with orphaned socks – all single socks are put in a bag in case their twin turns up. Once a year I get fed up and throw them all away. Sod's law dictates the missing ones turn up the next day.

The final seal on adulthood for any teenager is that magic moment when you pass your driving test. I've never much minded bumps on the bodywork of the family vehicle: if it gets tipped in the ditch, the war wounds stay. Thieves are inclined to choose less customized transport, and you get more respect on traffic roundabouts. But with four learner drivers clamouring for lessons and private roads round the estate for a playground, we made an investment in an old banger. Whatever happened, it had to be cheaper than paying for everyone to get their initial experience at driving school. Learning to drive is a hairy business at the best of times. Anything can happen – from small arguments with a wandering bollard to major territorial disputes with a breeding bull, to the moment when the engine and the clutch finally part company for good.

Being a teenager is hell for everyone intimately involved. The curious thing is that other people's teenagers are invariably charming – just as charming as other people find yours. Other people's teenagers are polite, civil to their elders, help with the washing-up and never set the bedclothes on fire when smoking in bed. As a solution, I have long proposed a teenager exchange: you get other people's and they get yours, and everyone has a much nicer time until they all reach adulthood and turn back into human beings again.

It comes to every family, the knotty problem of co-habitation, the establishment of house rules to govern that which comes most naturally and vigorously in the teenage years. To put it delicately, that particular expression of affection which leads to extraneous bodies in the kitchen at breakfast. Mine was never a liberal household – in these matters at least.

With a father of the family who was perfectly capable of waiting up all night, rolling-pin in hand, behind the front door to repel boarders, I didn't reckon that tolerance was a likely option. It's a curious thing about fathers that they are only too delighted when their sons sneak home with a girlfriend – but when it comes to daughters, it's another matter altogether. So I simply announced that there was only room for one mating couple in any household – and that was going to be *me*. However, when we were away for the weekend, we would announce this well in advance, together with time of departure and estimated time of return – and those at home would be notified of any deviation. What the eye doesn't see, the heart doesn't grieve over. Anyway, I hate surprises, particularly when I have to deal with the irate males and furious females who are the inevitable price.

Intergenerational spats were inevitable throughout the teenage years, but I knew the daughters who had run away from home could usually be found lurking in my sister Marianna's spare bedroom. Bless her: every family should have one. The tacit understanding between all parties was that those who ask no questions are told no lies.

Anyone over the age of consent – eighteen in our household – could do their tom-catting elsewhere. Taxi money was left out for returning night-owls who had missed the last bus – although it was understood this was to be treated not as a windfall, but strictly for emergencies.

Until the exam-taking years, Sunday lunch had always been the main meal of the seventh day. Not any more. There comes a moment in every mother's life when it's simply not worth winkling the teenagers out of bed. The stress level on both parties is too high. That's the moment to introduce Sunday dinner, taken sometime between six o'clock meat-tea and the acceptable adult hour of eight-thirty. This, whenever possible, remains our family get-together – a chance for those who, making their separate ways in the world, can check in on each other's lives, providing an informal opportunity to introduce new friends to the family circle.

Over the years, we have acquired a wide range of young honorary family members – their interests ranging from poetry to carpentry. Everyone's preoccupations and friendships are reflected in the mix, giving all of us access to those who might not otherwise come our way.

Through this gathering – irregular as it now may be – we are best able to preserve a strong family identity. I have no doubt that the sharing of a meal serves not only to remind us of the past but gives us faith in the future.

CHAPTER TWENTY-ONE

Clan memories

'Don't expect too much of life. Live as well as you can.'

The Reverend Sydney Smith*

THE FIRST TIME I WAS AWARE THAT WE WERE A CLAN RATHER THAN just a family was when we were on the road between Andalusia and London.

We had left Poppy behind for a week to keep her friend Emma company — she was due to return to London by air. For the entire journey I felt a nagging sense of betrayal. Every time we stopped for a meal in a café or restaurant I would confidently order a table for six, only to realize immediately that one of our number was lacking.

*Advice to a young lady in low spirits (c. 1830).

245

Ever since then, there has been no question but that significant rites of passage demand the presence of the full clan – whatever the occasion and however numerous the other guests.

The first major landmark was Nicholas's fortieth birthday – celebrated in our Andalusian valley, with, to paraphrase the policeman in *Casablanca*, a round-up of the usual suspects. We had told everyone to bring something favourite to read, an oral commonplace book delivered in the language of the guest's choice. Naturally, we feasted until dawn – quails and quinces and all those things which might be considered fortifying for a man passing into his prime.

As the first of the four to claim the key to the door, Cas's twenty-first birthday marked a watershed in family life. He had spent his eighteenth birthday at one end of a disused sewer pipe in Alice Springs: no place to hold a party, even if the itinerant Aborigine family camped at the other end were willing to share their supper with him.

The guests numbered twenty-four – the maximum I could possibly seat. I've never liked buffet suppers – fork suppers are uncomfortable, bad for the digestion, and things get spilled on the carpet. And the toasts and speeches essential to such an occasion need to be punctuated by standing up, sitting down and falling off – for which chairs are indispensable. The dinner was therefore declared a four-course, black-tie, sit-down event.

The meal was planned to reflect our wanderings. Four years at an Andalusian school came first, so the guests were greeted with cold manzanilla from Sanlucar – home of the best Spanish sherries – and plates of *serrano* ham and *chorizo*.

Then, for the serious business of the dinner itself, we began with *fruits de mer* for his year at school in France. Next, to mark the wanderer's return, a pile of good British roast game – saddle of hare, pheasant, partridge and the like. Bread sauce, game chips, rowan-and-apple jelly and bowls of watercress were provided to mop up the juices from the birds. With it was served a purée of swede just for the earthy taste of it with the game. Simmering and reducing all day, a stockpot with shin of beef, onions and carrots. This, with the pounded livers of the birds, their cooking juices and a spoonful of rowan jelly, made excellent hot gravy. It also diverted the two resident rat-catching moggies and provided lunch next day for left-over guests. The usual chocolate birthday cake provided a triumphant conclusion. And then it was time for champagne and speeches, with English Stilton, French chèvre, Spanish grapes and port – one wonderful bottle of Taylors '53 stowed away for those who were still sober enough to recognize a decanter. Strong Aussie billycan coffee was provided for the rearguard.

The arrival of the champagne galvanized all twenty-four guests into speeches – most of them emotional and some of them more than once. These were followed by all twelve verses of 'D' ye ken John Peel?' including the echoing bits with the horns. At that, the cats and the Chilean butler borrowed from my mother retired simultaneously into the comparative safety of the streets.

All important birthdays – those involving a zero – need a focus. For his thirtieth, Cas followed his father's example and marked it with a literary event. By now a City man, working for a major Japanese bank, the food, by special request, reflected his recent travels in the Far East. The readings were delivered hesitantly at first, but with increasing confidence as the evening got into its stride. Although it hadn't been planned – each guest was invited to bring a favourite poem or short literary extract to last no more than three minutes – it somehow followed naturally that the readings reflected the relationship between each reader and the young man himself. Fran, as the eldest sister, organized a ballot for the order of reading – with two family members taking the first turns to encourage the others.

I thought it sensible to choose simple food which could be eaten with the fingers and does not demand to be consumed instantly: Chinese dishes, *tapas* or *mezze*. Plenty of wine was provided to loosen up the vocal chords, and the entertainment declared open, with a short pause at ten-minute intervals for the participants to refuel.

Five years earlier, we had celebrated our silver wedding – a clan celebration with only the family and our oldest friend, Venetia, present. Mindful that four of the guests had not been there at the event whose twenty-fifth anniversary we were celebrating, I served as close as I could remember to the original wedding breakfast, cake and all. The centre-piece of the table was a remake of my bridal bouquet.

Bang Bang Chicken

This is a classic Chinese party dish. The steaming of the chicken and the preparation of the sauce can be done a day ahead – convenient when you're throwing a party.

─────────── SERVES 10 AS PART OF A BUFFET ───────────

1 small chicken
Salt and white pepper
I small piece root ginger chopped
(or 1 tablespoon powdered ginger
and a little grated lemon rind)

4 spring onions, cut into short
lengths
1 tablespoon light oil

─────────── FOR THE SERVING SAUCE ───────────

1 tablespoon roasted ground
sesame seeds (or roasted peanuts,
crushed)
1 teaspoon ground Szechuan
peppercorns (or grind together
half black peppercorns, half allspice)
1 teaspoon sesame paste (or smooth
peanut butter)
2 tablespoons sweet chilli sauce

(or tomato sauce with a pinch
of cayenne)
2 tablespoons plum sauce
(or plum jam, sieved)
2 teaspoons light soy sauce
2 tablespoons Shaoshing wine
(or sherry)
1–2 garlic cloves, crushed
Salt and white pepper

Lettuce
*1 tablespoon chopped spring
onion*

*1½ teaspoons roasted sesame
seeds (or crushed roasted peanuts)*

1. Spatchcock the chicken: cut down the length of the breastbone and open out the carcass. Season with salt and pepper.
2. Lay the opened-out chicken in a shallow heatproof dish with half the ginger and spring onion tucked underneath and the other half on top. Pour the oil over the chicken. Steam on a rack over boiling water in a wok or saucepan for 35–40 minutes, lidded, until cooked through. Allow the chicken to cool in its juices.
3. Combine all the sauce ingredients in a food processor.
4. Skin and bone the chicken, and cut the meat into fine strips and dress it with the sauce. Arrange on a bed of lettuce leaves in such a way that each leaf can be picked up in the fingers. Sprinkle with chopped spring onion and sesame seeds.

Prawn Toasts

This Chinese delicacy – very popular as a starter in Chinese restaurants – is the best of finger food. It's not nearly as fiddly as it sounds.

---MAKES 12 FINGERS---

6 oz/175 g raw shrimp, peeled
1 oz/25 g diced pork fat
(or green streaky bacon)
1 level teaspoon cornflour
½ teaspoon salt
White pepper
½ teaspoon chopped root
ginger or 1 teaspoon powdered
ginger

1 egg white
3 slices brown bread, crusts
removed
2 tablespoons sesame seeds
(finely chopped nuts will do
at a pinch)
Vegetable oil for deep-frying

1. Put the peeled shrimps in the food processer with the pork fat, cornflour, salt, about half a teaspoon of pepper, ginger, egg white and a tablespoon of water. Process to a coarse but smooth paste. You can do this with a knife – the Chinese are very good with knives.

2. Spread the bread slices evenly with the paste, using about 1 tablespoon per slice. Cut each slice into quarters. Trim the edges neatly. Take each slice and press into the sesame seeds to coat them thoroughly.

3. Heat the oil in a wok or deep-fryer.

4. Fry the slices, coated side down, for about 3 minutes, until lightly golden. Turn and fry for another minute. Remove with a draining spoon onto absorbent paper. Serve hot.

Looking back now across those years, we seem to have covered a lot of ground. Not one of nature's natural policemen, I have never tried to prevent my offspring from doing anything as long as it is not illegal and did not actively damage others – and that includes smoking, drinking and choice of love-object. I try to keep confrontation to the minimum. Life is anxiety-ridden enough in young adulthood without mother popping the last straw on the camel's back.

Bringing up a family has never been anything but a tough row to hoe – anyone who pretended otherwise would be a fool. As parents and children, we need all the help we can get. Bearing in mind that romantic love is a comparatively new notion in human relationships, the family unit was never intended to be limited to a single generation of parents and their children. I can only think it is the accelerated breakdown of this arrangement, the disappearance of the back-up group, in the form of the active grandparenting generation, even the support of unmarried relations, which causes much of the current confusion.

The result is that, at the last resort, what was once a shared inter-generational responsibility devolves on the mother alone. Even a young mother with a career cannot escape her role without abandoning everything. But the young father has no such practical limitations. Unencumbered by pregnancy, he can be in Tierra del Fuego by next Tuesday with ne'er a birth pain to show for it.

The reality of the matter is that, whatever intellectual decisions may be taken, young men are programmed to be efficient sowers of wild oats – and that is where their practical responsibilities end. Nature has not provided the young man with any real incentive to stay around and see the harvest gathered in. In other words the young male is perfectly equipped for fatherhood, but not particularly for being a good parent – that is, an adult who takes care of the offspring. What we understand to be fathering is in reality grand-fathering – the role which comes naturally to the clan patriarch. At the time of life when he is ready to be a grandparent, a man might naturally be expected to have done his roaming and be grateful for the comforts of home.

In the last few generations, we have dismantled this practical social structure – at its best, a mutually supportive institution where family members could benefit from each other's skills and strengths. We no longer live as household clans. Our social services – however essential they may now be – encourage us, by taxation and legislation, to form separate small units. So even if a man's children have obligingly provided him with grandchildren – and mine seem in no hurry to start producing offspring – a grandfather needs proximity if he is to fulfil his role.

Nature is hard to fool. When a man who has previously shown no particular enthusiasm for active fatherhood reaches the time when he feels he should be a grandfather, he may well abandon the mother of his first batch of children, and set about acquiring another. You see it all the time. To his abandoned spouse's bewilderment, he then proceeds to make the most excellent of parents – patient, home-loving, settling down to read the bedtime story, the very model of fatherhood. If it's any consolation, such a man is not behaving like a father at all – he's simply being a grandfather.

This is a pit into which the most sturdy of marriages can tumble. Short of countenancing serial polygamy – for the wife with the golden wedding in her sights, there's no easy solution to what has always been the most obvious manifestation of the male mid-life crisis. And it's certainly not the best of reasons for attempting to persuade your mutual children to procreate on schedule. Marriage is no battleground – unless the protagonists have more long-term stamina than I. Nevertheless, a little stragetic planning never comes amiss. Forewarned is forearmed. There's no sense in waiting until the horse has bolted to shut the stable door, but there's an outside chance that if you can feed in a subversive notion or two ahead of time, any romance might be nipped in the bud. No red-blooded mid-lifer likes to see himself portrayed as the victim of an attack of the grandfather syndrome.

One precautionary measure worth contemplating when family upheavals threaten is to move house. Relocation is supposed to rank second only to divorce as a prime cause of nervous breakdowns. But I found it had the same effect on family politics as Mao Tse-tung's state of permanent revolution: if you keep the population on the hop it won't have time to protest.

Everyone has a limited period in which it is possible to live the high-speed city life. Bedsits and shared flats are the best when you are single and footloose: modern city apartments can only – should only – be treated as hotel rooms. I would reckon twenty years is the maximum. After that the lead in the petrol at pavement level begins to addle the brain.

So, true to our established pattern of drifting with the flow, we exchanged a large family house in south London for a smallish city-centre flat, and a cottage with a derelict garden in the Hebrides, on the beautiful island of Mull. The Hebrides is in Nicholas's blood – his grandmother was a Mulloch born and bred, and his father lives there still.

The islands, the silvery sisters of the Hebrides, are like no other place on earth. Ask anyone homesick for the Western Isles, and you will be told, not of turreted castles, but of wild skies and gun-metal seas, of scarlet sunsets and clear white dawns. Ask after island hospitality, and you will be entertained with stories not of grand banquets, but of simple things – the flavour of a new-laid egg, the taste of a scone baked on an iron girdle, the silken sheen on a cloutie-dumpling rich with fruit and darkened with molasses.

It was thirty years ago, newly married and already expecting our first child, that Nicholas took me to visit his childhood home. We had been loaned his father's croft house, a little stone dwelling overlooking the gentle island of Ulva, which the explorer David Livingstone once called home. His childhood companion Jessie ran the sheep on the hillsides all around, and Gaelic was the lingua franca of the islands.

It was long before the days of tourist buses and the huge ferries which now link the island to the mainland. An elderly smoke-blackened puffer landed the handful of crofting wives and ourselves, the only visitors that day, at a rough stone jetty under the lee of the ruined fortress of Duart, the ancient stronghold of the Maclean. On the crossing, the ferryman, a fisherman at heart, heaved-to for a moment to check a lobster creel, threw a line overboard in the hope of dogfish, or skate, or even a late-running salmon. At the end of the journey, mindful of my condition, he assured me that if I cared to send a message with the postman, we would not lack for a bite.

That kindness was the first of many: hospitality comes naturally to those who once depended on such generosity for their very survival. There were eggs to be had from my crofting neighbours, with maybe an old hen for the pot, and a batch of scones or gingerbread for tea. Among the islanders who fished, there was a view taken about what was properly a trade item: crab and mackerel could be had for free, but lobster and prawn went to the traders, as did the haul of diver-gathered scallops which I made vain efforts to intercept for ready money at the quayside.

But Nicholas knew where to gather barnacle-crusted mussels and oysters from the rock pools beneath the waterfall which fell in a white-mare's tail into the bay – skills he took delight in passing on to his children. Since then, over the years, I have learnt to add my own wild-gatherings to the larder. The consolation for summer rain is a fine autumn growth of edible fungi. And in the proper season I could gather carragheen seaweed to set a jelly, sorrel and watercress for salads, raspberries and blackberries and blue-bloomed sloes for pies and preserves.

The house we bought on the north-western corner of the island was tiny but beautiful. It had been a holiday home, so its facilities were minimal. Nestled on the hillside where Jessie ran her flocks, it was a stone-built cottage with a rattling but and ben made of corrugated iron, snugly lined with wood. Perched on the lip of a great walled garden, centred by a tall cyprus tree, many years had passed since the garden had seen love and care. The cot once housed the gardener of the Quinish estate, and there were family connections with those who had once owned the land.

Nicholas set to work with a will, and I threw in that mixture of jerry-building and recycling that characterizes my own school of interior decoration. The islanders do not see any particular reason to do more than is strictly necessary in the line of paid employment. As is the way with self-sufficient communities, everyone does a little of everything – and a dram and a slice of cake will do more to see the plumbing connected than a fistful of the Queen's currency. For the more sophisticated carpentry and such, we looked to the incomers, the only craftsmen on the islands.

We converted and mended the house, ploughed and planted in the garden. For both of us – me in the potting shed, Nicholas in a little wooden hut up the hill among the foxgloves and bracken – it was a fine and peaceful place to write, and I began my first novel, *Emerald*. Once again, as in the Languedoc and in Spain, we took pleasure in the passing of the seasons. In autumn, the beech woods blazed red and gold. In winter, the tall trees which fringed the garden danced in the gales and we would wake late in the frosty mornings to find the turned earth of the garden white with snow. In spring, Jessie would come to fetch one of us to help with the lambing – a robust chore, since the island sheep are a hardy breed and do not care to be coralled. In summer the hillsides were bright with harebells and there were blueberries and blackberries for the picking. We scarcely needed sleep at all when the soft twilight reached right round until morning.

We turned over the flat to Cas, now working in the City, and spent less and less time in London. Mull soon became our new family home. It was far from the lights of the city, but the children loved the islands and thought it no hardship to make their way by train and ferry to join us whenever they could. They came often to visit with their friends, or simply scuttled home to recover from love affairs or discuss the new directions their careers might take.

Our particular clan has never needed bricks and mortar to declare its identity – we can pack up and pitch camp at will. For more permanent shelter, all we need is the proverbial roof beam, a fire in the hearth, and a kitchen table – that same broad stretch of board which first accommodated us in Spain.

Which was why, some four years after we had settled in Mull, when the death of a generous godmother delivered to our care the small estate of Brynmerheryn in the far western corner of Wales, we moved again. We knew the place was coming to us years before it claimed us, but Nicholas was doubtful at first. He is heart and soul a Scot – a man for the sparkling Western Isles – and he thought he had come home at last. But then, say I, what's the difference? It's all Celts and sheep and wind and weather.

Brynmerheryn – the name means 'hill of the rams' – is as isolated as any place can be, even in Wales. Some ten miles inland from Aberystwyth, at the end of a long bumpy track lined with bilberry shrubs and clumps of heathery scrub, you'd never know there was a house there at all, so buried is it in its own little patch of watery woodland.

The house itself is of no particular architectural distinction. Like our two relocated London moggies, its charm lies in its lack of pedigree. Nobody can say when the first shelter for man and animals was built, but there has surely been a dwelling-place here for a thousand years. Good-natured and amiable, the house adapts to the changing requirements of its residents. Like an ancient mariner adrift on a sea of change, it rambles.

The heart of the building is the old farm dwelling – a bare two rooms stacked one on top of the other, built of thick rough-hewn stone. Beneath the floorboards are cobbles laid on bare earth. Dark as a womb, tiny deep-set windows protect it from the cold east wind. Tacked on the front of this ancient house is a little Georgian rectory, four-square, with six windows, two of them blind. The old panes of glass make beautiful reflections, tipping the view a little this way or that, each pane trapping a miniature landscape. The twin dwellings are linked by a sloping slate-floored passage hacked through yard-thick walls. Behind, reached through a glassed-in corridor, is a huge barn converted into an airy studio which I have chosen as my workplace.

Most ancient of all, down by the garden gate stands a little guardian dolmen – a cromlech, a pillar of stone, unmarked, tall as a teenager. Under the benevolent eye of this Celtic talisman, Nicholas has pitched camp. His workroom is the snug little wooden hut he had brought down from the Hebrides, shadowed by a tall Scots pine to remind him of his beloved islands. The peat-marsh of Tregaron spreads out below and there is all the sweep of the Cambrian mountains beyond.

We spent our first Christmas in our new abode. We had warmth and shelter, we had good food on the table and blazing fires to keep out the winter cold.

We had no notion of what was to come. Later I was to remember that it was in 1986, the year I had published *European Peasant Cookery*, the book with which I made my name as a cookery writer, that I first heard the warning. It was no more than a secondary item on the news, a quotation from a report issued by the World Health Organization on the spread of a new disease for which there seemed to be no cure: 'By the year 2000, this plague will claim one in four.'

It was the familiarity of that number which caught my attention, the bleakness of the statement which sent shivers down my spine. I had four children – the youngest still at university and the other three launched into the market-place. All were shining and healthy and making their way in the world at their chosen careers, no longer in need of their parents' or anyone else's protection. Surely they could not mean one of us?

No family is immune from tragedy. Immortality is no part of the human condition.

By now you will perhaps have guessed what is to come.

Before Francesca begins her story, I should like to introduce my eldest daughter not as a child, but as she is in adulthood – at the moment when she embarks on what she herself describes as the second part of her life.

I will be brief, but, like any mother, I am proud of my daughter, so you will have to forgive a parent's subjective eye.

Physically she is beautiful. She is fastidious, loves clothes, takes pleasure in luxury. Yet hers is not the kind of beauty which needs powder and paint – although when she has decided to make an entrance, she can give herself the kind of glamour which silences a roomful. She is slender, not overly tall, dark-haired and dark-eyed, well-proportioned, with a curvaceous figure and long shapely legs.

Her height, small feet and delicate hands (with which she sometimes earns money for modeling) come from her father's side of the family. As a little girl she was not considered beautiful but something of an ugly duckling – but always with grace and the promise that some day she would be a swan. The promise was well-fulfilled. She has the clarity of skin, the broadness of forehead and brightness of eye, the fine bones which would have allowed her to be as beautiful in old age as in the bright youth she now enjoys.

But it is her mind which is the most striking of her attributes. Her beauty hides a formidable – and formidably idle – intellect. She is clever, funny, sharp-witted and heart-stoppingly perceptive. Sometimes I think she is the cleverest of all my children – although there's no doubt that her very brilliance has sometimes worked against her. She sailed through her schooling without having to lift so much as a finger to pass exams. She played chess for her country and decided not to play again the following year. Friends from university complain to this day that she could win herself a first in any subject by doing half the work that anyone else would need to earn a doctorate.

Her great gift – unusual in one so clever – is her kindness and her affection for her friends. Francesca, my sweet daughter, has a remarkable capacity for giving and receiving love – most of all

257

when she is not romantically involved. She can be difficult, quarrelsome, even harsh with those she loves – but her anger is a storm which quickly passes. She does not judge her friends on intellect – like all the naturally intelligent, she does not put a high value on such things. Instead, she looks for other qualities which she values more: a capacity for happiness, a particular skill which she can encourage and admire, an enjoyment of life which she can share. And once she has found these things in a friend, she will not easily lose them.

I promised brevity. Now it's time to meet Francesca in the flesh. As you might expect, she is more than capable of speaking for herself.

CHAPTER TWENTY-TWO

Meeting Francesca

AFTER MUCH SOUL-SEARCHING AND MORE THAN ONE FALSE START,
maybe this is what I am meant to be doing: telling my story. For no better
reason than to get it off my chest, so that I don't think about it any more.
Maybe it will also help others.

I have not found many women's points of view on this subject. It is
always possible that I have not looked hard enough. But anyway, here is
mine. I am a young heterosexual woman infected with the HIV virus. It is
1992, a year since I was diagnosed. Since then I have learnt to live with it
in my own way.

Let me sketch in my life to date – the person I have become twenty-seven
years after arriving on this planet, born what's known as a blue baby on a
bitterly cold January night.

I am unremarkable except for the fact that I believe myself to be truly remarkable.

Nothing in my life would make me a candidate for this kind of thing. I have never touched drugs, nor do I belong to any of the groups medically 'at risk'. My sex life had been extremely low-key. My longest relationship was my first – a kind, gentle boy who saw marriage at the end of the day. But I had other plans – university, work, a life of my own. I had no intention of becoming a suburban housewife in Northampton, where he lived. These days, sometimes I think maybe I should have taken him up on the offer. At least I would have had a lover and maybe some children. I still kind of hope to have children – although I don't know anyone fool enough to go for it. But stranger things have happened.

I did a biology degree at London University. I specialized in parasitology, tropical diseases and immunology. At the time I attended lectures on this new disease, they were still trying to understand it. It was fascinating. The National Geographic *ran a colourful guide to the life of the virus. At that point in my life I would leave the lectures, go home, whip on a miniskirt, and head off to one of the nightclubs that my lover ran – jumping into bed with the guy I can only assume passed on the infection to me. Ironic (or stupid) to think that I was probably better informed about the whole thing than most of my contemporaries. Maybe I should have paid more attention during those lectures.*

You can survive the shock at first. Friends, family rally round. Later you have to learn to live with this thing every day. It is not a case of learning how to die with it, it is simply learning to live with it – whether because of it or in spite of it. I haven't found any miracle answers, I have just learnt to cope.

In this country, the most famous angle on AIDS to date is the director Derek Jarman's. I admire him very much for what he has done. He came out and faced the prejudice and hostility of a world that doesn't understand and is populated by latent and overt homophobes. Already well-known for his films and his homosexuality, by taking that decision, he has laid himself open – and I wonder if he regrets it sometimes. A little privacy would be nice occasionally – for people to look at you and talk to you and not know. I can only guess at the problems he might face, and read what he says in his books. My problems, however, differ from his.

AIDS has been touted as the homosexual curse. Some absolutely ludicrous things have been said and are still being said about it. As a journalist, I read the press coverage of it with interest and am often dismayed to see in print the description of someone who is HIV positive as having AIDS (or even 'riddled with AIDS'). It might be a minor point to those who don't have to face the problem personally, but there is a distinction between being HIV positive and having AIDS. A fact of which we should all now be aware. A lack of forethought can often result in sensationalist, inaccurate reporting.

I don't know the answers to all the questions. I don't know how it has affected me and those around me and how I have learnt to deal with it. Most of my family have been very supportive – and because of them I have edited out quite a lot of their reactions because I think it is probably unfair to draw conclusions about how they feel and how they reacted. They too need some privacy.

How it began

It is January, 1991. Britain is deep in recession. In the early hours of the day following my twenty-sixth birthday the West went to war with Saddam Hussein. By the end of the week, my Great-Aunt Peg had celebrated her eightieth birthday at a large family dinner in Camberwell. My paternal grandmother had persuaded me to visit her in Sussex. A doctor had told me I have AIDS.

One minute my life was following its natural course, the next minute everything had changed. Part two of my life had begun. The questions going through my mind: What happened? Why me? Who is responsible? Why didn't I know about it? Have they made a mistake? And the answers . . .

The strange thing is that it immediately became part of me. It felt like my destiny – part of the tapestry of my life. I believed that the hardest part was going to be the first few days, and that if I managed to get through those, then I could go on to deal with the rest as best I could. Something had happened and it was impossible to envision what might follow. I did not feel that it was my place to fight it. At first you accept it, later things change, maybe.

It was a shock – to me, my family and anyone who knew me. I had been suffering from tuberculosis the previous year. I had probably picked up the infection early in 1989 and had been slowly getting very run-down until I finally went to see my GP in early 1990. A friend at work noticed how swollen the glands in my neck looked and almost had a fit. At that time you would have been forgiven for thinking that I was a close relative of the 'Elephant Man'. She said it looked like glandular fever and I should go and see my doctor immediately. He took one look at me, sent me for a chest X-ray and referred me to a specialist.

I went to see the lung specialist a couple of days later – the earliest possible appointment. He examined me and said he could see I should not be at work. I looked terrible: run-down, my neck glands were horribly swollen, and I had lost a lot of weight. I had no energy at all, could hardly climb the stairs and *was pretty grumpy to boot. I returned to work to pack up my things and burst into tears. It was such a relief to have someone confirm that there was actually something medically wrong with me.*

The specialist sent me for some blood tests and diagnosed tuberculosis, formerly known as 'consumption'. That was quite fun. Many of the great artists had had it, I was in good company. I didn't have any old disease – I had a big one. But it was all right, because in this day and age, you just take some medication and you're fine again. I was put on a heavy course of antibiotics which seemed to do the trick, and after a couple of months I returned to work. Shortly after that I lost my job. The industry was in recession and cut-backs were being made all over the place. I had only been half the person I normally am for about a year, so I was the one to lose my job. I can't blame anyone. In my employer's position, I would have done the same.

I continued the course of antibiotics for some months. The recommended length of treatment is between six and nine months, and after six, I felt well enough to want to come off them. I wasn't really suffering side-effects, but I couldn't drink, even at parties, for fear of interfering with the effect, and it was a bore to have to take them every day. Anyway, I was feeling better each day. Just before Christmas that year, I was allowed to stop taking them.

Christmas passed and I was starting to feel a little slow and tired. A couple of weeks into January, my glands were swelling up again. I was relapsing, and when I returned to the specialist he decided we should check and see if there was anything else going on that might be making me run-down. He suggested it might be a good idea to test for HIV, just in case, so that we could clear that possibility and begin to look for some other reason for the recurrence of the TB.

Sure, I said, good idea, and trotted around the corner to have my blood tested.

The specialist was a private doctor, so he sent me to a private laboratory. I knew the place already. The number of staff and the cleanliness spoke of money. I handed in my forms at the desk, and took a seat in the waiting-room. I was summoned by a man in a white coat. I followed him down the corridor to a boxroom containing a single chair, where he took a blood sample. And that was it. Home.

From everything I have heard since, I was the exception. The way anyone is tested for HIV now is very different. Before the test, you are given counselling to make sure you understand the implications, and that you are strong enough to be able to handle a positive result. You have to convince the counsellor you will not be alone when you get the result. You are then given the test and return later for your results and further counselling if necessary.

For me it wasn't like that. I had no counselling. Nobody spoke to me, except the accountant to ask me for the fee. It wasn't until I had given my blood and walked out of the building that I began to worry. I thought the possibility was there, however remote, that I could come out with a positive result, and maybe I should be facing it. I called my sister, who hopped on a bus and came to meet me for coffee.

The next day, I started to worry in earnest. I wasn't desperately anxious, just uncomfortable. I kept thinking it's always possible the test will come out positive. Finally, I decided that I would continue to worry until I knew the result. I called the specialist who said my anxiety was quite understandable, and he would let me know as soon as the results came through. At the time it crossed my mind that this was slightly strange because it obviously meant he would have to give me the result over the telephone. He said he would call me by eleven o'clock the next morning.

The following day, I was pottering around my flat. At ten-thirty the telephone rang. It was my mother. She wanted to know if I had heard anything. I said, in all honesty, that I wasn't really thinking about it and anyway he wasn't due to call me until eleven. I put the telephone down and shortly afterwards it rang again.

It was the specialist.

He said, 'It doesn't look good.'

Silence from my end of the line. 'I want you to come down and see me at the Brompton Hospital at two o'clock. It sounds worse than it is.' I thought – what are you talking about? How could anything be as bad as having AIDS? I put the telephone down.

My flatmate Joe was hopping about nervously, asking me if I was OK, a slightly desperate note in his voice. I was keen to get out so I didn't have to answer his questions. I grabbed my things and jumped into a cab. By this time, there were tears in my eyes.

I sobbed quietly in the back of the cab all the way to my parents' house. My mother wasn't at home – she had popped out to the shops. My father was sitting there, a glass of wine in front of him. 'It'll be all right,' he said.

'Well, it won't be if the doctor now tells me I have AIDS,' I replied.

My mother returned shortly afterwards, and as she walked into the room, her face went completely grey. She aged ten years in the second that she saw me. It frightened me more than anything. Maybe I was slightly in shock. There was a calm atmosphere, not hysterical. When my mother recovered a little we decided to go out for lunch to kill the time before I was due at the hospital. I put on my dark glasses to try and hide my red swollen eyes. By a ghastly coincidence at the wine bar we were served by my last lover's ex-girlfriend. She may not have recognized me.

Before we left the house, my father repeatedly asked my mother to buy some boxer shorts for him on our way back. People later explained it as some kind of displacement activity to avoid facing the real issues. Later he said that it was to try and take our minds off the situation by asking us to do something slightly ridiculous.

Bellies full of chips and wine, my mother and I trotted off to the Brompton at the appointed time. I had bought a copy of Hello! magazine on the way and sat my mother on the bench outside the doctor's office with it while I went in, hoping it might provide some distraction.

In that poky little room, the doctor told me I had AIDS.

I asked him how long I had, and his reply was – well, two to four years, and, because I was young and relatively healthy, I would be at the long end of the spectrum. He gave me a new prescription for my anti-TB drugs and the telephone number of a nurse at the hospital who is used to dealing with people like me. He told me not to take any important decisions, no drastic action for three or four days, until I had calmed down. I realized he meant suicide. Funnily enough, at that point, it hadn't crossed my mind. What was going through my head repeatedly (and I was saying to him) was that it can't be great for him to deliver that kind of news. He said no, but that it was worse for me to hear it.

Towards the end of the consultation he left the office to get something, and my mother, who had been sitting on the bench outside, leapt up, wanting to know what was going on. She was looking at the doctor with hate in her eyes. I said: 'Look mum, it's not his fault.' The look stayed there.

We left the hospital arm in arm, and nipped into the pub for a whisky mac, to warm my insides. When we walked out of there and started heading home back up the Fulham Road, we bumped into my father. He said he wanted to make sure we went to buy his boxer shorts.

Afterwards, we nipped into the off-licence, and then into the record shop. I wanted to buy some mood music – Al Green. In the record shop we bumped into three friends of mine (male).

'Hi, Fran. How are you?'

'Fine. Meet my mum and dad.'

I must have looked pretty odd hidden behind my RayBans on a cold overcast day in a dimly lit record shop, stinking of drink. Later, when the young man I had spoken to heard about me, I think he saw the humour in the absurdity of that exchange.

Back at home, I was crying in my mother's arms, and I said – if it doesn't get any harder than this, I can deal with it. The toughest part was putting my family, my brother and sisters through it. I know they love me. My sister Poppy drove over from her flat to my parents' house to join us. I suppose she must have known what had happened, but I don't think it's the kind of knowledge you can really take on board unless you are there to see it and hear it. Her face just crumpled up in tears when I told her.

In the early evening my brother Caspar came home from work. I took him into the sitting-room next door and told him. He just said, 'Oh, my God,' over and over again. His face was serious and composed. Everyone will have their own way of dealing with it, and this is his. I don't think I have ever seen him looking more handsome. My youngest sister Honey was in India, so she would not learn about it until she returned.

That evening we were all due to attend a large family dinner, and my mother was cooking for a Burns' Night supper. We decided it would be best to all go out because otherwise we would sit in a kind of morose huddle, looking at each other, not knowing what to say. I must have looked absolutely ghastly. I hovered in the background trying to avoid the dozens of family who were there to celebrate my great-aunt's eightieth birthday. It was a fairly jolly evening after all, and probably took everyone's mind off things for a while. My cousins were all looking tall and dashing.

That night I slept in my flat, my sister curled up on the sofa next door – my guardian angel. It was a comfort to have her there. I needed people around me. I did not want to be alone at any point during the day or night. The presence of other people around me reaffirmed the fact I was still here – alive. It's like a human mirror all around. That evening I started my diary from which this account is taken. I eventually fell asleep when it was light outside. I slept well.

Taking it in

I awoke at five-thirty the following morning when the birds were already singing on the branch outside my window. I lay in bed thinking. By the end of the century, I had read, everyone will know someone with AIDS. Guess who?

I was worried about my flatmate, Joe. He knew something was afoot, but didn't quite know what, and I wasn't quite sure how I was going to tell him. Not long ago a close friend and mentor of his had died from sickle-cell anaemia, and this would be another hard blow for him. I didn't want to tell him until the dust had settled – as the good doctor had kept repeating: 'Don't do anything for the first few days, at least three or four. Or else you might do something rash.'

The key phrase that kept going through my head was *'from the time of first infection'*. I had had the first infection. It was downhill all the way from here.

In my diary I counted down the days. Day Two. It's very much like the Gulf War: they flash up the numbers on News at Ten. The Gulf War, Day Five. When I finally emerged from my bedroom, my sister had some coffee on the hob, and she had managed to shoo Joe off to work. I tidied up. I had picked up some leaflets from the London Lighthouse, and was worried I might have left them lying around.

It had already crossed my mind – it was bound to – walking down the street looking at children and pregnant women, I thought I would never be pregnant, never have children of my own. People talk of being old and complain about birthdays, but I wonder if I will even manage to reach thirty.

I always suspected there was something slightly wrong with the way my life worked. I always wanted to have children, lots of them, a home and a husband. Now I'm all alone with this body of mine full of these little viruses swimming around. It's quite extraordinary how quickly it becomes a reality. You are not given the choice. You are presented with a fact, and have to deal with it.

In a way – mad, black and twisted – it's very romantic. There you are in your prime. Young, pretty, with a perfectly good body, a fine pair of legs, but with this terrible thing inside you. It's like being a walking Trojan horse. I can only assume this means no more sex. What with one thing and another, it's been a long time since I have engaged in that particular activity – and they say you get used to anything.

Presumably at some point I am going to have to take a decision on how to tackle this. Almost forty-eight hours since the big bang, and strangely enough, it's still all right. I love my sister and it is hard to put her through this.

So I head off to Wales with my parents, stopping off en route with an old family friend, Venetia. She has known me since I first appeared on the planet, probably always thought I was a nightmare. She says she used to feed me sleeping pills when I was a baby. I was a bit of a screamer in those days. Well, I still am.

My third day and I'm still alive. It kind of settles in slowly. I don't think about the reality of it: the physical illness. I assume that I can deal with that when the time comes.

I was happy to be in Wales, in the big rambling stone house. It was cold. I was so used to my father turning the heating down that I assumed he had done so. If this thing doesn't get me, my father will! If I malign him, it's not *that much. In Wales, my mother and I are already making black jokes about the whole thing. It eases the atmosphere.*

I had always missed my cat since I emigrated her to Wales; she was going mad climbing up the walls of my flat in London without access to the great outdoors. At the time I was too ill and hadn't the energy to feed her or clean her litter as often as I should. I was delighted to see her. It might sound stupid, but to her I am the same person I was when she last saw me. She has no prejudice, except of course when it comes to who feeds her.

That weekend, my brother arrived bearing a large box of my favourite chocolates, which I devoured immediately. My mother watches everything I eat. She believes diet will be the key. She would — she's a food writer.

The plan for the immediate future was to sell the cottage in Scotland if we could get round my father, and buy me a little flat in West London, all painted white, with a nice thick carpet, a large bay window and a window-box filled with hundreds of geraniums.

I spoke to the family doctor, a GP who has looked after us for as long as I can remember. We talked a bit and he told me about a patient of his who had been infected when she was at university, so at least I'm not the only one. He made an appointment for me to go and see a specialist at the Middlesex Hospital. He recommended that the rest of my family get themselves tested. He also told my father that I was the bravest girl he had ever met and that he felt small beside me. My father was probably using poetic licence, but it made me feel good. My sister said it was going to make me unbearable.

I was very much looking forward to seeing my specialist. I thought it was going to be very interesting. At that moment, I was getting pangs in my chest, but on reflection I think they were minor anxiety attacks. You become acutely aware of every twitch in your body.

I noted in my diary that evening: 'The only thing that matters is now. Tomorrow and yesterday are of quite secondary importance.'

Life seemed to be settling down to some kind of normality. My father had fed the information into the family grapevine. My aunt revealed that my cousin had had a test on his return from Thailand. Anyone stupid enough to put himself at risk in a country like that needs a sanity test, not an HIV test. My grandmother — Nicholas's mother — called, and said that everyone might think she was an old dingbat, but she watches a lot of television and knows what she is talking about. I can believe that. My father's sister Priscilla wrote a good letter — sound and practical as always.

Sometimes I feel like I'm in a movie — it's very strange.

Meanwhile my sister was busy in London planning a ten-day holiday in the sun for us. My brother and I bought a mug for me in Aberystwyth that afternoon, my special mug so that no-one uses it and gets my horrible, lurking, all-consuming thing. One of the daft things my family doctor said was that, for the moment, it might be best if I had a mug of my own and cutlery and stuff to avoid passing on the infection to anyone else. So I now have a lovely big mug. My mother painted a little red heart with nail varnish on a glass for me. I thought it was completely absurd, so I painted little red hearts on all the glasses and mugs in the house. They are still there – the marked glasses, me and my family.

It was lambing time, but Will, the farmer, still hadn't got any lambs. The idea of telling people was getting more distressing as the time approached for my return to London. The words seemed difficult. I was worried. I didn't think I would be able to take the pressure if people started to tell me to fight it, or to be the first survivor, or to write a book about it.

'Time is running out, you know.'

I headed back to London. I didn't want to face my flatmate. I didn't want to tell anyone until I had spoken to my doctor.

My mother said she would travel the world if it were her. I just want to be safe, to have a home where I can lock myself away and the world out. Somewhere that will always be there for me. Like a security blanket.

I'd like to take my cat to my new home.

Telling my friends

It was Day Ten of the Gulf War. Maybe we were all going to die anyway.

I was diagnosed exactly a week ago. I must surely be heading for some kind of breakdown because everyone keeps offering me counselling. That must mean I need it.

Back in London I have an itchy scalp, and I'm scratching away at it in a kind of self-destructive fury. I am exhausted from being strong for other people and saying things like 'low-level infection' and 'years and years'. But do I believe it? Maybe I can't handle it – but it would be unfair on them to say so. People don't want to know that kind of thing. They want to know that you're tough and can cope. I have always been very private with my feelings, and I still don't know if what I write is really how I feel. Sometimes it feels as if there's no-one inside.

I was looking forward to seeing the specialist on the day after I returned to London. He was the only one who could answer all my questions. All at once — maniacally — I wanted to tell people. If I had not told anyone, it would have been harder for me. I would always have had this deep, dark secret inside me. Whether or not you tell your friends or whether you keep it within the family is not a decision you take, it's taken for you. It's just the natural course of events.

On the Sunday night I telephoned my friend Marielle and asked her to come over. She was just on her way out to meet some of our friends. My sister was with me, and she was not at all sure that I was doing the right thing in telling Marielle, but I felt I should. Marielle was cool and calm about it, listening with her hand on her hip, trying to work it out in her head.

I persuaded them both that I wanted to go and have a drink with the friends in the wine bar. I went up behind a close friend, put my arms around him and told him. I was holding his hands and they just went stone cold. Maybe that was unfair of me. I might have been playing games with my friends — but I needed to know what their reaction would be. I wanted to see it for myself — sometimes it's quite dramatic. We bought several bottles of champagne and talked for a while. It wasn't gloomy or miserable, but I did have the advantage. I had had time to get used to the idea.

It seems strange to me that within my large circle of friends and acquaintances, I am the only one. Maybe there are others and they don't know, or maybe they are not telling. At the end of the day one thing is certain, you're no longer just one of the crowd. On the whole my friends were supportive. I think I probably expected too much of them, but on the whole they came through.

I called Amy, one of my closest friends, and told her on the telephone. She almost didn't blink — it makes you think people don't care, even when you know they do. Maybe people just don't know how to show it. My friend Gary was the same. People carry on regardless. My flatmate Joe didn't need to be told. He put two and two together, poor guy. He told me a story about this friend of his who had died, a story he wouldn't otherwise have told me.

There were obviously different reactions from different people. You could split the crowd in two. One half — those I was with at Westminster (an exclusive private school where I did my A levels) — were very restrained and had great difficulty showing their feelings. That is the way you are taught to behave if you are brought up in that sort of environment. I had some problems with them because they would say inane things — 'any of us might get knocked down by a bus' and so on — to cover up the fact that they didn't know how to react or express what they felt.

The other half – those from Pimlico Comprehensive days and my working life – found it easier. They gave me a lot of support, mainly well-wishing messages. A few days later I made one of my first mistakes, of which I have now made many, I think. I had dinner with an old acquaintance, and I told him. He said, 'I feel terrible for you'. Maybe that was what he meant, but it sounded woefully inadequate. It seemed to me that he didn't feel it himself. If you care, you feel terrible for yourself. Maybe I was too hard on him. The trouble is it's really quite hard to keep control of yourself, and no-one else can do it for you.

One day I returned to my flat to find thirteen messages on the answering machine – people I hadn't seen or spoken to for a while, including relations and family friends. They were all just checking that I was still here and to ask when they were going to see me again. It was kind, but completely exhausting. I felt like I was constantly on parade, presenting myself to people just to prove I hadn't come out in green spots. At times that was depressing. The nicest things of all were the couple of cards and letters I received in the post. It felt like these things were for me alone, the senders didn't expect anything in return. Writing this now, I veer between tears and anger. On the whole, I prefer the anger, you feel less helpless.

These days, doctors can predict illness and diagnose infections before someone is really ill. You have to learn to live with the knowledge. As things stand at present, I would not advise anyone to have the test unless it is strictly necessary. It doesn't help to know. People cannot necessarily handle that knowledge. Government campaigns to encourage people to get tested are strictly for the benefit of modern medicine – naturally the authorities are keen to know how many people are infected. But they are dealing with millions of people, and to the individual the knowledge that you carry the virus can be damaging in itself.

I went to see my specialist in his private room at the Middlesex Hospital. He was patient with me. That first meeting started at three p.m. and I didn't get up to gather my things until four-thirty p.m. I hadn't noticed a minute pass. At no point did he attempt to end the consultation. He talked and I listened. Afterwards, he answered all my questions. He explained to me that if what I had been suffering from earlier was really TB, then as things stood, I was only HIV positive, I didn't have full-blown AIDS. On the other hand, if what I had last year was this other infection, then what I have is an AIDS diagnosis. This was quite a dramatic turn around from the two to four years the lung doctor had given me. Although everything is relative, this had to be good news. But it does raise your hopes when you've already accepted the big one, so maybe I'd rather not.

The specialist said he would find out from the lung doctor whether or not he had got a re-test for the TB. In the way these things work, you tend to believe the worst. I remembered at the time the lung man saying that it was a 'peculiar presentation of TB'. So I immediately assumed that it hadn't been TB at all but that lethal form of pneumonia to which people with AIDS (known in the business as PWAs) seem to succumb.

That day was my last brush with private medicine. My BUPA insurance had just run out, and they wanted me to complete a new application form. Over the past year I had been claiming quite a lot because of the TB, and I would have to say I had never been tested for HIV. So it was onto the National Health.

That evening I went for dinner with two friends, Toby and Ingrid, and their little girl Lotty was there. They must have thought it strange that I wouldn't let her have any food off my plate (maybe they never noticed). But I didn't want them to find out about me, then worry that I might have given something to Lotty. Maybe I'm being ignorant. I don't know.

The next day, I spent a long day shopping with Marielle, a very able shopper, for the truly tropical holiday. My brother had come up with an all-in holiday for my sister and me in Mauritius. If I was going to crack, I'd rather do it lying on a beach somewhere. I was rapidly reaching the point where I was all talked out. I had nothing left, I felt like I'd given all my strength to other people. They seemed to need it more than me, but maybe I didn't keep enough for myself.

The following day it was time for a radical new haircut. At that point, shopping had become my main occupation. If you come home with a new item of clothing, something pretty or sexy, it makes you feel good. Things never looked so bad after a successful day's shopping. Except the bank account, which was taking quite a hammering.

Medical matters

Doctors and dentists have taken on a special significance in my life – I have to learn a new vocabulary. On my return from Mauritius, my specialist doctor told me that he had checked with the lung specialist and the TB test had come out positive, so I didn't have full-blown AIDS.

I was surprised. He is a kind and honest man who makes me laugh and tells me silly stories, and I think he only tells me as much about my condition as I really *want to know. There is never really any bad news. My visits are now monthly and last anything from half an hour to an hour. Originally he had said I wouldn't have to see him more than once every three months, but because I was still taking the TB drugs, I had to see him once a month. Except of course when I up and go.*

In the beginning, every time I went to see him he would tell me about this guy who had been coming to see him for years and was still as fit as a fiddle. He said that most of the research is aimed at keeping the virus under control, rather like diabetes.

At that time, my monthly visits were at the James Pringle House, part of the Middlesex Hospital, the most depressing buildings I have ever entered. Grumpy uninterested staff greet patients at the downstairs reception. The women's Sexually Transmitted Diseases Clinic has a series of cubicles where the women are examined. The walls are painted a dirty colour. The place feels dirty all over.

I'm surprised anyone actually bothers going for treatment at all, considering the indignities we have to suffer. To the doors of several of the cubicles are clipped the charts of the patient inside. On the chart a diagram of the vagina is printed. On it is marked in biro the problem area – vaginal warts and so on. It's hardly dignified. Often the nurses are too busy gossiping about their sex lives to treat the patient until long after the time of the appointment. The only time I am ever seen quickly is if the doctor comes down with me. Maybe I'm being unjust, maybe the nurses are overworked. Whatever the reason, it's not conducive to the patient's peace of mind. You do not leave feeling happy and well.

Every month on these visits, one of the nurses takes a blood sample. Among other things, my doc has to check liver function – the drugs have a tendency to zap that poor little organ – and a full blood-picture is done to cover all eventualities. Every two or three months, he also does a CD4 count – expensive at ninety pounds a go – which checks the level of my white blood cells. A dramatic drop, and I'm in trouble. After the first test, the lab had no record of ever having received my blood sample, and everything had to be done again. The next trip, they lost my X-rays. My chest X-rays are a legacy from the TB – shadows on the lungs and all that. I had them redone and delivered them personally to my doctor's secretary.

The other day, when my doc gave me a quick physical while wearing rubber gloves, I asked him what they protected him from. He laughed and said, 'Nothing really, it's just that it's more pleasant for everyone if I have to do gynaecological checks and under arms. People sometimes don't wash.' And then he patted me without his gloves on to show he wasn't afraid of me. That was sweet, and it made me feel less like I was carrying the plague.

My previous dentist, made aware of my condition, was willing to clean my teeth, but refused to treat me for fillings or any major work. The absurdity is that he cannot know whether some of his patients are infected and don't know, or simply haven't told him. There are rules which govern procedures when dentists treat special patients like me. Additional precautions have to be taken – double gloves, extra-strong disinfectants and so on. Yet we are all potential HIV carriers, and the extra precautions just serve to alienate the patient – encourage us not to reveal our hand. If those who treat me support the campaigns to remove prejudice and ignorance which exists when it comes to AIDS, they should give some thought to this.

My new dentist has his surgery in a little basement room in the dental school. He's young, and on my first visit he introduced himself. He is a sweet-faced jolly young man, and he likes to shake hands before he starts his treatment. Naturally, I asked him why he is doing this kind of work. He said that in the early days, while he was still training, he saw some of his friends suffering from AIDS and he could see that there was going to be a need for this kind of treatment. I always ask people why they are involved in this field – it seems important.

The waiting-room is tiny. It is physically impossible for two people to sit opposite each other – there is not enough room for two pairs of knees. The walls are paper thin, and you can hear the grunts of pain in the surgery with frightening clarity.

On my first visit, the dentist said I had a minor infection on my tongue, and he could give me either this drug or that. 'I think I will give you these tablets to suck because we like to keep these others for when you are ill.' There is never an option. It is always 'when' and not 'if'. They give you no room for doubt. Yet there is always room for hope, isn't there?

It's not all distressing. The dentist thought whatever I had on my tongue was interesting and he wanted to take some photographs to show his students. People don't usually have their tongues photographed. The nurse yanked and the dentist bore down on me with a huge camera only an inch or two away from my face. I defy anyone not to laugh in that situation. Then, of course, the flash didn't go off, and he had to start all over again.

The doc said the first symptom of AIDS is hypochondria. Of course he's absolutely right. Any little twinge and I go into a panic, a drastic decline. It takes patience and reassurance from my sisters and my mother to stop the worry.

My worst fear is and always has been gynaecological treatment. Recently I went to have minor attention. I was terrified, tense and nervous. Tears were welling up in my eyes more from fear than pain. The specialist explained he had opted for a minor treatment rather than a more major one which would produce a lot of bleeding, which is dangerous. For him, not for me. By the time I left his surgery I felt positively dirty, infectious and completely miserable.

I feel this is all wrong. The NHS should be there to care for me, not make me feel like I am demanding something I should be grateful to get and never complain about. There should be more respect for the patient. If there were a more sympathetic approach, patients would recover more quickly and everyone would be happier. How many times do you have to read about miraculous recoveries by people who are kept in comfortable, friendly surroundings and treated with care and affection before someone takes notice and realizes it would save money?

We all respond to affection. My favourite story is one I read in one of those self-help books that you tend to turn to (I think they are subtly planted in my way). It's about a bunch of laboratory rats in which the scientists are trying to induce cancer. Not very nice, I know, but that is not the point. At the end of the experiment all the groups except one had developed the required cancer. The scientists couldn't work out why this one particular group had managed to come through unscathed. They had been kept under identical conditions. Finally, they questioned the lab technician who had been looking after them. He admitted that at feeding times he had taken them out and stroked them for a while. Just that was enough to keep them alive. I love that story. Although I'm still looking for someone to stroke me every time I get fed.

Mind and body. The only time I get religious is when I'm very unhappy. I place myself in God's hands as if I were a baby, and I feel safe.

It seems kind of strange writing my life story at such a tender age. Not presumptuous, just strange. I know that there are some people out there who are like me, and interested in what I have to say and how I feel.

In the early days, everyone was telling me to go to counselling. It wasn't really something I felt the need for, but I went to see one of the resident female counsellors at the James Pringle. My doc was keen for me at least to make contact in case, at some later date, I needed to speak to someone. She said some interesting things. Her advice was to have sex – even one-night stands – and don't tell, but use a condom. Otherwise, tell them and it soon sorts out the men from the boys – you'll find out if someone really loves you or not. To date, no-one has taken that decision, or that risk. As for casual sex, I've never been very good at that anyway.

Even before I went to see this counsellor, I had visited the London Lighthouse which is just down the road from where I live. It wasn't very welcoming – in fact, it was frightening. The three women receptionists at the desk were talking and laughing together. No-one looked up or even paid the slightest attention when I *walked in and approached the desk. I asked them what happened in the building. They looked at me as if I was dim-witted. They said it was a hospice, with a residential floor upstairs. I was embarrassed, mumbled something about the leaflets probably giving details, gathered up a handful and beat a hasty retreat. Subsequently, people have told me the place is more suitable for middle-aged homosexual men. I can well believe that it doesn't cater for young heterosexual women – and to me that smacks of discrimination.*

I also attended a seminar, a kind of positive-thinking group, hosted by a slightly peculiar little man, always smiling, with small naughty eyes. It was held over the weekend in his spacious Fulham flat. The room was packed with pretty young girls. You could see where he was coming from – it's a great deal more fun to help an attractive young lady than it would ever be to help an ugly old man. The seminar seemed to be mainly about people's problems with relationships and trying to sort them out. He was a bit of an amateur psychologist, which can be dangerous. Talking to one of the girls who said her father had died of cancer, he asked her if her father had been an unhappy man. When she replied that he was, our enlightened amateur pronounced that we tend to bring all illnesses on ourselves. That may be his view, but it is not mine. I'm sure he meant no harm, but it made me very angry and I ran for cover.

You can't let this thing take over – you must be the one in control. This was brought home to me sharply one evening when a friend who had been working with one of the AIDS help organizations, took me out for a curry and told me a story he had heard about a patient who went to see his doctor. On his arrival, the doctor expressed surprise at seeing his patient again. The patient took this to mean that the doctor thought he would be dead already. He became hysterical and made himself ill. The doctor merely meant that he didn't think their next appointment was so soon. That seems to embody what it is all about. I have to remember I am still the same person, the only difference is that I have this thing lurking inside me.

I just have to try to believe it. It's the only sensible course.

The danger in reading too much about it is all too clear. It's fine and interesting for the first couple of paragraphs and then you suddenly hit the point at which an article will start talking about the awful things that happen to AIDS 'victims'. You begin to believe that there is a set pattern to what is going to happen to you, that fate has your future mapped out and there is no hope but to prepare yourself for the inevitable.

Does it really have to be inevitable?

FAMILY LIFE

Looking for the source

After that first appointment with my doc, I felt it was time to track down the source of the infection. This didn't seem to be something I desperately needed to do — just something which should be done.

In my saner, calmer moments, I never felt anger towards whoever it was. Although shortly after I first heard, I was walking from my flat towards the Portobello Road, and I thought if anyone spoke to me, be it a stranger or a friend, I was just going to let rip. Luckily I didn't bump into anyone, because I dread to think what might have happened. I was full of fury. But later, I felt no anger.

I began my search. Other people have different attitudes, but I don't think I found it too difficult to call my previous lovers to tell them I had had the test and come out positive.

The first partner I called, I knew I had to let him know quite quickly otherwise it would have filtered back through mutual friends. He was worried and went for the test. My reasons for calling him had been to check that I hadn't passed it on to him; it never occurred to me that he might have infected me until someone suggested it to me. All the time, I had been certain it had been another — a heavy cocaine user. It didn't strike him that I might want to know what his result was, and he didn't call me until he was nudged into it by his former girlfriend who knew I wanted to know — so she had called to tell me he was clear anyway. I was relieved he was OK. I bet he was too.

The next one of my previous partners I tracked down was the coke-head. It took a few calls, and I didn't really stop to think about it, so it didn't make me uncomfortable. Nobody asked me why all of a sudden I wanted the number of someone I hadn't seen for a couple of years. When I found him, he was sweet and said he had had a test already and come out negative.

I have shared a bed with fewer men than I can count on both hands, so the remaining possibilities were fairly limited. As my doc says, it's not as if I had such a great time while catching the virus. Of the only two men of recent years, with one I used a condom (the first and only time, the last time I had sex). London is not that big, and he must have heard about me on the grapevine anyway. The others were a long time ago: one is now married with two children and living in Los Angeles.

That left one other real possibility. It was a bit surprising, because I really did believe the culprit was the coke-head. So now I had to turn my attention to finding him, the last candidate — I shall call him Fred, although that is not his real name, my boyfriend of a few years earlier, although he was more of a

276

regular-irregular lover than a boyfriend. We had separated a few years back, and he had set up home with a girl who made crocheted hats and tops. One evening when I was particularly upset after we had split up, we went out for a drink and he told me she was pregnant and he loved her, so he was staying with her, which upset me even more. When we left the pub and were walking down the street to the tube station, I had turned towards him, talking – and walked smack into a lamppost. That brought me straight back to reality with a very sore face.

Over the years, we occasionally used to meet for a drink. The girlfriend hadn't had the baby, but they were obviously still together. The last time I saw him, we had gone out for lunch and he was talking about going holistic – practising Buddhism, meditation and all that. At that point I was very ill, run down with the undiagnosed TB and still working. Shortly after that I went to the doctor and was told to take time off work.

When I finally returned to my job, I paged Fred. To my surprise he returned my call instantly. I suggested that we meet up for a drink at some point. He said he would call me the following week, and rang off. The strangest thing is that, at the time, what had gone through my head was exactly what I now believe. I imagined he had found out he was HIV positive and thought that I had too, and that was why I was calling him. At the time, I didn't know I was positive myself.

After that, none of the telephone numbers that I had for him produced any response, although I left a good hundred messages on his pager. When I finally got an answer on his home telephone number, it appeared to be a pay phone in the middle of the street. This didn't strike me as too strange, because everything I knew about him led me to believe that if he wanted to avoid everyone (or someone in particular), he would go to great lengths to ensure he couldn't be tracked down. It is likely he has moved – he never stayed in one place for very long.

Fred is from Lagos. Maybe he visited some time in the past decade, and picked up the virus while he was out there. If he had had sex with someone, that would immediately put him in a high-risk category. I don't believe he mainlined drugs, but it's possible he had bisexual tendencies. At the time it was fashionable for people to intimate that they had homosexual relationships, and he had a very unsavoury close male friend at the time. The two of them have fallen out and on the occasions I have run into this friend of his, he claimed they hadn't seen each other for ages. He said he had been up to his house and had bumped into his girlfriend who had tried to throw him off the scent. They were close once, so it seems a shame.

Anyway, it is all speculation. Just because I haven't managed to find him, it doesn't necessarily mean he is the source (I like that word!). I would still very much like to see him, but short of hiring a private detective, there is nothing I can do. All the same, I would like to know. I'm curious. I would like to see whoever it was to find out how they themselves are coping with it. Having not attended any of the therapy groups, I don't know anyone else in my situation, although by the law of averages some of my friends – at least one – must be carrying the virus and remains in blissful ignorance. I now understand the meaning of that expression.

Maybe I'm wrong. Maybe it wasn't Fred. Until I track him down, I can never know.

There is a very pretty chapel at the Middlesex. The walls are covered in mosaic. Every time I go to the hospital for my check-ups, I light a candle for whoever infected me. Maybe the message will reach him and he will contact me.

Living with the virus

Today, for the first time in many, many months, a young man took my fancy – I had butterflies in my tummy. I suppose I've been too wrapped up in morbid thoughts to have had any notions in that direction. The object of my affection probably had no idea (at least I sort of hope he didn't). I dread to think how fast he would run if it had crossed his mind that I was looking at him in anything more than a strictly friendly way. I believe he was actually flirting with me, without really thinking what he was doing. It gave me something to toy with – and I toyed with it for a few days in my diary.

I often think about having children. They are still compiling statistics about infected women giving birth. It looks hopeful. The original batch of figures was compiled for African women, which gave a false picture. The mothers were malnourished and on the whole ill. For Europeans it looks better – as far as I know, women have given birth to children who are not themselves infected. I think the figures are about one in four in favour. But the babies cannot actually be diagnosed for a few years, since the baby is always born with antibodies to the virus which come from the mother's blood. It is only several years later that these disappear and you know whether the child is going to live or die. Infected children die quite quickly, and it would be unbearable to watch a child to whom you had given birth die – knowing that it had never had a chance from the beginning.

I've been doing a lot of mind-travel lately – sudden visions of all the wonderful warm countries like Spain, South America and Africa that are out there waiting for me. I have decided to buy a huge map of the world for my wall so that I can plan my journeys. The only problem is I seem to get stuck in a circle and suddenly everything turns in on itself and I'm in a black hole, unable to get out.

It was on a particularly bad day that I started writing the diary on which this account is based. I was lonely. I felt let down by everyone. It was the first night of two really bad weeks of consistent deep depression.

It was June. It was raining. Whoever coined the phrase 'flaming June' must have been out of their flaming mind. I had le cafard. Apparently last Thursday was black Thursday: the world was meant to end – sharp at three-thirty. All the planets were lined up to make catastrophe. For myself, I wouldn't say Thursday was the worst day of those two weeks – but it certainly wasn't great. By then I believed I knew the meaning of despair.

At the moment, there does seem to be a kind of all-pervading misery hanging over everything. People are depressed, unemployed and single. I might lead the lemmings off the cliff – there seem to be enough people ready to follow me.

It's hard not to lose sight of what you're doing. I found this poem somewhere:

> As I walked by myself
> And I talked to myself,
> Myself said unto me:
> Look to thyself
> Take care of thyself,
> For nobody cares for thee.

That's how I was feeling. It was a Sunday – always a bad day – and I was feeling scared of myself. I am a very strong person – but that can make you very destructive. Sometimes I cannot control what I do. I feel like I'm growing harder, closing myself off from people. The grim weather affects me more than anything else. Sometimes I can't help but be angry and want to find Fred. One always thinks things will be better, that something might hold the key – but it never does. I can feel myself swinging up and down from one extreme to the other – from lethargy to anger. I put a lot of pressure on my mother – too much, maybe.

That day I lunched at the house of my friend Simon's parents. His dad gave me a pink rose which he cut from a bush in the garden, the first rose of summer. It was lovely – I felt a little special.

Friends called me – it helped me through. Amy called. Gary called. They do sometimes call at the right time, say the right things. Rebecca has rung me every day since the blues set in – and it's not so bad after all. That particular day Rebecca was full of her own miseries. Everything is relative. Your problems are only as bad as you let them be – you realize after a while, yours are never the worst.

The other day someone was telling me a story they had heard from America about a woman who had called up her local radio station and said she was HIV positive. She had picked up the virus heterosexually, and she said she was going to sleep with a different guy every night – presumably to get her revenge on the opposite sex. I can imagine that is the kind of thing which spins through your head.

It's incredible how quickly this thing just becomes a part of you, how you learn to live with it. Self-pity and anger don't help you – they simply alienate other people. It sounds terribly smug, but that's the way I see it. It doesn't help to let others know you are handling it well, because they then withdraw the extra support. You can't have it both ways. People will start to treat you normally. They forget about it and load you down with their problems instead. That's when you know life has got back in balance – it makes you feel better. People tend to believe that because what you are dealing with is so enormous, anything that is making them suffer pales into insignificance. But it's not like that. Everyone can only see as far as their own experience, so their problems are just as great as yours and can make them just as unhappy – more so, sometimes.

In the end, people do forget. The other night I was out having dinner with some friends. We were talking about a young girl who had died. She was a heroin addict. It was a strange, confused story about her taking an overdose in her flat, passing out and because she was locked in the flat with her dog for days, the dog started eating her. I asked if she had committed suicide, but the girl replied, 'No. She had AIDS.'

'That's not a reason,' I said. 'Did she get ill?'

She looked me straight in the eyes and said, 'No. You know if you get AIDS you die.'

She knew about me, as did most people around the table. I think they noticed and felt uncomfortable – but she didn't. She does make a habit of saying the first thing that comes into her head without thinking. A few days later, she telephoned me to apologize. She said her sister, who had been at the dinner, had pointed it out to her the following morning. At the time, she had completely forgotten. It's a comforting story, in a way.

It took a long time for people to come up to me and just say hello without that extra hug or squeeze of the arm they give to communicate sympathy. People would give me a tremendously big hello and tell me how great I was looking. I felt like saying, 'It's OK. Just relax. And anyway, how do you expect me to look? I'm not ill. I'm merely carrying around this virus.'

It does work both ways. It has taken me a long time to relax about it myself and accept compliments for what I'm sure they are meant to be – just that I'm looking good at this moment. New haircuts on a regular basis, plenty of shopping and the old George Hamilton tan – year-round because I prefer to spend my time in sunnier climates. I like to see the sun when I look out of the window, not rain.

The key seems to be mind over matter – it stands to reason. When I get depressed, I can almost feel my body going downhill. Body and spirit work together hand in hand.

In the early days when I was first diagnosed I went to see the Westminster school chaplain. I hadn't seen him in years, but I knew he was a kind man and he had looked after the boys. Someone had told me about a boy who had died of AIDS and had been comforted by him, helped through it. I wanted to know what the chaplain had to say. I went to see him one morning – he fitted me in between engagements, after school prayers in the Abbey and before a meeting at the Palace, where he was due to take over as Royal Chaplain. I think I made him nervous – I have a habit of making people nervous. Maybe he felt inadequate as well.

He gave me a cup of coffee in his little bachelor pad just at the back of the Abbey. He seemed fairly ignorant about the whole thing, but then, on the whole, people are. But he gave me his time, which is what I needed. He told me about a former pupil, a boy younger than me, who was a haemophiliac and had picked up the infection from a blood transfusion. One of this boy's parents had died of cancer. I don't know what the timing was: maybe the parent had got ill when they learnt about the child. The boy developed AIDS shortly after the parent died. The son died. It's all linked together – grief brings on illnesses. That's why looking after yourself, mind and body, and maintaining the right attitude is essential. You must look at it all and take the positive, forget the negative. The old story that you might get run over by a bus tomorrow is true enough, however silly it sounds and however much I object to that as a response to my condition. So while you've got your health, keep it that way and enjoy your life as much as you can. It's common sense, after all.

This is easier said than done. But even though you go through the bad times, so does everyone else, so you must enjoy your good times just that little *bit more than everyone else. Enjoy the extra freedom you have – with no constraints; you can do whatever you like, partly because of what you know that others can only guess at, and partly because people are on the whole more tolerant. That sounds a bit spoilt, but you've got to have some advantages over other people in this whole thing.*

Working things out

Sunshine, the key to my life. Nothing looks so gloomy in the sun.

Having exposed myself fully in London, I decided to decamp on my own to a little village in southern Spain. There was no telephone, and the sun shone most days, but above all no-one knew anything about me except what I cared to tell them. Blissful to be ignored.

Spain is the home of feria and fiesta, where life is to be enjoyed. Money is necessary only for survival. Greed is not important, and alegria – being happy – is what matters. Enjoy your work, or don't do it. I have tripped myself up on more than one occasion. Coming as I do from a super-competitive environment, multi-media-mad London, to a small village in the hills of Almeria, it is odd to find that no-one is impressed or even interested in what I do. They accept the person and ignore the rest.

There is another side to the story, of course. For all Barcelona's hosting of the Olympics, Seville's Expo and Madrid's claims to be the City of Culture, the citizens of Spain are still just crawling into the twentieth century. They have a serious heroin problem in the country at the moment and many of the bourgeoisie are up in arms about it.

With a backward mentality comes ignorance and prejudice. The other day, there was a story in the local newspaper about a little girl from a nearby town whose mother, a junkie, had AIDS. The mother was in prison and had the child in with her, and one day for no apparent reason she stuck the needle of the syringe into her daughter, passing on the virus. The mother has since died, and instead of the child's plight tugging at the heart strings, the matrons of Spain have turned against her. The child could not go to the local school – other parents threatened to boycott it and remove their children. In an attempt to get them to change their minds, the little girl's grandmother (with whom she was living) appealed to the national AIDS commission to send letters to parents and teachers of the school to reassure them that no-one had ever been infected at school. It wasn't enough, and the child had to be educated at home by a private tutor. It must be pretty hard for a six-year-old to hear the taunts: 'You're going to die. Don't touch us, or we'll die too.' For the children taught those things, such ignorance doesn't bode well for a caring humanity.

I haven't had to face that kind of prejudice in my own life. Although of course I am aware that, as things stand, I am not allowed to enter the United States – an absurd situation since the number of people moving in and out of the country who are infected and do not know or simply don't admit it must be enormous. It is doubly ridiculous in a country that prides itself above all on the freedom of the individual. I was delighted to hear the other day that a conference on AIDS due to be held recently in the US was moved elsewhere as a protest.

I am guilty of prejudice myself – and I should know the reality. If I hear that someone (not obviously homosexual) is HIV positive, I assume that they are either promiscuous or mainline drugs. Take Tina Chow, the glamorous wife of a famous restaurateur; I was surprised to read a couple of months ago a short piece in a national newspaper saying she had died of AIDS. Since she was an incredibly beautiful, elegant woman, I immediately assumed that, as a model living in the fast lane, she was promiscuous and probably mainlined drugs. These assumptions were not justified: I found out a bit about the background to her illness only recently from a piece in Vanity Fair magazine.

There is still a tremendous amount of ignorance about the whole thing. Before I was diagnosed myself, when I first saw the pictures of Princess Diana holding the hands of an AIDS patient (I hate the word 'victim'), I remember thinking, 'Oh – so it's all right to touch them, then.' I'm no royalist – not by a long chalk – but I do know those pictures affected my own attitude, and God knows how many others saw the photographs and thought the same thing. I truly believe that single thing did more to help people like me than anything else anyone has ever done.

We are confronted almost daily with absurd comments in the newspapers. Columnists enquire why we are spending money trying to find a cure for this disease when it will die out of its own accord if everyone uses a condom. For sure it will die out. It kills. But how would you feel if it was your daughter who had the infection? Sometimes I wonder how the Daily Mail, my previous employer, would react if they knew about me. I read in the Mail on Sunday that pompous old fool, John Junor, complaining about the time Princess Diana had spent at the bedside of a man who had died of AIDS. 'Does she want to go down in history as the patron saint of sodomists?' he asked. It made me want to cry. I am no sodomist, Mr Junor.

To this day we haven't had a 'straight' celebrity come out and admit to having AIDS. Rock Hudson was a homosexual, and because of his fame his death shocked a lot of people, but basically it didn't change their attitude to the disease. We need a famous woman, a non-drug user, someone who cannot be explained away, to come out with it.

There was a time when rumours were spreading about Madonna in the media world in which I moved. If it were true, it would do a great deal of good. People think it is somehow the wages of sin – that those who get it deserve it. But, as I pointed out before, I have never been promiscuous, nor have I taken hard drugs. We must be many in the world. Perhaps this is why I declared myself – why I came out. It shocked everyone that knew me. To them, it didn't seem fair. But life is not fair – we all know that. The only thing I would say is it seems most of us who carry this thing are not really the right ones.

What's for sure is that someone made a mistake when they chose me.

CHAPTER TWENTY-THREE

Of love and angels

'Her mind was lithe and quick and muscular as a leopard.
Passion, tenderness and pain were all equally unable to disarm
it. It scented the first whiff of cant or slush; then sprang, and
knocked you over before you knew what was happening. How
many bubbles of mine she pricked!'

C.S. Lewis*

THIS IS THE END OF FRANCESCA'S STORY, THE MOMENT OF COLLISION,
that part of it which I must tell because she is no longer here to tell it
for herself. It took only a week, that final gathering of the spirit which
was and is hers alone.

Just as she offered her own thoughts in the hope that it might help

*Remembering his wife in *A Grief Observed*.

others, this is my own attempt to define the moment when the mortal debris releases the immortal soul.

Even so, I can only tell what I know to be true for myself. Francesca's knowledge is her own, and she keeps it still.

As she explains in the previous chapter, in her own words, the vulnerability of her immune system was discovered after a bout of TB picked up on a climbing trip in the Himalayas with her brother and her father.

The thing had a terrible logic to it. She was always the brightest and the best – so it was right, if such a thing can ever have a rightness, that her light should be extinguished in that great darkness.

She knew what the consequences must be of the coldly clinical diagnosis. Two to four years. With fair weather and a following wind, she was to have her four.

Her sister Poppy said that it was Francesca's secret that she was going to die. This was not to say that she did not reach out for love and comfort when she understood that her particular star was set on a collision course with what is defined as the great plague of our time.

We could not avoid the knowledge – but still we had hope. There is never a day when the newspapers do not report some new breakthrough in treatment, when some celebrity is not hosting yet another benefit to raise money for the care of its 'victims'.

Yet Francesca was no victim. There was no blame to be apportioned, no dark secret to be hidden, no secret vices of which others did not know for which she might expect to pay a price. Knowing the inevitable, she made certain that everyone who knew and loved her understood perfectly what had happened to her – and then she set the matter aside and went about reorganizing her life.

Even as a small child, she had always known exactly what she wished and needed. At the time of the diagnosis, she was working for the *Daily Mail*, putting her name to a regular shopping column in the 'Femail' section. There were those among her friends and family – myself included – who thought she should carry on with the journalism, that it would divert her and that the money would be useful.

Fran was adamant. 'Life's too short to write about shopping.'

Hearing her decision, we had a practical problem on our hands. The earnings of writers do not come regularly or plentifully. But we made the necessary arrangements so that she had a modest income which would keep her independent of state hand-outs. There was no room in her life for hostages to fortune, for form-filling beyond what was necessary for her medical care. And, since she was certainly capable of quarrelling ferociously with both of us, it had to be paid in such a way that we couldn't stop it even if we wanted to.

First came a holiday in the sun with her sister Poppy – her brother's gift. It was February, and the choice had to be the southern hemisphere. They chose Mauritius, in the Indian Ocean – looking for music and sunshine.

Back in Britain, the summer came, and with it, more of the healing sunshine. All through that first autumn after the diagnosis, she hid out in a hill village in Andalusia, gathering strength from her memories of childhood, reading and walking and taking comfort from the familiarity of people, language, landscape. It was here that she explored the meaning of what had happened to her. On her return, she wrote her own account of her feelings.

And then she came back to us at our farmhouse in Wales, and in the beauty of these upland valleys she left her diaries behind, and with it her desire to communicate through the written word.

Instead she began to paint. With a degree in biology and a career as a journalist behind her, this might not seem the obvious choice of self-expression. Yet it was natural enough. As a family we have always expected to be able to do everything – writing, painting, performing, whatever is necessary to communicate our feelings.

The use of brush and paint on canvas came easily to her. For the first time in her life she had found something which truly engaged her heart and soul. Those first paintings were only of herself. In a few weeks she produced more than a dozen self-portraits, head and shoulders only, wearing different clothes and with different backgrounds. All were painted with a glowing intensity, as if by capturing the living image she could fix her understanding of her own existence.

Now she was ready for her new life – and this time she had nothing to explain to anyone. She took the portraits to an art school, the Byam Shaw in London, where I had once studied, apologized for her lack of portfolio, and told the interviewers that she was ready for admittance. Faced with so single-minded a passion as her paintings displayed, they had no choice but to agree. At the beginning of term, she heard that she had been awarded a scholarship.

She borrowed her brother's empty flat in Stockwell – by now his employers had moved him to New York – and set to work to learn her chosen trade. From then until some three years later, when she fell prey to a rare cancer of the blood, her choice and her talent engaged her completely. At school she was disciplined and vigorous. She needed and soon acquired the skills to communicate her feelings, and in the long holidays she put what she had learnt to practical purpose.

From that moment on, she painted whenever and wherever she found herself. It was her choice to travel whenever she had the chance – and if her friends or family were making a trip, she would pack her paints and buy or beg a ticket – usually from her brother, the source of all such life-enhancing expenditure. She was cheerfully decisive. 'Have sketchbook, will travel. I'll go wherever I'm wanted.'

The travels bore glorious fruit. The best things she made, the most natural and beautiful, might be traced back to her memories of childhood: swiftly graceful oil-crayon sketches of the bullfights she went to with her father and brother. Pamplona for the bull-running, the great Roman arena of Arles for the Easter fights, the ring at Béziers for the annual festival. There was something about that confrontation with death in the ring which reached into her soul.

In between, she holidayed in Switzerland and came home to paint huge white snowscapes, vast and empty, with brooding forests. Cuba and Jamaica produced joyous jungle paintings, garlands of flowers, a passion for Gauguin and Rousseau. In Provence, where we borrowed a glorious house for a long spring sojourn, she painted the same sun-drenched landscapes which had once delighted Cézanne and Van Gogh.

It was in the summer after her second year at college that the cancer crept up on her. We had not expected it, and did not even recognize it when it came. She and I – and her sister Honey who kept her company all through that time – only knew that she was weaker, her limbs less agile, that there was an ache in her bones and she couldn't manage to do the things she had once done. We hoped that it was nothing, that soon all would be well.

We had scheduled our annual holiday in the Hebrides. No longer owning our little cottage, we rented a house near my father-in-law – familiar territory in which we had pitched camp many times before.

Fran drove up with her friend Pete – comfortably cocooned in his Mercedes. Honey drove up with me. Nicholas arrived from an appointment in Edinburgh, and Poppy, working on a film in Fort William, crossed over for Sunday lunch. Cas had fallen into the habit of telephoning regularly from New York at the weekends, so we did not feel depleted.

So the gathering was no different from many such gatherings, except that this time Fran was always a little tired. We walked in the sunshine. She had found a lump, a tumour, in her breast. We returned to St Thomas's. She was assigned to the cancer ward. The doctors watched her for a week, and then the surgeons operated. The operation was a success. The tumour was analysed, pronounced benign.

'A storm in a B-cup,' said Fran. Reassured and knowing that Honey was there for her, I left for a working week in Morocco. There was Nicholas to take over the hospital duties. In the aftermath of the operation, scans were arranged, discussions held, tests made. Wandering cells were discovered elsewhere – a shadow, nothing more. Malignant, perhaps. The hospital offered a little hope, a little treatment, talked of chemotherapy when she recovered her strength, prescribed a three-week course of steroids. We took courage – such drugs could not be dangerous. Athletes take them to increase their strength.

It is November 1994. November is the worst of months for the old and the sick. Dark days, long nights. We are in Wales again. Three weeks pass. We do not yet understand that this is already the end. By day, we walk in the woods, along the broad track which crosses the marshland. We rake and burn the leaves of autumn, light bonfires. Here is home – good food, blazing fires, her cat for comfort.

Francesca understands what the rest of us do not. She reads the signs and holds her peace. Her body is already betraying her, there is a warning in the broken sleep, in those strange dips and peaks of temperature which characterize her illness. She takes telephone calls from her friends, speaks to her sisters, her brother – she is cheerful, inconsequential, nothing to worry her long-distance communicators. Wales is a haven – five hours from the big city, we fear no casual visitors. By the end of these three weeks, she is bird-thin, weak as a kitten.

Monday. We return to London – hospital appointments are scheduled. Even then no-one knows anything for sure. More tests – for what? 'Something else to kill me.'

Cartoon-crazy images survive. Don't drink, don't dance, don't smoke. My Lady Nicotine brings comfort. There is laughter to defeat fear.

A terrible journey to hospital – stomach churning, the cancer has spread to her liver, her kidneys, her body is a minefield. I have a mobile phone in the car to call for assistance. I call the house doctor we trust, asking her to meet us with a wheelchair by the emergency entrance. A hearse blocks passage, the driver vanished. The car-park attendant swears at us, a Cerberus guarding the gates of Hades. I have entered the wrong channel, broken rules. Two mini-cab ambulance drivers, watching the diversion, collide. Mayhem rules. Recriminations reverberate through the rain.

I am unmoved, immovable. My daughter is dying, the world can go hang. She reaches sanctuary. She waves merrily from her wheelchair. The system bends, breaks. Ridiculously, I am admitted free to the consultant's car park. Passers-by marvel. No-one has ever done such a thing before.

T-cell melanoma is the name of the cancer, and its progress is so fast, so all-consuming, that it seemed impossible that it could be real. Not even the specialists at St Thomas's have any notion of its speed. In the young and vigorous it is known to travel more quickly than in the old and feeble. They are most at risk who are well-nourished, who daily renew their cells on which the cancer feeds. All this we discover later. Meanwhile, the specialists follow timetables, take samples, grow cultures.

Wheelchair-bound, tea-sipping, we take our place in the queue for the cancer doctors – monarchs of this shadowy glen. Beside my angular daughter perches a trainee specialist, plump as a partridge, his accent thick as chickpea soup. He tells us her raging scarlet skin is a reversible condition, drug-induced, no more. We nod politely, relieved and credulous. We believe in the knowledge of medical men. At this moment we would accept the reassurances of the devil himself. Instead we are to await the opinion of The Specialist. He takes in the situation at a glance, retreats: in this case cancer is but a scratch on the paintwork of the *Titanic*. He vanishes to more treatable bedsides.

Poppy arrives. We do not know it yet, but we are already complete. There is a balance to our trilogy. We form a single organism, three-sided for strength. This is to be ours for the dark time to come.

We wheel ourselves back to the day ward where the nurses bustle. Francesca's regular doctor, the kindly HIV specialist who has cared for her these past four years, greets us warily. We feel his anxiety, his sense of defeat. We are walking wounded, soon to be out of his care. Later that evening, the house doctor we trust finds us a bed. The first circle of the *Inferno* perhaps, where we may drift with the other lost souls. Not so: a small side ward welcomes us.

Yet all the while, we are moving towards the rapids. Beyond, unseen, the waterfall roars. We tumble downwards, free falling. The precipice offers no handhold. Rocks tear flesh. Beneath, a fathomless pool.

Francesca sends us home each evening. 'Off you go, sweetnesses. Sleep well. No man-with-a-sickle tonight.'

By day, we are three in my daughter's space, in her bubble of love and angels. Poppy makes circles on her sister's forehead with her finger. Touches hands.

Francesca's body burns. Her body is weak as a newborn baby, her muscles useless. Yet her mind is strong and sharp, her beauty glows. Nicholas, knowing we need him but unable to find his way through the wall of her bubble, patrols the perimeters.

Thursday. The houseman appears. He is Indian, or maybe Pakistani. We feel his detachment, his curiosity, his pride. He is the right-hand man of The Consultant into whose empire Francesca has been admitted. We have been listening to *Bhowani Junction* on tape. Francesca christens him Mister Govindaswami, half-remembered as the all-powerful instigator of Indian insurrection. She has never been awed by authority at the best of times, still less at these.

This new doctor is young and ambitious. He has research to prepare, a career to carve, boxes to tick. Francesca is courteous, considerate – she too has been a student of medical matters. He wants answers which fit his questions. She has no time for word-bending. He has printed words to define her pain – is it sharp, or dull, or stabbing, or bruising? Patience, she says. There is discomfort certainly, but not the pain that he seeks. She talks of aching limbs, a recalcitrant digestive system, an ache behind her eyes. Her vocabulary is rounded, offering unsuitable pegs for rectangular holes. She searches for truth, he for unticked boxes.

It is Friday, and still we tumble downwards. Her little room has grime-streaked windows, a view of Big Ben, the Houses of Parliament. The room fills with flowers – messages tucked among pink roses, white carnations, tiny yellow autumn narcissi.

Three white-coated students appear at our door. They are two silent young women and a nervous young man. The young man is the spokesman. He is yellow-haired, bespectacled, earnest – University Challenge meets Emergency Ward Ten. The girls are mice, submissive.

I am impatient, but Francesca beckons them in. This is a teaching hospital, she is willing to accept their curiosity. They put their questions to her, invasive, insulting to my ears. Serene in her dignity, she answers all with thoughtful care.

At the end: 'Do you want to specialize in my disease?'

A nervous laugh and a shake of the head.

Fran smiles gently. 'How wise.'

We have a wheelchair. She can still sit upright – tomorrow it will be impossible. But for today, we whirl round the hospital, trailing the drip on a mobile coat stand, scaring the visitors, shopping. She is hungry for shopping – like a passionate reader faced with nothing but the cornflakes packet at breakfast. We acquire newspapers and magazines, tissues, scented soaps. We are like wild-haired pilgrims scouring the markets for trinkets.

Back in the ward, the dermatologists want photographs for their records. We are flattered. At least we have something they need. We wait three hours. Four hours. A porter and a chair appear. Francesca selects Poppy for company. I am despatched for a coffee break. 'Get a life, mother.'

We all three return to the room simultaneously. Poppy is wheeling the chair with the coat-stand drip wedged beneath it. She has abandoned the porter to his mobile phone. The trip had turned into black farce – the photographers were out to lunch. The sign on the door read, 'Back in ten minutes.' Francesca, says her sister, did not have ten minutes in her. Staff nurse is sent to remonstrate with us. We will get no medicine, no treatment, until we follow the rules.

Rules only apply on weekdays. Friday afternoon is the start of the weekend. Wards empty, the specialists, chemists, photographers, go home. The vast hospital drifts rudderless, the *Marie Céleste* with a skeleton crew. Agency nurses man the HIV ward – the plague waits for no man. We have lost our small identity, our computerized notes, our box-ticking housemen, our trio of students.

Saturday passes multi-layered – tiny meals, sips of water, news read from the papers, the bustle of the nurses. There are vanilla-scented strengthening drinks to be sucked through a straw. Such things are expensive, kept in a locked-up fridge – they have street value. Fran struggles to empty a single carton. She must have seven a day. We watch the lottery on television. We have no numbers to check. Poppy says, 'Never mind. I'll buy you a ticket next week. Win a million.' Fran smiles. 'Not necessary, sweetness. Next Saturday I'll be in the Caribbean.'

Her father appears, struggling for cheerfulness. It is his chosen role to bring us diversion, widen horizons. He is to chair the launch of the new Wilderness Trust at the Royal Geographical Society. Sir Laurens van der Post is to be the star. He has attended a meeting at the Ministry of Defence – a climbing expedition is planned for the Himalayas.

Fran glows palely from her bed. 'Speed it up, Dad. I'll come too.'

Our room is all our own now. We have draped the chairs with brightly coloured stuffs. The television rumbles in a corner – a plaque proclaims it a gift from the Friends of St Thomas's. God bless the Friends, but they might have provided a remote control. We watch a panel game on which celebrities make jokes. It is AIDS Awareness Week, and we notice red ribbons on every lapel. All but Ian Hislop, editor of *Private Eye*, who wears a large white L. We hope it is for Learner: 'Bless him,' says Fran. She does not approve of red ribbons. Those who care, care anyway.

All Sunday long, through the soot-streaked window, across the wintry Thames, flicker the lighted windows of the Mother of Parliaments. The sparkle reflects in the river beneath. Time for a story – something familiar. Oscar Wilde's *The Little Prince*. Fairy stories should have happy endings. This one is unbearably sad.

It is very busy, this physical hospital world. Each night we are worn out with the hustle. Decisions must be taken about what is to be brought for breakfast, for lunch, for tea, for dinner. Roast beef and Yorkshire pudding, shepherd's pie, side dishes of jelly and yoghurt. Trays are brought and removed untouched. We talk of Chinese take-aways, pizzas from her favourite bakery, we read recipes in glossy magazines – chocolate truffles, caramel baskets with vanilla ice-cream. Poppy is despatched to search the canteen for baked potatoes with cheese, chips with tomato sauce. We steal space for reheating the chosen delicacies in the nurses' microwave. Forbidden, but stolen just the same.

Francesca pecks at our offerings, smiling encouragement. 'The mind is willing, my sweets – but the body— ' This is part of the game, the game which protects her secret.

We are busy as bees under Fran's direction. We settle down together in this small world, this bubble of my daughter's making. There are angels here. We feel them all around us. We bring nothing into this bubble but ourselves, no mathematics or chemistry or poetry. There is no room for sentiment, or tears, or doubt.

Beyond our bubble, out in the corridor, we have visitors. Poppy or I go out to greet them, familiar faces drawn and anxious. Arms thrust sheaves of lilies tall as palm trees. Fran will not see these friends, but her touch is light for them, for those she loves, 'Say to Joe, come back later – tell him he knows how moody I can be. Tell Pete he'll soon be on the pizza run.'

Although we have raised no alarm, the word has spread. But Fran will have none of it – for now. Now is to be no wake, no all-night vigil. We mean no exclusion. We belong to each other. It won't last long. That at least we understand.

The *Marie Céleste* drifts on. The weekend crew is overworked, underpaid, regulation-hemmed, computer-screened. Reality fades. I buttonhole a nurse, explain what we need for my daughter's comfort. The pillows to ease her breathing, the creams to soothe her skin, the aspirin to bring down her soaring temperatures. I am impatient, a mother protecting her child. I fail.

Poppy leaves the bedside and makes a bridge: 'You don't know my sister, and you don't know us, but let me tell you so that you can help us.' She sees herself in these young women – understands their bewilderment. Hearing her, they are gentle with us, and kind. They no longer glare as we pass, but break rules for us. They give her soothing cream baths, a soft bed which will move as she turns. They speak gently, talk of special diets and strengthening supplements.

In the neighbouring ward, a Nigerian family attends a young boy. Sombre black faces throng the empty spaces. By evening, there is a choir, a priest, a knot of small children, be-ribboned, Sunday-bested. We watch the little faces through a narrow gap in our lowered blind. Innocent faces, bewildered by things they do not understand, nor as yet do we.

Small things divert. We find laughter in absurdity, in the unpredictability of our situation, in the curiousness of the half-world we share. In the Albanian cleaning lady, tiny and angry and buzzing like a wasp, who pushes a threadbare mop around our debris. In the staff nurse, upright and formal, who takes an anarchic pair of scissors to the string which had prevented the sunblind from descending. In a pretty Indian girl from down the corridor who persuades Nicholas to bring her back an order of Peking duck with pancakes from the Chinese restaurant. At the cashpoint, neither mine nor Poppy's cards will yield the necessary. So we use Fran's, absurdly the only one of us with a reliable income.

But beneath it all, something new. Francesca is making pictures in her mind. Words define the images. The pictures are for Poppy – some for us both. They are very simple, very primitive – images drawn in sand at the edge of the ocean.

Francesca shuts her eyes. 'We are in a garden. I see two women on a swing. Between them, a little girl, smiling.'

Later as night draws down, a darker image, most poignant. 'Another picture. I see two mountains with a rope stretched across. There's a man on the rope, but the rope is weak and dips in the middle. He may not make it to the other side.'

Next morning, an exchange between the two sisters: 'Another picture for you, Poppy. I see you holding out a green box to me. Inside is a silver box.' Hopefully from Pops, 'Am I giving it to you, Fran?' Confidently, the reply from her sister, 'No. You are *showing* it to me.'

And then again: 'Poppy, I see you with your head bowed; you are sad and bewildered. There are spirits all around.' Gently Poppy asks, 'Are you a spirit, Fran?' Impatiently the answer comes, 'No. *You* are the spirit.'

The weekend-duty houseman slides in. He is fresh from medical school, young and green. He has a list of questions – all have been asked before, but no-one can read anyone else's handwriting. Name, age, sex, symptoms, pain on a scale of one to ten. Absurdly to us, there is a box to confirm that the family is 'Aware'.

Monday comes. We have been here now for five long days. We have not yet caught sight of The Consultant into whose care my daughter is given. He is a busy man, The Consultant, other hospitals share his brilliance. He reads the notes before entering – we hear his murmurings beyond the door, the restless shifting of the white coats. He is tall, well-tailored, a dandy. The nurses flutter.

The Consultant needs to be alone with the patient in bed fifteen. It is a courtesy that he remembers my daughter's name, even if only briefly, so that he may greet her. This is the nameless ward, its turnover swift – Abandon hope, all ye who enter here. But now, at this moment on a Monday morning, Francesca belongs to him, and he to her. We, the Aware Family of Bed Fifteen, sit on a bench by the triple rank of lifts. There is no waiting-room for families, no space for us in this vast ship of dreams. Hope and despair are in other hands than ours.

We have no notion of time, only of its passage. The Consultant strides towards us at last. Busy as he is, he scribbles notes. A vacant room beckons. The door says, 'Strictly Private, Staff Only!'

'We won't be disturbed. One has to be decisive.' We are privileged. We know we should be grateful.

The room is not designed for interviews. Medical stores, sterilizing ovens line the room. Shelves are loaded with the now-familiar paraphernalia of bedpans, drip bags, boxes of surgical gloves, disposable masks, plastic aprons. In the centre, a table and chairs.

'You must be anxious to know who I am. I am The Consultant in charge of the patient's treatment.' He raises eloquent eyebrows at Poppy. Grown-up talk, say the eyebrows. Siblings excluded.

Nicholas's reply is swift. 'Poppy is almost Francesca's twin. She is the best means of communication with her sister.'

The Consultant sighs, shuffles papers. He has a speech to deliver. It defines the role of doctors, patients, families – Aware and Otherwise. It is a good speech, an adaptable speech. It has been spoken a thousand times to a thousand families. So that we will understand him more clearly, he compares himself to the consultant in a television hospital drama. 'Think of me as the man in the white coat who makes the ward rounds in *Casualty*.'

We apologize. None of us watches television at that time of the evening. He adapts. Perhaps we read books, are concerned with schooling. 'Let's say I'm a bit like the headmaster. I am in charge of the other teachers. My business is to listen to all the experts and make a decision based on their opinions. I am here to protect the patient's interests, to decide what is best for her. If all these busy people can find a window, we shall hold our meeting next Wednesday.'

He talks on. We listen. Life or death in his hands.

'My patient is considering the possibilities of the options we might offer.'

What options? Nicholas enquires.

'Her team will decide. They will communicate their decisions to me. I will confer with the patient.'

He speaks of choices. Chemotherapy. Curative or gentle.

Poppy, slumbering until now, wakes up. '*Gentle* chemotherapy?' Later she tells me she thought it a euphemism for painkillers. Any painkillers. Opium, heroin, pethidine, send for Nurse Beverley Allitt, that one-woman Reaper jailed for bringing death to the wards. Every hospital should have one. Dear Lord, such grim humour.

But no. The choice is blacker by far. Noxious drugs in one strong blast, or noxious drugs in small and regular doses. We do not need to be told of the side-effects. No need to explain the sickness, the weakening of the body's defences, the baldness. Knowing this, Fran has already had her hair cut short like a boy's. 'Halfway there already.' We have already collected a prescription for the wig-maker – it's cheaper on the Health.

The Consultant shifts uneasily. 'And now, if there's anything, anything at all. Such an anxious time for all of you. You must be full of questions.'

For the first time, I meet his gaze. We are in the country of the blind. I see no one-eyed king.

'No thank you,' I reply.

The eyebrows arch. 'I must tell you I had a long and useful talk with—' he glances at his notes – 'Francesca. And there are certain things she has told me which might hurt you.'

The interview is nearly over.

'Tell us,' says Poppy.

'She needs time to be alone. To work things out for herself without interruption,' he is frantically improvising, he is lying. 'Without – her family.'

'We understand.' Poppy's blue eyes blaze. 'We understand, my sister's Consultant, that your name is written above my sister's bed – but don't ever try to deceive us. Don't try to pretend – even to *hint* – that you know something about my sister which you are keeping from us.'

The Consultant seems startled by her passion.

Poppy decides to help him. I marvel at her. In this, she is far more generous than me. She tells him about her sister's pictures. She tells him that Francesca is very intelligent, very determined, very sure of what she needs and wants. She tells him her sister has a secret which she is keeping from her family and her friends. Her secret is her approaching death. She has strength only for her own preparations, certainly not for ours. We – and he – must respect this.

She explains that this brings a problem. We don't know if we can be strong enough for long enough. She fears that we, her people, may lose our nerve, or her sister will get frightened, or there will be pain. For this we need the hospital's help – and we need to know that that help will be there.

The Consultant's voice is smooth. 'The patient's interests and those of her family do not always coincide.'

We hear him loud and clear. He invokes regulations, ethics, rules. Poppy will have none of it. 'Rules do not apply to us.'

The Consultant's eyebrows seek support from Nicholas.

I rise, walk to the door. 'Please talk to my husband. He understands these things better than us.'

Poppy follows immediately. Behind us, we learn later, the great doctor backs out of the room almost before Nicholas can address a word to him. We have scared him half to death.

We hurry back into Francesca's one-room kingdom. She greets us cheerfully. The light hurts her eyes – she is wearing a white bandana to shade them. She questions us about the interview. We tell her. She nods her understanding. 'Up to a point.' She taps the chair beside her bed.

'Sit here, Ma. Don't move. Send Nicholas and Pops away for the afternoon. Get a life.'

She pauses. *Get a life* is her usual instruction when she thinks she is being too hard on us. 'Poppy, be back here at seven. You can go then, Ma, and play. Nicholas looks lost. He's your man. He needs to know you love him.'

We breathe again. Fran rules her space. The dragon who is Her Consultant slinks away.

The afternoon passes.

We keep good company, my daughter and I, and busy. There is cream to smooth on her raging skin, drops to put in her eyes to relieve the ache, a new nightie to lay out and admire, pure and white and embroidered with pearly beads. We talk of gentle things: of Christmas to come; of Honey and her Indian adventures, her latest postcard from Thailand; of the possibility that Caspar might drop in from New York. Fran will countenance no thoughts of emergency – but I know, and so does she, that her brother is already on his way. Nicholas is searching for Honey, swallowed without trace in the islands of the Indian Ocean.

It is time and past time for the whole clan to gather.

Poppy returns for the evening's vigil. Afterwards she tells me that she and her sister talked little. No need for words, they shared a companionable sweet silence. In my mind's eye I see the two sisters dreaming, dozing, drifting together through the dusk of that last night.

Tuesday dawns. I wake at seven in our borrowed flat. I telephone the ward sister. Francesca has had trouble breathing, she had to have oxygen. I leave immediately. Cas is due in to Heathrow at eight, and Nicholas will have to wait to bring him down to the hospital. In the car, I telephone Poppy. She, too, is on her way.

Nine o'clock. The three of us once again in Francesca's bubble of love and angels. She is yellow now, yellow as mustard, her features angular, her breathing laboured. Her eyes are luminous and dark – her beauty shines from these bright windows.

Her brother is at the door, and her father. She welcomes them in. Her brother loves her, and she him. Her face lights with happiness, the two dark heads, brother and sister, bend together and murmur. I leave briefly. She is not mine to guard – she belongs to us all.

Doctors and nurses bustle, The Consultant lurks. I take my place beside my daughter again, her sister guarding her flank. We are quiet now, and peaceful. Her voice is so low that only Poppy hears it.

'Have you packed my bag?'

'Yes,' Poppy answers. 'Some new things too. Special things you like, for you to take.'

'Good,' Francesca says. 'Now dress me in my white shirt – the pretty one with the frills.'

'I've done it. Let me do up the buttons.' Poppy's small hand moves down the covering sheet, her fingers tender, making the movements as if it were true.

'And my new white skirt.'

'You're wearing it.'

Smiling, Francesca smooths her coverings.

A brief flurry follows when Poppy confronts The Consultant. Worried that her sister may find pain, her blue eyes relentless, Poppy demands that the appropriate drugs are to hand. Five minutes later, a young nurse comes in. She whispers we have all that we need outside the door.

Francesca has no such preoccupations. She is supremely gentle, loving, marvellously calm.

'Tell me where we're going,' she whispers.

We talk softly of sand and sunshine, of sea and soft breezes. Poppy's finger-circles soothe her forehead.

Francesca's body is still, her skin bruised blue, her face tranquil. She says, 'Is it far?'

We reply, 'Not very far. Not far at all.'

She turns her body to me, small as a child. She comes into my arms. I bend over her, shielding her with my body. My arms are strong around her frailty. Four years ago, when we first knew of what was to come, she sent me a postcard. On the reverse were written three words, 'I love you.' The picture was a Leonardo pencil sketch, a mother with her daughter, head resting on lap, tender in each other's arms.

My strength flows into her, linked through me to her sister by touch. She holds tight to my body, an infant at the breast. Strength flows through us like a current. Her hands reach up to my face, pulling the life-force she needs for her journey, drawing the breath from my lips. Her body is cold as ice – not a dead thing, but a living cold which freezes all it touches. But at the core I feel the burning flame, as if all the warmth in that brief life is sucked into a single red-hot core.

Her breathing calms. Her sister's litany of love is in her ears, my strength within her. I rock her in my arms. 'Sweet baby, my baby, my baby, my baby.' I am carrying her now, cradled in her cloud of love and angels. Here is no dark river, no tumbling waters, no fathomless pool. We move together towards that far shore. The breeze on our cheeks is soft and sweet.

As yet I have no tears – Francesca would not have permitted such sorrow in her presence. A phrase from Virgil, a clumsy translation from school days, comes to mind. Odysseus on his journeyings, musing on the certainty of death: '*Sunt lacrimae rerum* – there are tears in the nature of things, but mortal things touch the mind.'

Afterwards, I cannot tell the exact moment when her breathing stops, when her spirit leaves her body. I only know that I am permitted to carry her across, to give her into gentler arms than mine, that there is not a single instant when she is alone. No time of fear, or pain, or loss.

This for comfort, for hope, for peace – my daughter, my sweet child. Light candles for her spirit, her bravery, her tenderness. At the end, in that moment of final triumph, was nothing left but joy.

CHAPTER TWENTY-FOUR

Facing the future

'And while the customs slept
I crossed to safety,
And what I would not part with
I have kept.'

Robert Frost (1874–1963)

BELOVED FRAN WAS LAID TO REST IN THE LITTLE CHURCHYARD AT Ripe in Sussex, near her paternal grandmother's house, where she spent the first Christmas of her life.

In a tiny chapel nearby, she, her sisters and brother were privately confirmed by the monk, Peter Ball, then the Bishop of Lewes. The view from the churchyard is of the Downs – and distantly, as suits a wanderer such as she, to the grey sea beyond, the English Channel, beneath whose waves her infant brother lies.

Trees and hedgerows of wild roses, green fields where horses graze, surround her.

The men of the family, her father and her elder brother Caspar, arranged the funeral – we women could do no more than keep her company on her last journey. The little church was full – the word of her death had spread quickly among her friends. There were poems and readings, hymns and simple prayers. Nicholas read from John Donne, Robert Frost and Christopher Logue, Poppy's godfather. Two of Honey's friends, on Fran's absent sister's behalf, from Shakespeare. Sunshine bathed her at the last: no less could be expected. Out in the churchyard, slender shafts of golden light threaded through the grey November day, falling on the pale lilies and black earth which covered her.

O Come All Ye Faithful

O come all ye faithful
Here is our cause:
All dreams are one dream,
All wars civil wars.

Lovers have never found
Agony strange;
We who hate change survive
Only through change.

Those who are sure of love
Do not complain.
For sure of love is sure
Love comes again.

CHRISTOPHER LOGUE

On her coffin Nicholas placed a little pottery emblem of the white dove, *la Blanca Paloma*, giving her into the care of the little doll-faced Virgin of Rocio in the marshes of Andalusia.

Then we returned to our house in Wales. Once again, thirty years later, we live now, as we did when the children were little, in a beautiful place, with woods and water for our playground. We have

picked up the tangled threads of our lives, and returned to work –
both of us – at our chosen careers. These too have evolved over the
three decades. Nicholas continues as a novelist and travel writer, but
he is now deeply involved in matters of conservation – the
husbandry of wilderness and the preservation of wild land for
future generations. As for me, after a decade of cookery writing,
I have just published that first novel which was begun on Mull.

The little estate needs love and care and plenty of attention, and
for the first time in our married lives, there are just the two of us to
share it. Like any married couple after the children leave home, we
have to look for a new accommodation with each other.

After all these years together, we have a deep well of memories to
share – the old stories are always the best. We find, too, that the
division of our labours means that we have neither grown apart nor
together, but in parallel. Perhaps because of this we still find each
other surprising and interesting. Unexpectedly, after three decades
of independent living, we can still learn from each other. We know
one another's weaknesses and strengths – and, after all these years,
take care not to tap too hard on the cracks.

Who knows but we may yet make it through to the golden
wedding.

With this in mind, I am happy to report that Nicholas, always a
Capability Brown at heart, is restoring the garden. He has lately
become very knowledgeable about soil types and pest control. He is
bossy about drainage and has firm opinions on trees. True to my
housekeeperly nature, I keep a low profile in the garden, contenting
myself with weeding the borders and planting unfashionable things in
pots. There's always the outside chance that geraniums and marguer-
ites may turn my damp Welsh courtyard into an *andaluz* patio.

Like my beloved daughter, I am a creature of the sun.

There are no rules for the future. We still have no game plan to
carry us further than dinner or tea. Access to the big city remains
important to both of us. But just the same, I can't help hankering
after a medieval citadel, a clan stronghold full of all ages and
occupations, with woods and fields and common grazing, hens,
pigs and a cow or two in the yard. I'm sure that my hankerings are
for a life that was nasty, brutish and short; that the Black Death raged
unchecked by the National Health; that the roads were terrible and

only the rich had any fun or a life expectancy beyond thirty and three-quarter years.

These are modern times – the Wife of Bath has a mobile phone and Nicholas threatens to link us into the information superhighway. No doubt I shall soon be able to hold daily conference links with all my children – they will know when I haven't washed my hair, and I shall know when they have dragged unsuitable partners back to their lairs.

Naturally, I hope in due course for grandchildren. As Poppy, frustrated in a date at the age of fourteen, once memorably said to her father, 'If we're not allowed boyfriends, how can you expect us to have babies?'

For the moment at least, the daughters and son are too busy making independent adult lives to think about delivering the goods. As for me, I'm still years short of claiming the bus pass, but I have warned my children I fully expect to be a burden to them in my old age. Heaven protect me from an old folk's home.

Meanwhile, whether in the big city or the country, I deliver Sunday dinner on demand. The non-resident family filters in any time after six, grabs the newspapers, and sometimes, depending on their leanings, helps with the tattie-peeling. They like to plug into each other's news, as well as that of the nation. They are all engaged in quite different activities, so, like any working couple, they go through the 'Good day at the office, dear?' routine, and check out any likely amusements for the coming week.

These weekly get-togethers have always been moveable feasts – with the children's friends joining the gatherings. This has had the unexpected bonus over the years of moving us beyond the narrow band of our own generation, and Nicholas and I have acquired a new circle of friends who illuminate and enrich our lives. Some of them, but by no means all, you will have met in these pages – and we hope for others yet to come.

Like any family, we have our triumphs and disasters – and only the future can tell us which is which. We have always faced these things together – using each other as the need arises and geography allows, for support, affection, or merely as a sounding-board for working out our problems.

Looking at the admirable adults my children have become, I cannot judge them, I can only love them. And then I cook them dinner, which I see as the greatest earnest of maternal affection.

Even so, however healing time may be, we can never escape the knowledge that we have lost one of our number. Perhaps we don't need to. She told us where she was going – not so far after all, just off for a bit of Caribbean sunshine. We are used to such absences. We'll see her again – no doubt of that.

I have in mind a new family celebration, although in truth it is not new at all. I remember, as a young woman in Mexico, going with a friend on the Day of the Dead to the cemetery where her family was buried. It was a very merry occasion; nothing sentimental or sad was allowed to disturb the festival. There must have been thousands of us there – old men and young, toothless grannies and new mothers, infants at the breast, toddlers, teenagers. Lanterns blazed, stews bubbled on braziers, there was music and song; on the sandy paths, children played with sugar skulls. We cooked our meal and picnicked companionably on the family tombstone, sipping cactus-wine and discussing the good times shared with those within.

Ethnologists would dismiss this celebration as ancestor-worship – but I am not so sure the ritual does not fill another more immediate necessity. After the acceptance of death, we need to celebrate the lives of those we have lost – mourning alone will not suffice.

Such ancient rituals are not confined to what might be considered primitive cultures – the relics of similar pagan ceremonies can be found in our own Christian traditions. I was reminded of this a year or two ago, when, finding myself sharing the Easter festivities with a community of Ukrainians on the Slovak border, I accompanied a Russian Orthodox family to the churchyard with their baskets of eggs, ham and sweet bread to be blessed. Although we took the food home to consume it, I was told that, in the old days, the feast would have been shared out in the boneyard with the dead.

I think I'm beginning to talk myself into an annual family picnic. We would have to be circumspect about it, of course. No bonfires or loud music – but maybe a little strumming on Fran's guitar, a click or two of the castanets. Flowers certainly, beeswax candles of course, and naturally something delicious to eat and drink. Caviare perhaps – she learnt to like it, just as she promised. And wild strawberries with one of those honeyed wines she loved. Francesca would not find anything but the best acceptable.

Such a celebration would certainly not suit modern notions of decorum – perish the pagan thought. We'd surely upset the pastor and no doubt frighten the neighbours.

But then, when all is said and done, I've been doing that for years.

Index

(* indicates recipe)

307